SOME GOOD IN THE WORLD

Edward Piszek

SOME GOOD IN THE WORLD
A LIFE OF PURPOSE

A MEMOIR

By

Edward J. Piszek

As told to
Jake Morgan

University Press of Colorado

© 2001 by the University Press of Colorado

Published by the University Press of Colorado
5589 Arapahoe Avenue, Suite 206C
Boulder, Colorado 80303

The University Press of Colorado is a cooperative publishing enterprise supported, in part, by Adams State College, Colorado State University, Fort Lewis College, Mesa State College, Metropolitan State College of Denver, University of Colorado, University of Northern Colorado, University of Southern Colorado, and Western State College of Colorado.

The paper used in this publication meets the minimum requirements of the American National Standard for Information Sciences—Permanence of Paper for Printed Library Materials. ANSI Z39.48-1992.

Library of Congress Cataloging-in-Publication Data

Piszek, Edward J.
  Some good in the world : a life of purpose : a memoir / by Edward J. Piszek as told to Jake Morgan.
    p. cm.
    ISBN 0-87081-627-6 (hardcover : alk. paper)
  1. Piszek, Edward J. 2. Mrs. Paul's Kitchens—Officials and employees—Biography. 3. Polish Americans—Biography. 4. Medical assistance, American—Poland—History—20th century. 5. Tuberculosis—Poland—Prevention—History—20th century. 6. Poland—History—1945–
I. Morgan, Jake. II. Title.

  HD9460.P57 A3 2001
  338.7'6649453'092—dc21

                                                                    2001002738

Design by Daniel Pratt

10 09 08 07 06 05 04 03 02 01   10 9 8 7 6 5 4 3 2 1

To Oddie
and my children, Ann, Ed, George, Helen, and Bill,
who helped make me who I am

Contents

Foreword
by James A. Michener

I have a double pleasure in writing this introduction to the autobiography of my friend, Ed Piszek. First, it puts on record some of my deep personal regard for a most unusual man. And second, it provides me with the opportunity to speak again of my own friendship for Poland and its people, a friendship that he shares and that has bound the two of us together.

My first visit to Poland was in 1972, when I was traveling with President Richard Nixon on his historic trip behind the Iron Curtain, and the impression made on me at that time by the hundreds of thousands of enthusiastic people who lined our route from Okecie International Airport to downtown Warsaw was unforgettable. Those were difficult years for the United States, and an American president was not always well received, even in the capitals of some of our allies. But here in the heart of a communist-run nation, in one of the coldest years of the cold war between East and West, the warmth of our reception would have melted icebergs.

Since then, I have returned to Poland many times—to make a film documentary for American television, to reacquaint myself with Poland's rich culture and its one thousand years of recorded history, and to research my novel *Poland*, which helped to introduce that country and its people to millions of Americans. During these journeys, I have met some of Poland's finest sons and daughters: writers, journalists, intellectuals, and spiritual leaders, including Karol Cardinal Wojtyla, now Pope John Paul II, and his friend and mentor, the late Stefan Cardinal Wyszynski. I met with the leaders of the Solidarity movement—men whose work, courage, and endurance led the process that liberated Central Europe from Soviet domination—including Lech Walesa, whose friendship I continue to treasure. I traveled the length and breadth of Poland, meeting men and women from all walks of life, and getting a powerful sense of the country.

But this long acquaintance with the Polish people began long before, through a friendship I had formed with Edward J. Piszek, an amazing Philadelphia industrialist and a devoted American son of Poland, whose stories about Polish life and history sparked my early interest, and who tells his own remarkable story in the pages that follow. It is a story that imparts exactly what makes America unique among nations, where any man or woman may start life with few advantages and then—through courage, brilliance, endurance, and hard work—achieve not only great material wealth but also turn that life into the greatest treasure of them all: a life filled with purpose.

My great respect for Ed, and the depth of friendship and esteem that exists between us, have surprised some people now and then. We are not alike. We do not tread the same paths. Our interests are not always similar. There have been moments when we have disagreed on some important issues. But we have learned to know each other so well through the years, and we have shared so many concerns about the world we live in, that this mutual regard has grown rather than been diminished by our differences.

Edward Piszek was born in Chicago on October 24, 1916, the son of parents who had emigrated from Poland to America at the break of this century. The senior Piszeks (whose family name was *Piszczek* before an American immigration official decided to simplify it for them) were farmers from the rural neighborhood of Tarnow, a heritage that would later impact immensely on their son. Young Edward's father eventually brought his family to Philadelphia, where he opened a small retail grocery, a footstep in the food industry that his son was destined to follow.

Growing up in a poor, working-class neighborhood, the lively, curious, and hardworking lad soon learned the value of a dollar and the pride to be taken in a job well done. These traits enabled him to work his way through the University of Pennsylvania at night, paying his tuition from the wages of day labor and ultimately earning a degree in business administration. The path that took him from these small beginnings to the position of founder and president of a major American corporation is the core of his book, and I shall not intrude my thoughts into it. It was, however, that same position, and the material means it brought, that led him back, in the most unexpected way, to his Polish roots and forever altered his life and the lives of everyone around him.

This story, in a way, belongs in a novel, and perhaps someday a skillful novelist will take an interest in it. I can see that such a tale, told as a work of fiction, would capture the imagination of many and inspire many more. It is an exciting story. What happened and how it came about he will tell you himself, and I do not wish to anticipate this telling. But for a novelist like myself, who must look beneath the surface of every human being to find the nuggets of gold in the straw and sawdust, a minimum of essential facts suffices.

And what I see is this:

A simple man who has never lost the common touch, but who is the intimate and friend of presidents and the pope in Rome, as welcome in the White House as in the Belvedere in Warsaw or in the private chambers of the Vatican.

A man who set out single-handedly to eradicate tuberculosis in Poland, saving the lives of millions, and who continues to invest his drive and resources in other humanitarian projects of immense practical value to the welfare of people all over the world.

A complex, often difficult and elusive figure, at times almost painfully uncertain of himself and anxious for affection, who is at the same time a man of such great drive, courage, and imagination that he can simply overwhelm the obstacles that arise before him.

And finally, I see the most curious and challenging blend of all: an essentially straightforward, decent human being of great spiritual resources who, at the same time, insists on absolute control over his own life, sometimes over other lives as well, and always over the course he has chosen for himself; a man who is wholly dedicated to Christian principles of charity, brotherhood, and sharing but who insists that people earn everything they get; an idealist of great vision and passionate devotions who sometimes gives way to anger and impatience with people who cannot see as far as he can, nor respond as quickly to the call of opportunity; and—finally—an eminently practical businessman and financier, who hates to be known as a philanthropist but whose profound commitment to the doing of good has given him the real secret of success.

Reading his book may not provide an automatic guide to power and riches, but that is not what he intends. What he shares here is much more than that. Told from the heart, his story is an inspiration and a lesson of another kind. For if the purpose of life is living a life of purpose, then we all have a lot to learn from Edward J. Piszek.

Prologue: A Drive in the Country
by Jake Morgan

I am a writer, a writer for hire. If there's a sentence you need written, I'm the man for you. I take orders for words the way a tailor makes a suit. I inquire: What size sentence, exactly? Adjectives? How many? Do you plan to use this sentence for formal occasions or just around the house? Here, let me measure.

For fifteen years I have been making my living in this peculiar way. My philosophy, a practical one, is this: *You bet I can write that.* What have I written? A freelancer cannot always be choosy any more than a man can choose which molecules of oxygen to breathe. I have written everything from fact to fiction and all the gray areas in between; I have written novels and stories, smarmy editorials and elegant obituaries, "thought pieces" about nothing and everything, history books, travel books, book reviews, how-to's, profiles of people famous and obscure, even a speech for a presidential candidate (which he didn't use; he wasn't elected, either).

Who knows why? I started out with the ambition to write just one beautiful sentence. In college, I would sometimes read a story or novel and be so moved by it that I would have to lie down for a day. For graduation, my father bought me a crate of blank paper, with these words on the side: "Contents: Unwritten writing. Handle with high hope." I moved first to Hawaii, then to Los Angeles, then to Iowa, thinking these would be the right sorts of places for a writer. I bought a computer with borrowed money and stared at the blank screen, its serenely blinking cursor waiting for my one beautiful sentence to arrive. It may have already happened. I've written so many sentences, I can't tell.

But of course, a writer also needs a story. One of my teachers in graduate school explained it this way. Being a writer, he said, was about maintaining a state of readiness; you wrote and wrote to keep yourself sharp, but what you were really doing was waiting, he said, for the good story to come. When I asked him where they came from, he smiled—a mysterious and happy smile—because he had written three wonderful books, and I had written none.

"They come from above," he said.

The life of Edward J. Piszek is one such story. It is an amazing tale, deeply American in a way few stories are anymore, and rich as the life it contains. It is amazing not least of all because it is, in fact, true. And it began, for me, one bright, cold day in Philadelphia in April 1996, when I found myself, of all places, in the backseat of a gleaming, gun-metal Lincoln Continental, as plush as a parade float and as overpowered as a fighter plane, gliding north from the city's well-heeled suburban edge into the Bucks County countryside, looking for a river.

A serendipitous chain of events had brought me to this moment. Six months before, I had been working in my office—I was just finishing up a long project, a history book for Reader's Digest—wondering in a nervous way where the next checks would be coming from, when the telephone rang. I recognized the voice on the other end of the line immediately; it was my old graduate school professor. I smiled to think he had found me just where he had always told me to be: at my desk, writing and waiting. We spent a few minutes catching up—complaining, as writers will, about money and time and how little we had of each—and then he told me he had a favor to ask. There was a man, he said, an important and interesting man, who was trying to compose his memoirs. He didn't know the details. It would be a lot of work. The man lived in Philadelphia—probably not far at all from me—although that wasn't why he had thought to ask me. He needed a *writer*. There was a story here, my teacher said, maybe a great one. Was I interested?

I looked at my final check from the Digest, sitting on my desk beside the phone. As far as I knew, it was the last such check I would be receiving in my life. Was I *interested*? I told Frank he could count on me and wrote down the information. I recognized the town: Ft. Washington was fifteen minutes away, just over the Philadelphia city line in Montgomery County. The place was literally right under my nose.

"This man. What's he like?" I asked.

"Mr. P?" Frank paused, hunting for just the right phrase, the perfect comparison. "Well. Do you know those Horatio Alger stories?"

I did. As a boy, I had devoured them, slender, sentimental novels with titles like *Tattered Tom* (1871) and *Luck and Pluck* (1869). Alger, a clergyman from Massachusetts, had written nearly a hundred of them in his lifetime, and the plot was always the same, a lightly retooled version of that durable and ancient formula: poor boy makes good. They were classic rags-to-riches, up-by-the-bootstraps tales, told with an innocent purity that I associated with an America long gone, and as a child I had loved them at the same time that I had seen right through them. Sentimental or not, the message they contained was one that any kid in any century could stand to hear: work hard, and you'll do well.

"You're kidding," I said.

Frank laughed. "Go see for yourself."

And so I did; I dialed the number without delay, made the arrangements, and two weeks later drove out to Ft. Washington to meet the man who, as I had been told, had stepped straight from the pages of a nineteenth-century novel for boys.

I had done a little homework, too. Ed Piszek—"Mr. P" to everyone who knew him, the "fishcake king" to those who did not—was a commanding, even mythic, local figure. Typing his name into the correct database, as I had done, produced dozens of stories from the Philadelphia *Inquirer* and *Daily News* (and their predecessors), as well as an assortment of regional and national magazines, spread over a forty-year period. Just as Frank had said, the tale I assembled from these articles followed the precise and handsome arc of the all-American success story. But it was also a story that seemed, to me, the very essence of the city itself.

Summarizing Philadelphia is not easy. It is both as worldly as San Francisco and as parochial as Des Moines; as glittering as a miniature Manhattan and as run-down as Buffalo. In some ways, Philadelphia is America's smallest major city or else its largest town. Although a million-and-a-half people live here (six million if you count the extended metro area, a triangle roughly connecting Allentown, Atlantic City, and Wilmington, Delaware), it seems, at times, as if everybody here knows everybody else, like some enormous club. To an amazing extent, Philadelphia is a city of lifers; if you were born here, the odds are unusually good that you'll die here, too. Philadelphians rarely seem in need of new friends, beacause they have so many to begin with, and people who move here from somewhere else tend to report identical feelings of displacement and alienation. One recent newcomer told me that moving to Philadelphia felt like walking into a difficult class halfway through the semester.

The difficulty is compounded by modern Philadelphia's striking contrasts—of high culture and low, of grinding poverty and soaring wealth, of southern lassitude and northern snarl. The saying goes that Philadelphia is a "city of neighborhoods," which is certainly true enough. But it is also a city of centuries, laid layer upon layer, like an open-air archeological dig. Even the smell of Philadelphia—a potpourri of smoke and sewage, of wet stone and dank vegetation and river water—is the smell of age itself. Center City Philadelphia, with its discordant visual mix of eighteenth-century colonial houses and modern skyscrapers, is by far the most prosperous part of the city, the heart of William Penn's "greene countrie towne," and the Philadelphia that most tourists see. But in terms of land area, most of the city is classic industrial rust belt. Though some of these neighborhoods have remained viable, many others have not. Once the humming heart of nineteenth-century immigrant life in the city, the downtrodden neighborhoods of North Philadelphia are a textbook case of what happens when an entire economy is made obsolete. The sausage and hat factories, the ball bearing plants, the tool and die works, the breweries and slaughterhouses and munitions plants—by the thousands, these once-thriving concerns, mini-powerhouses of the free market and human warehouses for whole generations of Irish, Italians, Poles, Germans, Czechs, Russians, and all the rest (including vast numbers of African Americans, many the descendants of slaves who migrated north after the Civil War), are today no more than rusting shells, not always even recognizable as buildings. Much of North Philadelphia seems as empty and desolate as North Dakota. People who can avoid it rarely go there, but anyone who has ever ridden a train on Amtrak's Northeast Corridor has seen it from the windows. The irony is that North Philadelphia is actually one of the greenest parts of town. Nature is actually reclaiming it, pulling it down house by house, factory by factory. From the cool, detached comfort of an Amtrak Metroliner gliding north to Manhattan, the effect is like looking at a lost Mayan city peeking from beneath a gauze of vines.

Beyond this zone, of course, is where most Philadelphians have ended up. Like the rest of America, Philadelphia is now a city of suburbs, less a discrete place than a hodgepodge of places cobbled together. Statistically speaking, the city itself is dying. Since 1950, its population has fallen nearly every year; 500,000 fewer people live here now than when Dwight D. Eisenhower was president, enough to populate the entire city of Nashville. And yet, Philadelphians seem as sentimentally wedded to this place as the residents of any city I have ever lived in. To say that they love it is only half the story, for their love is also tragic; they pine for its forgotten glory and its unrealized, finer self. Which is to say, for better or for worse, Philadelphia—city of the Eagles and the benumbed Phillies, of Main Line Ivy League–educated lawyers and punch-drunk Rocky Balboa, of haute cuisine and the hoagie—is home to them.

The story of Ed Piszek is, truly, a Philadelphia story—a tale that, to my mind, could not have happened anywhere else. It is a working-class story for a working-class town, and though it takes place entirely within one century, its spirit belongs at least in part to another. And so, it is also a kind of ghost story.

Here is what I read:

Ed Piszek, the fishcake king, was born in Chicago in 1916, the son of Polish immigrants. As a child, he moved first to the Pennsylvania farming community of Quakertown, then to Philadelphia, settling in the working-class Polish-Irish-Catholic neighborhood of Nicetown, where his parents owned a corner deli. I cannot help myself: I imagine him, as a kid, rather like one of the characters from the *Our Gang* movies, a little wiseguy in knickers, pocketing a stolen apple or carving his initials into a telephone pole. (Nothing about the man himself, in fact, dispels this vision.) He got into trouble, like many kids; he also worked hard, like many others. At eighteen he married his high school sweetheart, began college at night, worked as a traveling soup salesman, then on the assembly line at a General Electric plant during the Second World War. His life might have been the same as thousands of other lives in this city—a story of modest, hard-working prosperity in the first half of the twentieth century.

But that, of course, is not what happened at all.

It is said that the truth is always stranger than fiction, and the chain of events that propelled Ed Piszek from ordinary obscurity to international prominence is something you could not pass off in a novel if you tried. How does a man rise from nothing to become one of the century's most successful entrepreneurial capitalists, sole owner of a business worth nearly half-a-billion dollars? It is axiomatic to the American psyche that such things happen, but the truth is, they almost never do. The company he founded—and later lost in an equally dramatic twist—was more than a case of the right thinking at the right time. Like Apple Computer (or even Standard Oil), Mrs. Paul's Kitchens was the first of its kind. In effect, Ed Piszek had invented an entire industry.

But Ed Piszek's business triumphs were only half the story. As I looked over the clippings, I noticed a change; by the late 1960s when his company was well established, most of what was written was not about Mrs. Paul's at all but about Poland. There were articles about something called Project Pole, and an effort to cure tuberculosis in Poland, and trips to meet an electrician in the Gdansk shipyards—a man named Lech Walesa. The tone of these pieces was different, too. There was a suggestion of eccentricity; the writers, whoever they were, seemed uncertain what to make of a Philadelphia capitalist who spent most of his time in a country that was (as people said at the time) "behind the iron curtain." No one came right out and said that Ed Piszek was a Communist sympathizer or a mole for the CIA. But it was clear to me that in midlife—just when many men of good fortune have settled into an early retirement—Ed Piszek had embarked on a whole new kind of search. And it wasn't a story that anyone had managed yet to tell.

I arrived that first morning in October 1995 full of questions and a set of expectations that proved, to a one, completely wrong. Based on what I had read, the image I had constructed in my head of Mr. Piszek was decidedly romantic. What did a captain of industry turned global philanthropist look like? I didn't know, but mentally, I had prepared myself for some amalgamation of J. Paul Getty and St. Francis of Assisi, perhaps with a dash of James Bond. But the man who met me at the door could not have been more different, and he instantly defeated my second expectation as well: that I was about to meet someone quite elderly. Numerically, this was true enough—at the time of our first visit, Ed Piszek had just turned seventy-nine—but he gave no hint at all of his age, nor of the deflating grief that I had prepared myself to find when I had learned that Olga (whom he called Oddie), his wife of more than fifty years, had recently passed away. He met me at the door with the firmest of handshakes—a hale, bespectacled man with a sharply chiseled nose, thin white hair, twinkling green eyes, and large muscular hands. His dress, then as later, was startlingly youthful. In his brightly colored warm-up suit and brand-new Reeboks, he reminded me, for all the world, of a semiretired, Main Line Philadelphia banker on his way to a set of tennis at the Cricket Club. He seemed delighted to see me, and as we made our way through his enormous house from back to front—we were headed for the library—he produced from the pocket of his warm-up suit a reporter's notebook, fat with scribbling, in which he had jotted notes for our conversation. He wanted to tell me about a new project that excited him, a joint venture with the Peace Corps to make English "the universal language." I had to laugh; two minutes into the project, and I felt like I was being dragged from a horse.

We talked that first day for three hours and met regularly through the winter. Our ritual was always the same. I would arrive at Emlen House in the late morning, and we would chat in the library until lunchtime. We would then adjourn to the sunroom, a favorite of his late wife's, to eat and talk some more. Sometimes I would tape these conversations. Sometimes I would just listen, pausing only to jot down a few notes. My intention, in these early meetings, was simply to get to know him, to assemble some sense of who he was. Our conversations ranged easily over the whole of his life, from memories of his father (who had died when he was a teenager), to his five children (all grown and fully into their own lives), to the pressing projects that still occupied him. (For an octogenarian, Ed Piszek had the busiest calendar I had ever seen. I was most impressed—and who wouldn't be?—when his son Bill phoned me one day to say that we would have to change one of our appointments, because his father had been summoned to Washington, D.C., to attend the funeral of former Chief Justice Warren Burger.) I now know that the real purpose of these early meetings was social; we were learning to become comfortable with one another. If I was going to help him write his memoirs, we would have to trust one another.

And bit by bit, we learned to do this. The gaps between us were large; Ed Piszek lived in a world that most of us never visit, a world of presidents and popes, of late night flights across the international date line, of smoke-filled boardrooms and high-level meetings. He lived in a two-hundred-year-old house on seventy acres; by the roadside, where a pair of stone columns marked the driveway, was a bronze historic marker that said—rather casually, I thought—that the house had served as headquarters for General of the Continental Army George Washington in the months between the battle of Germantown and his winter retreat to Valley Forge. In other words, Ed Piszek's life was as remote from my own as it could possibly be, and I often returned from our meetings feeling a little dazed, as if, in just three hours, I had rocketed to the moon and back. But meeting by meeting, my sense of strangeness departed, and what emerged was my vision of a man—at bottom, a completely ordinary man—who had never lost the common touch, who was just as amazed by the events of his life as I was. Sometime before the snows had melted, we began to speak of the project as if it had already begun, and I knew the first test was behind us.

Yet, I still felt that something was missing, or that something lurked just beyond my grasp. I had begun my education in *what* had happened but not in *why*. A memoir that presents itself as a simple chronology of events is not a memoir—it's a list. A memoir, as its name implies, is a book of memory. Like a novel, it is organized around a theme—a theme of personality, if you like—but because it also needs to be true, this theme must emerge naturally from memory itself. A memoir tries to answer the question: what does this one life *mean?* Intrinsically, Ed Piszek's life felt to me as if it possessed such coherence—everything connected somehow—but I was yet to unearth that connection.

Instinctively I had begun to circle around one particular idea. I wasn't even aware that I was doing it, not at first; in hindsight, I'm certain that Mr. Piszek wasn't aware of it either. Seen objectively, the arc of Ed Piszek's life—from bucolic Quakertown to hardscrabble Nicetown to Warsaw and back—had a quality of *return,* of the immigrant's longing for home. This made sense to me, but it also did not. Ed Piszek was, after all, American born. He was fiercely patriotic, in fact; in the 1970s, he had actually commissioned a reproduction of Philadelphia's Liberty Bell to commemorate the bicentennial. His house was full of Americana—a bust of George Washington, copies of the Declaration of Independence and the Bill of Rights, and so on. What was it, then, that connected him to the Polish past, to a country he had never lived in, that by his own account, his parents had gratefully fled? What regret was there, what need to search, what excavation in the psyche that asked to be filled? Through those first winter months, while we talked about the Peace Corps and Lech Walesa and the pope and

Mrs. Paul's and all of it, I detected, at odd moments, a kind of wistfulness emanating from him. It was as if a ghost had entered the room. Frequently, I found the conversation, at these moments, drifting back to the Quakertown farm. I detected something more than sentimental nostalgia for a lost childhood home. More and more, I questioned him about his father, who I knew had died in a car accident when Ed Piszek was just fifteen.

Did your father speak Polish? I asked.

Some, yes, of course.

Was he kind to you? (A pause.)

I think I was his favorite.

How did his death affect you?

Well, very terribly. I was sad for years. For a while, my mother didn't even know what to do with me. I think I treated her badly after he died.

When you think of your father, how do you see him?

See him?

Yes, I said, *see him. It might help, Mr. Piszek, if you closed your eyes.*

In his chair in the library, Ed Piszek let his lids fall shut. I could tell he thought my request peculiar, which it was. I felt suddenly that I had transgressed a boundary—that I had come too close to something, or maybe close enough. For a moment, we just sat there, like two people at a seance.

Then, his eyes still closed, Mr. Piszek began to describe his father. As I had hoped, the image seemed taken from a photograph. He described a man in his late forties, wearing a wool suit, his hair tousled by the wind, sitting on a chair with water behind him. The water appeared to be moving.

"Is he on board a ship?" I asked.

Mr. Piszek opened his eyes. "Yes, I think so."

"You never told me your father went anywhere on a ship."

"I guess I'd forgotten he did. It was just before he died. He went back to Poland, to find his relatives."

Back to Poland, I thought, and I knew that I had found what I was looking for. What had I been seeing all those mornings, if not a son's search for a lost father?

"I think it's time we took a drive," I said.

So, at last, the scene.

A bright cold morning in April 1996; an inch of fresh snow had fallen overnight, smothering the newly budding trees and weighing their branches down like wet laundry. It had been a long, hard winter, and the night's surprise snowfall seemed like a bad joke. But by nine o'clock, the sun was out, and squares of green grass had begun to push through the white mantle that dressed the rolling hillsides.

I viewed the day from the backseat of the Lincoln headed north from Ft. Washington into Bucks County, the upscale, bucolic countryside northwest of Philadelphia. Our destination was Quakertown, and the farm where Mr. Piszek had spent his early boyhood. Driving the car was Mr. Piszek's youngest son Bill, a man about my age—thirty-five. I had gotten to know Bill pretty well in the four months since I had been meeting with his father. Bill acted as a kind of first lieutenant for his father, serving as president of one philanthropic foundation he had created, vice president of another, and traveling with him whenever he went abroad. The closeness of our ages made it easy for the two of us to become friends, and in fact, we had more in common then than either of us yet knew: we were both about to be fathers.

That morning, I watched Bill as much as I watched his father. If what I sought was a chain of meaning that connected fathers to sons, then certainly, the bond between Bill and his father would serve, in some unconscious way, as a replica of Mr. Piszek's own patrimony. Bill was no less an interesting subject in his own right. I did not envy his tricky role in life. It is a difficult thing, I imagine, to be a powerful man's son, and not just a powerful man, but a man whose ascent up the rungs of the class ladder had assumed, by the standards of the local culture, nearly epic proportions. Bill would always travel in that shadow, and as his father's right-hand man, he was linked to his father's fate with a day-to-day intimacy that would have driven many men crazy.

On Bill, though, the twin mantles of privilege and responsibility rode with a completely natural and easy drape. Beyond the coincidence of our simultaneous passage into fatherhood, our lives were, surprisingly, not so very different. I had gathered, without being directly told, that at the core of the Piszek family was an ethic of self-sufficiency, of making one's own way usefully in the world, and all five kids, Bill included, had done so. Their childhoods had been comfortable, with good private schools and upscale vacations and all the rest. (*Comfort* was too slight a word, really; how many children get to ride their bikes up and down a driveway nearly half a mile long?) But as adults, their lives had been their own to make. Of the five, a number owned or had owned small businesses (a Nissan dealership, a pair of sports apparel shops, a meat wholesaler); several had worked at various times for Mrs. Paul's before the company had been sold; and three of the five (and some of their spouses) still served as officers or board members of the family's various philanthropic enterprises. All lived within a ten-mile radius of Emlen House, but there were no mansions in the bunch, and their lives, though comfortable enough, suggested little more than solid professional-class achievement. Bill lived in a house I might have lived in; his wife had a job my wife might have had; he had gone to a school I might have attended if I had grown up in Philadelphia. His job had its exotic perks—his passport was fat with visas, whereas mine sat in a bureau drawer, unused for a decade—but he approached it with nothing more or less than the cheerful willingness of a good son to pitch in, and on a daily basis, our lives were consumed by the same things (such as where to buy a good infant car seat cheap).

So Bill drove, Mr. Piszek talked, and I watched. Our ultimate destination was Quakertown, about thirty miles distant, but along the way, we planned to pause at two other places, a pair of houses where Mr. Piszek and his wife had lived in the early years of their marriage, when he was still a traveling soup salesman working the towns of Bucks and Montgomery Counties. We arrived at the first one, in the town of Chalfont. On the main street, Bill slowed the car as we pressed a block of small attached houses wrapped in aluminum siding, and Mr. Piszek pointed through the window at one of them. We glided by before I was sure which one he meant, and I asked Bill to double back so I could have another, closer look.

"You lived here—now, when was that?" I asked, though I knew. Ed and Olga had lived in Chalfont for about eighteen months, in the late thirties; their oldest daughter Ann had been born just before they moved there.

"Well, I think it was in '38."

Bill pulled the Lincoln to the curb across the street, and I looked the place over. It was neat and spruce but decidedly unfancy. In recent decades, the farm fields around Chalfont had mostly been plowed under for upscale housing, and houses like this one, right by the main road, had become less desirable. Several had been rezoned for small business: a real estate office, an insurance agent, a thrift shop, a pet groomer called K-9 Kuts and Kurls. Someone had left a baby carriage by the door; a brightly colored plastic swing hung from the porch rafters. The whole building was small enough to fit in the living room and kitchen of Emlen House.

"It was all very different back then," Mr. Piszek explained. "Ann used to roller-skate right in the road."

We pulled away and drove ten minutes up the highway to Doylestown. Once again, the house floated past before I had a chance to look, and we turned around and found a spot to park out of the way of traffic. Like the Chalfont house, the structure sat just a few feet off the busy highway, but it was quite a bit older—a three-story farmhouse, probably built in the mid-1800s, with stone walls as thick as a bank vault's. Like many such houses of the period, it had been constructed to look larger than it was; behind its front edifice, the house was in reality no more than thirty feet deep, like a phony saloon on a movie lot. The interior would be cramped and dark and cool in the summers, as it was meant to be; behind it, marking the far end of the shallow yard, was a weedy creek.

We drove on. In the plush backseat of the Lincoln, Mr. Piszek and I talked about the early years of his marriage and the way the Bucks County landscape had changed since then.

"Did you like living here?" I asked. "It must have seemed very different from Nicetown."

"Well, I'd say it was." He nodded, allowing his gaze to drift past me to the window and the unfurling countryside beyond. "In those years, you see, this was the sticks. People still kept their food cold by putting it down a well."

I could not tell if he thought that the changes of the last fifty years were an improvement or not. Probably, like most people, he thought it was both. I knew that he harbored no special nostalgia for either of the houses we had visited—his years as a traveling soup salesman were nothing he sentimentalized—but I also understood that moving away from the city, as he had done in his early twenties, had possessed some of the qualities of return that I now believed were the controlling influence of his entire life. The old farmhouse, the weedy creek and backyard well, the cool, moist rooms within; I understood even then that the Doylestown house was in some ways a replica of the boyhood farm in Quakertown, which was itself a replica of some ancestral peasant farm in southern Poland where he had never lived. Emlen House, as grand as it was, was another link in this chain, possessing the same essential elements: a stone farmhouse surrounded by green, with running water sculpting the edge of the property. If you squeezed your eyes just right, its expansive, expertly manicured lawns became farmland (as no doubt they once had been); subtract the circular drive, the winglike additions to the main structure, the tennis court, and all the rest, and what you had was the same modest country house I had just seen sitting by the highway. Each setting of his life was a facsimile of the others; viewing them in order was like watching a train of identical boxcars rolling by.

But the most curious thing—and at first I found this vexing—was that Mr. Piszek seemed to have no conscious awareness of this fact at all. The psychological themes of his life were nothing he himself wished to name. Whenever I pointed out some striking similarity, some coincidence that the psychologists would say was not a coincidence at all, his eyes would widen, he would pause a moment, then say something like, "Well, think of that." Or, "I see what you're saying, and it makes sense to me." Or, "You know, that's interesting. I never thought of that before."

At first, I wondered at this reticence, thinking it was some kind of elaborate defense mechanism I would have to get past. But over time, I came to understand it as a deeply human response, necessary and natural, and axiomatic to the impulse to record his life. Consciously, Mr. Piszek was unaware of these themes, because he was still living inside them. Unconsciously, he was directing me—and himself as well, for the unconscious mind is always sly in just this way—to the doorstep of their meaning. It was he, after all, who had added Doylestown and Chalfont to our itinerary. On the surface, he professed only to think that such visits would be helpful; I ought to see the places he had lived, he explained, and they were on the way. But at some other, deeper level, he was asking me to help him understand his life—to turn it into narrative.

The Quakertown farm was, of course, a farm no longer, at least not as a going concern. Some of the land was still in cultivation, Mr. Piszek told me, but these acres were leased; the house itself and all the grounds were owned by a retired physician who kept horses and an apiary. "Gentleman farming," Mr. Piszek called it, and in his voice I heard for the first time a trace of bitter irony; his boyhood Eden had become an aristocrat's hobby.

Convinced as I was of my "theory of return," I fully expected the farm to bear some fundamental resemblance to Mr. Piszek's Emlen House estate. But even so, I was shocked by what I saw. As we approached the farm, the car crested a rise, dipped into a shallow valley, and arced in a gentle curve toward the entrance—an identical geometry to the highway leading to Emlen House. We turned right down the drive, disappeared into the trees, and emerged again into an open clearing, with muddy fields on either side, a millrace with a duck pond to the right, and a barn and old stone farmhouse at the end. Every detail matched; it was as if the Emlen House estate had been picked up and planted forty miles away. Even the ducks looked somehow the same. The resemblance was so striking, it felt like déjà vu.

I looked at Bill. "Holy moly," I said.

He shot me a smile, wagging his eyebrows. "You figured it out," he said softly.

Bill pulled the Lincoln into a space beside the barn, and the three of us got out, blinking in the late morning light and stretching our backs and legs. The sun was out, but the air was still crisp and laced with the sweet fragrance of horses and dirt. As Bill and his father removed rubber boots from the trunk, I looked at my own shoes—black loafers, their soles thin as paper—then at the muddy fields around us, with dismay. What had I been thinking? I pulled my jacket around me in the cold air and folded up the collar for good measure.

"They're all away in Florida," Mr. Piszek said. "So we can't go inside." He gestured toward the house. "It's all different, anyway. They've spent quite a bit of money on the place."

We approached the house from the front. The structure had been substantially enlarged, but the front rooms were clearly original to the house. Without saying anything, I put my nose to a window and cupped a hand around my face. Details emerged as my eyes adjusted to the light: the perfect smoothness of new Sheetrock; gleaming antique furniture and oriental rugs; prints of horses on the walls and, above the mantle, an assortment of ribbons and cups; a beautiful soapstone woodstove where an old coal grate had once stood; on the wall beside the stairs, a slim plastic pad with three blinking red lights, indicating that the house's security system was operating.

"Have you been inside since it was redone?" I turned from the window to find that Mr. Piszek was standing at the foot of the front steps, looking away toward the duck pond. An enormous RV was parked beside it, wearing a heavy cloth tarp streaked with black droppings. He seemed not to have heard me.

"Mr. P?"

He returned his eyes to me and nodded. "Once or twice. I thought it looked like a hotel."

I had to laugh; that's exactly what I'd thought, too. "Agreed. But otherwise, it's the same place?"

He gave no answer; instead, his gaze fell over the fields again. I looked at Bill standing beside his father. There was nearly half a century between them, but the family resemblance was still encoded in a thousand details: the same hooked nose, the same broad forehead and rosy cheeks, the same easy posture, one hand pocketed, the other riding a hip. For a long moment, we all just stood there, then Bill rocked back on his heels and gave his father a nudge.

"Pop?"

"Ah," he said, the trance broken. He waved over the grounds and gave a faint smile—a smile of memory. "Yes. Otherwise the same."

We crossed the lawn, heading for the woods beyond. I could hear the sound of the creek before I saw it—the full, swollen sound of running water in springtime. Whenever he had spoken of Quakertown, it was always the creek his thoughts returned to. I had looked through a gazetteer the night before and found it: a thin blue line, hardly worth the mapmaker's attention, a branch of a branch of a branch. With my finger, I followed its course. About ten miles south of the farm, it flowed into the Perkiomen, a pretty river where my wife and I liked to fish for trout on summer evenings, then through a reservoir and over a dam, into the Schuylkill, and on to Delaware Bay. I backtracked the other direction, following the creek to its source, but found that there was none: somewhere in northern Bucks, at the edge of the Pocono Plateau, the blue line simply disappeared. I understood this to mean that it was spring fed, and therefore, would be cool all year round. In the wet heat of mid-Atlantic August, a boy could stick his feet into it and feel as if he had stepped into winter.

We passed through a tangle of bushes, under a stand of hemlock shady enough for the snow to fill my loafers, then arrived at the river's edge. As I had expected, the water was running high. Although it would thin to a trickle in late summer, on that April morning at the end of a long, snowy winter, it had thickened to nearly thirty feet across, and debris raced down its course: branches, leaves, even clots of soil. On the far side, where I had expected to find another farm and open fields, there were only more woods, thick with brushy undergrowth and snow. We sat down on a pile of boulders at the edge—the same boulders where Mr. Piszek had spent a thousand idle hours as a boy and again years later as a young husband and father, when he had picnicked here. He had courted Olga on these rocks, I imagined, held his children in his arms, grieved the loss of his father, dreamed the thousand dreams that would become his life.

I did not know what to say, so I said nothing at all. Just seeing the river felt like I was learning something. The three of us rested awhile—the sun had come out again, warming our faces—then we hiked upstream along its banks. Where the tangle of brush became finally impassable, we turned back toward the farmhouse, though by then, we were far above it. We made our way through the woods again, and finally emerged in what Mr. Piszek called "the upper fields": a wide, open expanse, perhaps ten acres in all, muddy and full of cornstubble. Huge rocks dotted the field—the same blocks of intractable granite that we had been sitting on minutes before. Probably the fields were packed with them. With only a team of horses and a strong back to farm it—as Mr. Piszek's father had done—it would be murderous work.

"What did your father plant up here?" I asked. "Was it always corn?"

"I don't know. I think it might have been potatoes." He gave a little laugh. "The truth was, my father wasn't much of a farmer. He was born to be a peasant, but it didn't come naturally to him. It was always a struggle."

"Was he relieved when he sold it?"

"Well, some." Mr. Piszek frowned. "Maybe he felt he had failed. I was young. It was the end of the world to me. When you're young, and one place is all you've ever known, it's impossible to imagine leaving it. I don't think I cared how he felt. I hadn't really thought about it until you asked."

We headed out over the fields. The mud sucked at my shoes, and by the time I had gotten halfway across, Bill and his father were well in front of me. At the field's edge, Bill waited for me to catch up.

"It's quite a place, isn't it?" he said. His father had gone ahead, and Bill let me put a hand on his shoulder for balance while I scraped off some of the mud. "Sorry about your shoes."

"It's just a little mud." I released his shoulder, and for a moment the two of us stood side by side, watching his father. We had paused only a moment, but already Mr. Piszek was far beyond us. I thought briefly that he might have forgotten all about us.

"That's him all right," Bill said finally. He had a hand over his brow to shield it from the glare. "That's my father, right there."

"Tell me what you mean."

Bill thrust his hands in his pockets to think a moment. "Well, he's always gone his own way." He shrugged noncommittally. "The rest of us just follow along, really. I'm not saying it's a problem. It's just how it is."

"He's remembering his father, isn't he," I said. "That's what this place means to him."

"That's what everything means to him," Bill said.

We returned to the car, scraped the mud off our clothing and shoes, and headed home. The drive was forty minutes, and in the comfortable backseat of the Lincoln, it would have been easy to fall asleep. I felt strangely exhausted, as if I had traveled for days, and none of us said much. But I had one more question to ask Mr. Piszek—the question I had been saving all morning—and I waited until we were halfway home to ask it.

The road we were driving on was Bethlehem Pike, the same road where, in the spring of 1932, his father, returning from a weekend visit to the farm, had lost control of his car. The vehicle, a 1931 Nash, had slid off the road, rolled down an embankment, and struck a tree. His father had died instantly.

"You father was killed on this road, wasn't he?"

Mr. Piszek nodded. In the rearview mirror, I saw Bill's eyes rise.

"Do you know where?" I asked.

He waited, and I felt a little sorry I had asked. But I needed to know; I needed to travel with him to that moment. A few minutes passed, the highway markers clicking by, and then, without looking up, he said, "About here."

We drove the rest of the way home in silence. When we returned to the house, it was a little past noon. We ate lunch together in the sunroom, then Bill excused himself to the office, and I asked Mr. Piszek if we could use a couple of hours right then for some interview time. He was tired, he said, but two hours would be all right.

In the library we arranged ourselves on rocking chairs, and I set up my tape recorder on a small metal table between us. The walls of the room—

like so many rooms of Emlen House—were covered with shelves of books: so many books, their bindings so bent and worn, that I knew they had been read. Between them, interspersed in no particular pattern, were bits of memorabilia: medals, framed photographs, assorted objects whose nature I could not discern from where I sat. On the walls: maps and more photographs, a painted portrait of Oddie, assorted honorary diplomas and certificates of appreciation; on a wooden desk, tucked between more stacks of books and papers, a dour and elegant-looking bust of George Washington. Dust motes floated on sunbeams streaming through the wide windows. Outside, winter had ended.

I balanced the recorder on the table on a stack of books, angling its microphone upward toward Mr. Piszek, who sat patiently waiting for me to get my equipment in order.

"Testing," I said. "Testing one-two-three. Mr. P? Could you say something please?"

He smiled awkwardly. "What should I say?"

"Anything at all." I shrugged. "It doesn't matter. It's just to check the sound."

He considered my request a moment, not realizing he had already done what I had asked him to do. He rubbed his chin. "Good afternoon," he said finally.

I turned off the recorder, rewound it, and listened as our voices, clear as day, replayed the moment that had only just passed. I pushed record again. I gathered my pen, my yellow legal pad, my list of questions. I had typed them up the night before. There were over a hundred of them, just for starters—*when did this happen? what was so-and-so wearing? did X take place before Y?* They were the kind of questions any reporter would ask to get his bearings: sensible, reasonable, and as unimaginative as the points on a compass. I knew now that they would tell me nothing. I put them aside and sat back in my chair.

"Ready?" I asked.

From the rocking chair, a nod.

"Tell me the *story.*"

SOME GOOD IN THE WORLD

Chapter One
Quakertown

I believe that we are moved by larger forces, that there is a plan for us and for the world. But history? History is details; history is coincidence. And how far back should one go in telling the story of one's life? What detail— what moment of chance—is the starting point? It was 1917, a Friday night in a Chicago saloon, and a stockyard worker named Big John was getting drunk. I had been born eight months before, but this is when my life began.

The saloon was my father's. A Polish immigrant, he was still a young man, just thirty-four, though already a widower and a father to five. He stood behind the long wooden counter watching the Friday night crowd of men, their pockets fat with cash, for Friday was payday at the stockyards. They were Irish, Polish, Italian, Slav. Some barely spoke English, or if they did, they spoke it haltingly, their accents thick as buttermilk. America, to many of them, was still a new place.

It was summer, and though I do not know it for certain, I imagine it was hot, sweltering. Big John sat at the stool at the end of the bar. He was loud and liked to tell jokes, and he bought drinks for all his friends: a good customer. But he often drank his pockets dry, and the night before, as my father had closed up the bar, Big John's young wife had come in, pulling three young children behind her.

"Look at them," she had said to my father. There were two boys and a girl; they were tiny and wearing pajamas. "He's taking food out of their mouths. He drinks until there's nothing left." She looked at my father pleadingly, tears swimming in her eyes. All traces of youth were nearly gone from her face, erased like chalk from a blackboard by the hardness of her life. "All our money is yours," she said softly.

My father had five children: three stepdaughters, acquired when he had married my mother two years before; another young daughter; and me, his only son. He went behind the counter to the register and took out two dollars, about the same amount that John spent on an average night. He folded the cash into her hand.

"Here," he said. "Go put your children to bed. It'll be all right. I'll talk to him."

The next night, Friday, when John came in, my father watched him closely. He seemed as usual to be in happy spirits, a mood as large as he was, for his nickname was no lie. Broad as a barrel, he stood at least six foot three, with hands like bear paws, thickened and callused from heavy work. My father let him drink a whiskey, then another. When he ordered a third, my father asked him if he wouldn't mind having a word.

John followed him to the back room, which my father used for storage.

"What gives, Piszek?" he demanded.

"Listen," my father said. "I'm sorry, but I have to cut you off. Your wife came in to complain. She said you're letting your kids go hungry, and that's not right." My father shook his head. "I don't want any trouble, but that's how it is. You can drink in my bar, but go easy, will you?"

John poked a meaty finger into my father's chest. "How 'bout I go easy on you, Piszek? This ain't none of your business."

My father stood his ground. "When your wife comes in, that makes it my business."

"Is that right?"

"You bet it's right."

The fight was quick, explosive. My father wasn't a small man—he stood five feet eleven inches tall and weighed in at a little under two hundred pounds—but he was no match for Big John. A black eye, a badly wounded pride, some broken barstools: the damage wasn't bad by bar brawl standards, but for my father, it was enough. After it was all over, he closed up for the night, abandoning most of the mess to clean up later. His customers, who had fled when Big John tore through the main room, would be back the next night, and Big John's tirade would become another story to tell over beer and whiskey after work. No real harm had been done, but in his heart, my father knew he was through. A woman had accused him of being a thief; he had tried to do the right thing, and her husband had beaten him up and wrecked his place of business. Someday it would happen again—not Big John but somebody else, another drunk with hungry kids and a brokenhearted wife—and my father had no spirit for it. I see him walking home that night through the dark streets, past row houses and tenements, their windows staring darkly out; behind them children slept, or a woman lay awake, waiting for the sounds of a man's heavy workboots in the hall, stumbling with drunkenness. My father was a peasant, born to the soil. How strange the streets of Chicago must have seemed to him that night. He arrived home, checked in on his sleeping daughters; in the tiny bedroom he shared with his wife, an infant fussed in its cradle. My father had a black eye that was beginning to swell, a cut across his cheek, bruises. His right hand, still clenched, hummed with the force of the one good blow he had landed. He sat on the edge of the bed and imagined his future, and what he saw was not a saloon, the row of men nursing beer and ancient grudges. What he saw was a farm, and horses, and a stream flowing past fields into woods. He entered this vision as if walking into a room, and he knew that what he was seeing was his life. It was a future he understood, the one he believed in. He would find it, and take his family there.

What I do not know about my parents—the gaps in my knowledge of their history—tells me as much about the people they were as what I do know. The most basic, controlling fact of their lives was that they were born peasants. To many, the word is an unflattering one. A peasant, it is believed, is a kind of mule—a person without education, certainly unsophisticated, probably not very smart. His life is one of backbreaking toil that enriches others but not himself; his vision of the world is narrow and superstitious, composed of dull fact swaddled by a cloud of airy religion, and he carries into his days no hope for something better, no vision for a life other than the one he sees before him, like the plain dinner of hard bread, bitter vegetables, and chewy meat on his plate. When a peasant is asked to sign his name on a legal document—no doubt one he has not read and one that cheats him somehow—he holds the pen as stiffly as a fork as he draws his illiterate *X*. He lives and works and dies—dumbly, like an animal—on the same square of unforgiving ground, never knowing quite why, and his final thoughts are only of exhaustion.

None of this was true of my parents. Yes, their lives were bound up in work, and they were never rich, and the world was not always fair or kind to them. But they could read and write and think, and they saw more of the world than most of us. Born in Poland in the early 1880s, they traveled halfway around the world to make their home in the United States, and they did so at a time when such journeys were dangerous and complicated and took years of planning to accomplish. They were careful, smart, and capable people, and they owned their own lives.

What I mean when I say that my parents were peasants is that they were serious people who did not dwell upon themselves. It has become accepted today to speak openly about one's deepest feelings, to confess in the most painstaking detail one's private emotional history—even to tell these things to one's children—but my parents would no more have done this than believe that someday men would walk on the moon. To my parents, the past was the past, and the heart a private domain. Disappointments were nothing to dwell on, hopes not something to discuss. Their ambitions were modest: to keep food on the table, a roof above their heads and their children's heads; to live with quiet usefulness and dignity in a world that owed them nothing. In a word, to survive.

So what I know of my parents' early lives is limited to a string of bare-bones facts, and a few stories they liked to tell. But there is much between the lines.

My father, Peter Piszek, was born in 1883, my mother, Anna, just two years later, both in the tiny town of Tarnow, about sixty miles east of Krakow. My mother, whose family name was Sikora, was one of five children, my father one of ten. Both were born on subsistence farms, though my father's family's was significantly larger—thirty acres, compared to my mother's ten. In these numbers lay their fates; because their parents' modest holdings gave them no legacy, from the start, they were destined to emigrate. Much of the spectacular migration to American shores at the close of the nineteenth century can be accounted for by such simple geometry. Such farms as my grandparents' could pass only to one son; my mother, if she wished to be a farmer's wife, would have to find an oldest son to marry. Thus, of fifteen children—my parents and thirteen aunts and uncles—all but two immigrated to the United States, a story repeated in countless villages across eastern and western Europe.

They did not leave until their early twenties, and the precise year of their passage I do not know. (1904? 1905? Either could be true.) They had been friends in Poland, even dated for a time, but in the mad dash to America, they lost track of one another. To earn their passages, each had worked many years—my father as a farmhand, my mother as a housekeeper to her parish priest. No doubt there are records, somewhere, of my parents' separate entries at Ellis Island, the greatest of all doorways to American shores. They traveled with friends, unaware of one another, arriving months apart. But once arrived, their experience was, at least for the moment, the same: two more young Poles stepping from the floating nationlessness of a passenger ship into the spectacular chaos of Ellis Island's Great Hall. Some twelve million would eventually make the journey through that one cavernous room—even today, nearly half of all Americans can claim an ancestor who passed through the Great Hall—and at the time my parents arrived, the Immigration Station, just a decade old, was processing a million newcomers annually, nearly three thousand every day. For most, the anxieties of a treacherous journey across the sea were not soothed by what they found. No bands played, no flags flew, no trace of welcome was offered to acknowledge the great, hopeful gesture of beginning new lives as Americans; in the Great Hall thousands milled, clutching children and knotted bedsheets to hold their possessions, while a dozen languages and a hundred dialects ricocheted through the air like the sound of a terrible orchestra tuning up. A fellow Pole might have clutched at my father's sleeve, murmuring rumors of deportation; my mother, moving into the turbulence within and taking her place in line, might have heard whispers that some had waited for weeks, sleeping on the floor, only to be turned away. Idle rumors: for the vast majority, my parents included, the process was swift and successful. Forms were filled out, papers passed around; in a ledger book, their names were etched in ink by a grumpy, overtired clerk. They might have eyed him curiously, thinking: *That's all?* And it was. A door swung open, and they stepped into the bright light of America.

For Poles coming to the United States in the first decade of the twentieth century, there was really only one destination, one Mecca: Chicago. Again, my parents found their ways there separately. My father's route was more circuitous. His first stop was the anthracite region of Pennsylvania, near Scranton, where a strong man could find work in the mines. For four years he dug the ground for coal, and in that time he put aside enough money to buy the tavern in Chicago that Big John would later tear to shreds. He also married, though I know little about this, not even his wife's name. His first life in America as a Pennsylvania miner was one of those private matters he never discussed, though I am tempted to guess that, like so many women at that time, his wife may have died in childbirth. By age thirty my father was a widower and had had enough of mining. He was still strong and sturdy, but in some ways, he was already an old man: he had lost a country and a wife.

Chicago was his next destination—a sensible choice, for there, his loneliness might be cured among the legions of Poles who worked the stockyards and factories. And in Chicago, the story goes, he found my mother—or rather, found her again. I would like to think they simply bumped into one another on the street, as if their reunion were stitched in the stars, but the truth is probably less romantic. More than likely they reconnected through mutual friends, for in Chicago, my father would have sought out people he knew from the Old Country.

My mother, too, had already lived a full life in America. Indeed, her circumstances had become truly dire. In Chicago, she had met and married a Swede named Arthur Peterson, an engineer, and they had three daughters, my sisters Irene, Alice, and May. Together they had settled into a prosperous middle-class life. But then she, too, lost her spouse. How Peterson died I do not know; as with my father's first wife, Peterson passed unremarked into history. Still a young woman, my mother was left virtually penniless, with three daughters all below the age of five. When my father found her in Chicago, she had returned to work as a housekeeper, a trade that barely sustained her.

It must have seemed an act of fate that they were reunited and that such a stroke of luck was a reason to fall in love and marry. So desperate were my mother's straits that she even offered to give up her three girls for adoption if my father would marry her—an extravagant and desperate bluff, of course, and a test of his character that he passed. My father's refusal was swift. Thenceforth, he said, they would be his daughters, his flesh and blood, and from this principle he never once veered.

So, in 1914, my parents—a widow and a widower, ill-used but still hopeful that life in America would turn out as they wished—were married. A simple ceremony: just her daughters were in attendance and a few friends from their South Chicago neighborhood. Like so many immigrants, they had left their families behind and could only write to them of the news. En route to the church, they stopped at a photographer's studio to mark the occasion, and that image, which I still possess, seems to me the most eloquent document of who they were and of their lives before I was born.

It is a striking photograph, and if I were describing the image to someone who had never seen it, I would first say that it is an affectionate picture—that the two people in it seem to love one another, and that the formality of their pose amplifies this fact and dignifies it. Though many photos of that era reveal all too poignantly the hardness of life, bodies and faces worn quickly down by time, this is not the case with my parents. They are attractive people, even beautiful, and still young. Certainly my mother is beautiful. She has a soft, heart-shaped face—a Polish face—and her dark hair, thick and gleaming, is drawn up and away from her brow and cheeks and secured in place with a flowered garland anchoring the extravagant lace veil that cascades down her back. Only the flesh of her face is showing, and an inch or two on her upper arms, for her hands are gloved to the elbows, and her wedding gown, consistent with the era, is high-necked, riding almost to her chin. Perfectly tailored, its flowing skirt surrenders at a nipped waist to a bodice embroidered with lace and small white stones. She is every inch the bride.

The groom, my father, is likewise a handsome specimen. Looking at the picture, one might just as easily imagine him a banker, a railroadman, an heir to some great fortune, as the coal miner turned taverner that he was. He sits beside my mother on a low stool—the effect, again, is formal, although one can also discern that the photographer has posed him in this manner, because he is a good deal taller than his bride. He wears a tuxedo of early twentieth-century vintage, rather like a morning coat, and from his lapel bursts forth a plump corsage that complements the flowers wreathing my mother's hair. His face is what some might call an interesting face, with somewhat large and out-turned ears, a pronounced widow's peak, smooth cheeks, and jet-black hair oiled close to the scalp. Most remarkable of all is his mustache. It is the kind a child might draw, thick and bushy and waxed into delicate points at the tips. Hands folded, he sits stiffly, though not uncomfortably, and my mother stands beside him, both of her gloved hands perched on his right shoulder, forming a kind of loop. Behind them the eye discovers an ersatz wall of books—probably one of several painted canvases that newlyweds could choose as a backdrop. My parents, educated through the sixth grade, have chosen a library, no doubt the grandest thing they could imagine. They gaze into the camera with tight-lipped seriousness, almost without expression, but I imagine that the moment after the photo was taken, they blinked away the brightness of the flash and smiled; for it was their wedding day.

A year later, they had a daughter, my sister Cecilia. Two years after, I came along, my father's first and only son. Then, Big John, breathing 100-proof hellfire and dumb animal rage, tore up my father's bar.

The conductor said I was in a class by myself, the only child he had ever heard cry the entire distance between Chicago and Philadelphia. I was just a year old, and though I did not know it, I had nothing to cry about. We were headed to what, I still believe, is the very best place on earth.

These days, it might seem foolish to sell off a business and relocate a thousand miles because of one bad customer. But Poles—or rather, the kind of Pole that my father was—can be the most impulsive of people. And I believe, too, that it was a kind of homesickness, a yearning for the peasant life, that prompted our journey. Big John was merely the match that lit the fuse. With the help of his brother William, who had settled near Philadelphia, my father had purchased a sixty-acre farm in Quakertown, Pennsylvania, about forty miles northwest of the city in rural Bucks County. I would spend the first seven years of my life there among the woods and fields, living an existence that was in many ways a meticulous re-creation of nineteenth-century European agrarian life.

Today, the house and its fields look hauntingly untouched, though a closer look reveals that the enterprise has changed: the simple frame structure where we lived, with neither indoor plumbing nor electric light and the simplest homespun furnishings, has been refashioned as a gracious country home. Some of the fields have been returned to woods, and a marshy plot bordering the house to the south has been excavated for a duck pond. Like much of Bucks County, the age of the automobile and the suburban corporate corridor (several major drug companies are headquartered just a few miles from Quakertown) has recast my boyhood arcadia in upscale terms. But in 1916, the idea that someday my parents' sixty acres would be prime Bucks County real estate would have seemed absurd, and indeed, the land was not all that expensive. Beautiful as it was, it was not particularly good for farming, and my father got it cheap. Bordering a creek, perhaps a third of our plot was too low and wet for planting, while another twenty acres were thickly wooded with a tangle of trees and vines. The higher fields, though dry enough, were littered with rocks, some the size of steamer trunks. It was difficult land to farm, and my parents worked it for subsistence, following traditional European practices; we kept a dozen dairy cows, some chickens, a few pigs for winter meat, and with a pair of big Belgian horses, my father turned the fields to plant potatoes, rye, and wheat. Perhaps a few acres were given over to truck farming, and near the house, to a vegetable plot that my mother tended with the girls. It was a simple existence, in most ways more Polish than American, more nineteenth century than twentieth. Quakertown was the farm my parents could never have had in the old country.

I have no doubt that it was a hard life, for my father especially, but I do not remember it this way. What I do remember is this: picking potato bugs in the garden and chasing the butterflies that swarmed in summer; the aroma, dizzyingly sweet, of the apple and cherry trees in the old orchard that someone had planted long ago; the mad dash to the outhouse on cold winter mornings; the sour smell of the chickens and their insane clucking; watching my father push a fistful of mud into a horse's face, a trick he learned in Poland to make a stubborn animal behave; launching a kite high over our meadow, so high I believed it hung over the very world itself; walking with my sisters in winter dusk to the general store to buy kerosene for our lamps, each tree twisted into ghoulish shapes by the winter dusk; being whisked skyward by my father and plopped on the back of one of his draft horses, so thrilled and terrified all at once that I burst, predictably, into tears.

Brief snatches of memory, like single snapshots of the senses; my world then was as small as I was. Though we had neighbors across the road, a family named Heinz, and I was dimly aware that somewhere not far there was a one hundred–acre farm (I had heard my parents talking of it; surely its owners were rich), I had no sense that the world went much past the edges of our fields, nor beyond the old mill stream where I dreamily passed whole days, lost in games of the imagination. Of all the lush corners on my parents' farm, it was our stream, a branch of Tohickon Creek, that cast the deepest spell over me. It seemed, even then, to suggest the richness of the world beyond; it was a highway, a road to the future and my life, and now, three-quarters of a century later, it still courses through my heart, a memory as beautiful as Eden. Passing our house, it made a gentle bend where boulders formed a hole, and because sheep had once been washed there (How? By whom? I didn't know), we called it Sheep Hole. In summer, it formed a perfect basin for swimming, protected from the currents, and in winter, great flows of debris and ice would dam and lodge there, building a glittering palace of ice and stone that sent my mind spinning to thoughts of Arctic lands. Several years later, after my parents had sold the farm and we returned on weekends to visit (the owners were friends, childless, and invited us every Sunday for a picnic), I fashioned a fishing pole from an old branch and cast my bent pin and worm into Tohickon's lazy current and pulled, one by one, eight bass into the mist of a spring morning. Eight fish! I had just turned eight years old, and the coincidence dazzled me. I have subsequently fished all over the world, owned my own camp in Maine and spent years at another in Alaska, but never in all the years have I experienced anything like the thrill of that moment, standing in triumph with my homemade pole and eight smallmouth bass lined up before me on the banks of the Tohickon.

And once, another time, I was walking by the stream when I heard music, at a distance, from the woods on the other side. Someone was playing an instrument—a flute, or perhaps a clarinet. It was haunting, that sound, soft and lilting, never quite forming a melody. It was as if it came from another world, and I would dream about it often in the years that followed. I called out: *Who's there?* But there was no answer, and I never did find out, nor did I ever cross that river to see what lay on the other side.

I was not to be the baby long. That spot was taken, soon after we moved to the farm, by my sister Amelia. But I was the only boy, and for my father, the only son. Of Old World stock, he placed special importance on that fact, an emphasis that sometimes drifted into outright favoritism. No doubt today such preferential treatment would receive general disapproval, but back then, no; it was practically expected, and I hardly minded. How I would follow my father around! I had few other children to play with—my sisters, either too old or too young, held little interest for me—and when my chores were done (and later, when I returned from school, a half-mile walk each way), I would wander out to the fields to find him, to watch and learn. Like all boys, I understood instinctively that my father was the man

I would someday become, that his life would be mine. Sitting on a fence post while he plowed the fields or traipsing after him to the barn for evening milkings, I studied his every move. He was a self-contained man, never sentimental or outspoken about his feelings, but I understood I was his favorite; he would tolerate no interference from the girls, whereas he seemed pleased, or at least content, to let me bide my time in his shadow as he went about his chores. Not one for words, he treated me often to small gifts. Returned from town, he might reach into his coat pocket and produce for me a new ball of kite string, or a small toy, or else—and this he did often—a pile of bright pennies for me to keep. Perhaps the greatest thrill of all was to accompany him to the creamery in town to visit with the other farmers. I would stand and listen to them talk about their chores, about the prices of land and wheat, and wait until one of them might notice me.

"Say, Pete," one might say to my father, "what's that you have there?"

"There?" he would laugh. "Why, that's my son, Eddie. What do you think of him?"

An appreciative nod. "A fine-looking boy. Is he for sale?"

"He might be. If you come up with the right figure."

"Well, how much are you looking for?"

And so on, right up until the naming of a final figure (ten dollars at least), at which point my father would say: no, he guessed that he would keep me after all.

Pennies, kite string, voyages to town. Each was a part of the greater whole, the wonderful gift my parents gave me: a happy childhood, one as close to the natural world as their own had been. And thus a seed was planted. For although I was born within sight of Chicago's skyscrapers and factories, it was on that Quakertown farm that I met the world—a farm where Polish was spoken, the land was worked for subsistence, and life followed the ageless rhythms of the peasantry. I may be an American, but my roots are Polish roots. *Scotch, scotch,* my father would say to us kids as we set about our chores—a Polish word meaning "jump." Years later, in many, many business dealings when speed was important, I would find myself whispering "scotch"—and in an instant, I would be flooded by memories of those happy, simple times.

Happiest of all were summer Sundays, when my extended family of aunts and uncles—many of whom had also settled near Philadelphia—would drive out to the farm. In the era of the six-day workweek, when the automobile was new and marvelous, the grandest pleasure on a day off was to take a Sunday drive, and for my parents' friends and family, our farm was the destination. Sometimes thirty or more people would arrive; their Model Ts lined our long driveway from the house, food was unloaded, and soon the meadow would ring with the sounds of Polish mixed with English, laughter and talk, the squeals of children running everywhere. None of us had very much money in those days—butter, for instance, was one thing almost no one could afford—but no one cared. A great picnic was spread beneath the trees—ample, simple fare—and the afternoon would pass in a merry haze of games and songs and jokes.

I could have spent all my life there. But it was not to be. Nor was I to have my father as long as I would have wished. I would lose him when I was fifteen, far too soon—before I had really begun. So now when I remember those days on our Quakertown farm it is also with some sadness, and that sadness is etched in one final memory.

A day in spring: I had just returned from school, and as on so many other afternoons, I went looking for my father to see if I could help. I looked in the barn, on the upper fields, down by the slough, but found him nowhere. Dejected, I returned to the house, where my mother sat in the kitchen.

"Where have you been? Your father is looking for you," she said. "He's been waiting to see if you'd drive into town with him. Scotch, scotch!"

Somehow I had missed him. I tore out of the house in time to see the back end of his Model T heading out the drive. A quarter mile of soft dirt connected the house to the main road, and I broke into a run, hoping to catch him. "Pop!" I yelled, "Pop, wait!" But he didn't stop; the engine was too loud, or else he was ignoring me. Perhaps he was playing a game. I raced after him, always twenty feet behind. Whenever he slowed to negotiate a rut or pothole I would close the gap, then watch it widen with dismay as he accelerated once more. At one point, I nearly touched his bumper only to see it torn from my grasp. I yelled for him, again and again: "Pop, Pop, Pop!" At last he reached the end of the drive, turned, and chugged down the road.

I sat on the ground, breathless and half in tears, listening to the sound of his engine as it sputtered into the hills. He didn't hear me, I thought. If he had heard me, he would have waited.

Chapter Two
Nicetown

I remember the red of the bricks, the sound of my heart beating—then a voice next to my ear and breath so sour I gagged.

"Close your eyes! Close 'em I said!"

I did as I was told. I clamped my eyes and waited for the promised blow to fall, but instead, felt Loki's fat hand moving nimbly through my jacket pockets. With the other hand he pushed against my spine, crushing my face to the moist stone of the alley wall. "Stay up against that wall, Peez-a-wacker. Do as you're told or I'm going to put this fist right through your head!"

But the nickel that he wanted wasn't there; I had learned not to keep my money anywhere Loki could get at it so easily. Instinctively I curled my toes inside my left shoe, feeling the hard disc of the nickel I had stashed there. I collected such nickels by running phone messages up the block; my father's store had the only phone in the neighborhood. That number will be forever etched into my memory: Wyoming-10248.

"Turn around!"

Before I could obey, Loki seized my shoulders and spun me bodily and hauled me into closer view. He was an ugly kid, simply enormous, though perhaps my memory embellishes here; Loki was all of twelve years old. But I was just nine, small and soft—my sisters called me "butterball"—and it didn't take much to terrorize me.

He pushed his fleshy face into mine and snarled, "The shoes, Peez-a-wacker."

I feigned innocence. "My shoes? That's kind of low, even for you, to steal a kid's shoes."

A fat smile. "It's what's inside the shoes, Peez-on."

Defeated, I removed my left shoe—the one that held the nickel, for there seemed to be no point in prolonging my defeat—and handed it to him.

"Peee-ew, Peez-a-wacker. Don't you wash those feet of yours? And *saaaaaay* . . . what do we have here?" He turned the shoe over, and deposited the shiny coin into his hand. He held it up into the grimy light of the alleyway. "That's all? Just a lousy nickel? Cripes, it's hardly worth the trouble."

"That's all I have, I swear."

Just then my older sister, May, turned the corner and saw me pushed up against the wall, one shoe still on, the other in Loki's hand. She looked at me and frowned, her hands buried in the pockets of her apron.

"Eddie, where have you been? There's another phone call, for Mary Swenson up the block. Scotch! Scotch!"

Loki handed me my shoe. The coin had already disappeared into his pocket. "You're lucky this time, Peez-a-wacker," he whispered. "I'll see you later."

As I walked with May up the block, I turned to her. "Who's Mary Swenson?"

"No one." She smiled at me. "I made her up. I was just happening by and it looked like you could use some help. Was I wrong?"

"No," I admitted. "I'm glad you did."

"And you're all right?"

"Sure," I said. "Never better."

She shrugged helplessly. "Just try to be careful, Eddie."

Be careful. It was sage advice, though there was no way to follow it. Better to say: be smart. Run when you can't fight, duck when you can't win. When all else fails, be lucky.

And it wasn't the worst thing in the world, what had happened to me—that, at the age of seven, I had been plucked from the fields of my parents' farm and set down again, like a weed whose seed is carried on spring winds, in the concrete canyons of Philadelphia.

I think that my father had run our farm as successfully as such a farm could be, but I also know that he had tired of the effort, the grueling labor and nagging uncertainty that came with such a life. When would it rain? What price would his wheat and potatoes fetch at market? Though he was still young and strong, the strain had begun to show on him. Still, the day he told us all that he had sold it, I was crestfallen. The Quakertown farm was, after all, the only life I had ever known, and when he announced that we would be moving to Philadelphia—a city!—he might have told me we were moving to the surface of the moon. Philadelphia—that great, five-syllabled metropolis—was always out there somewhere, a gray smudge beyond the horizon of my consciousness. I had relatives who lived there, and my sisters had visited, returning with tales of the shops and offices and surging crowds, their eyes lighted with wonder at the many marvels they had seen. But to me, a child of seven, raised on butterflies and black-eyed Susans, such a place was beyond imagining. Not counting Chicago, the largest town I had laid eyes on was tiny Quakertown, and that just a handful of times. Philadelphia was something else entirely.

For my parents, the move also marked a return to the life they had begun in Chicago, a life of dollar bills and ringing registers. No tavern this time, but its opposite: as if to make up for the sins of that earlier venture (which would not have lasted anyway; Prohibition lay hard on the land), my father had purchased a small sweet shop in a neighborhood called Nicetown. A small brick row home on the corner of the block, it housed both the store and our modest apartment, above and to the rear. Quarters were tight, and we slept three kids to a room; I shared a bed with my younger sister Amelia, and to this day the rhythm of her breathing as she slept is stitched into my consciousness. We had no yard at all, just an alleyway of hard-packed dirt with laundry lines strung across it; standing at the front door, I couldn't see a single tree.

For me, the change was earth-shattering. I entered a world for which, in nearly every way, I was utterly unprepared. I didn't know how to play baseball or basketball or football or soccer; I didn't know how to skate or ride a bike or how to hit a ball with a broomstick or bang two eggs together while cracking only one. By the age of seven, a city boy was expertly versed in all of these tricks and many more. But more than games—which I could and would learn quickly—I was completely unacquainted with the very idea of competition, the ceaseless testing that boys faced at the hands of other boys. It is strange, but until that time, I have no memory of male friends or experience with boys, even at school. With four girls, our house in Quakertown was a house of women, and my interests—the woods, the fields, the garden—had a feminine softness, an easy relationship to natural things. I had no knowledge of machines or sports or war; I had never in my life pretended to shoot someone, or be shot, or raised a fist in anger (the very idea repelled me); I had never engaged myself in any activity in which someone would be the loser and someone else the winner. In sum, I had not yet been masculinized by the culture; I was, at the age of seven, a kind of girl.

I don't remember my first fight (my run-ins with Loki began a few years later), but it might have gone something like this:

"Oh, yeah?"

"Yeah!"

"You gonna make me?"

"You bet I am!"

And so on, leading to blows, bloody noses, and bruises. The subject of disagreement might have been nothing more weighty than whether or not it was warm enough to wear the collar of one's jacket down (we always wore jackets, thinking they looked tougher), or if someone had given over half his apple to share (*yakkies* was the term), or simply a random challenge, issued out of the unstructured boredom of an interminable summer afternoon. We needed no subject, really, to set our fists flying, and we fought as much amongst our friends as against our enemies, real or imagined. Despite its name, Nicetown was a rough-and-tumble place where the men scratched out a living in the factories and mills, and the kids scratched out a world of their own on the streets. Though we lived just a few miles from Center City, with its glittering department stores and hotels and halls of commerce and government, no one ever went there. Poking the heavens to the south, the tall buildings of downtown might just as well have been a diorama or a painted backdrop.

It was axiomatic to life on those streets that a boy belonged to a gang, for without friends to protect you, you had no chance. I quickly fell in with a group of boys on my block who called themselves, with romantic flair, "The Bloody Shirts." I remember just a few by name: Johnny Pete, who was, though neither the oldest nor the toughest, our leader; his first lieutenant, a rangy kid we called Droopy, who never picked up his feet when he walked; and last, a boy who never carried a handkerchief and so earned the unhappy nickname Snotty. Taking our cues from the gangsters we read about in the paper and saw in the movies, we went in for such nicknames, and I had my share, always some off-color variation on my name: Peez-on, Peez-on-your-leg. All told, we numbered about a score, with new members always drifting in just as old ones exited (often headed for real, grown-up trouble).

Within that world, there were rules we lived by. We were rug rats, ankle biters, wisecracking squirts no older than twelve, but we regarded ourselves with deadly seriousness and concocted a code of conduct as rigid as any I have ever known. The first rule was conformity. For instance, you never wore a hat or gloves or galoshes no matter what the weather, because not all of us had them, and on the most frigid days, I would hide my gloves in my pockets, as if the cold were nothing. There was no such thing as private property; woe betide the kid who set foot out of his house with a candy bar or apple without the intention to share. (On the other hand, eating it in the house would have felt like cheating.) In winter, the expression we used was "chip or get"; around four-thirty, darkness coming on, we would build a fire from scraps of wood in an empty lot, toss in some potatoes (usually pinched from the vegetable stand when the grocer was not looking), scrape off the skin, and eat away. Chip or get—chip in a potato or get out. Black stuff all over our faces. All part of the ritual.

Most formally elaborate were our rules of war. We fought with our fists only (a weapon of any sort was out of the question) and maintained a strict adherence to the Marquis of Queensbury rules. You never hit below the belt or hit a man after he had fallen; most important of all, you never interfered in another man's fight. (I use the term *man* as we did, for that was how we saw ourselves.) If your buddy was getting the worst of it, you might step in and try to stop the fight, but you would never gang up on his opponent. Perhaps it wasn't the best way to settle our differences, but at least it worked, and in the end, the damage we did to one another was small.

I was hardly the most courageous of my peers; at age ten, I had to struggle to chin myself but once, and even the most basic aspects of fisticuffs eluded me. Most of my friends learned to fight at home, but my father was no Joe Louis. (His virtues were many, but a knowledge of sports, especially American sports, was not one of them.) I took my licks, and if I couldn't win—and I almost never did—at least I acquitted myself honorably. A bloody nose would heal; in the eyes of my peers, it was far better to fight and lose than not to fight at all.

A gang of urchins needs something else to do besides beat one another up, and in our case, the solution to long, boring summer days and afternoons after school (where we barely paid attention) was petty crime. In those days, gangsters were glamorous characters; Prohibition, whatever its noble aims, had the effect of criminalizing a large portion of the American middle class (who drank anyway), and in newspapers and on the radio, men the likes of Al Capone, who kept the booze flowing, were hailed as "public servants." Popular opinion would eventually turn against them, but in the late twenties, tommy gun–toting gangsters were romantic figures to us, a new breed of gunslinger more compelling even than the cowboys of the Old West.

Thus, it was a small leap for us from the imagined criminal exploits of cops and robbers to the real thing. As a small-time thief, I began slowly, almost by accident—stealing fruit or candy from the grocery store, raiding someone's garden for tomatoes, "borrowing" a bicycle at the Logan Library (no one locked bicycles then; the trick was to ride it around for a day or so until the owner might notice, then trade it in at the library for a "new one"). We soon graduated to burglary. Johnny Pete, who seemed to have a flair for such things, cased the stores in our neighborhood, picking out the ones that the owners did not live above; a week or two later, we would sneak out at night, jimmy one of the skylights (Johnny Pete's father was a carpenter, and so we used his tools), and raid the place, filling our pockets with all the candy and cigarettes we could carry. The registers never had any cash in them; the owners were too smart for that. But they would leave the silver behind, and we would take that too, often returning the next day to buy candy with the same nickels and dimes we had stolen the night before.

We robbed so many stores I barely recall any of them in particular. But there is one I will always remember. The California Fruit Store on Germantown Avenue was more than a grocery—it was the neighborhood bootlegger. Rather than let old, unsold fruit spoil, the owners had set up a huge still in the back shed and were making wine by the gallons. (Most of it awful, I'm sure. But during Prohibition, people would drink anything as long as it was fermented.) For the Bloody Shirts, the cache of wine was too tempting, like a fat plum waiting to be picked. The summer I turned ten, a dozen of us broke in and stole as much wine as we could haul away. It was ghastly stuff, but there was no stopping us; we carted it to a vacant lot and proceeded to poison ourselves. Fortunately I knew when to quit (more likely, I was too small to put very much away), but most of my friends did not; challenging one another to drink more, more, more, they pickled themselves to unconsciousness. One more rite of passage accomplished.

Looking back, I'm amazed that we didn't get in more trouble than we did. We were kids, after all, and I don't see how our parents failed to catch on. But mine, at least, seemed cheerfully oblivious. Then came the summer I turned eleven.

It would be our greatest summer ever. Droopy and Johnny Pete had lined up over twenty different stores to rob, vegetable stands and mom-and-pops strung all the way from Midvale Steel to Simon Gratz High School. From the first warm day of spring we awaited the freedom of the final bell in June, whereupon we would unleash a reign of terror on Nicetown, steal every Zagnut and pack of Chesterfields that wasn't nailed down. We paced like caged cats, greedily thinking of our take. The loot was as good as ours. The Bloody Shirts would go down in history.

But then, the night before the final night of school, my father made an announcement. We had just finished dinner, and as he leaned back in his chair, he smiled at me, the same smile he always wore when he was about to bestow some gift or favor on me.

"Eddie," he said, "I have a surprise for you. Tomorrow is your last day of school. I thought this weekend, as a treat, we could all drive out to Quakertown."

This was nothing new. We visited the old farm at least once a month in summer, sometimes more, for picnic outings. All well and good, I thought. Our crime spree could wait a day or two, certainly.

"Fine, Dad."

"Oh, but that's not the half of it. You see, I know how much you miss it out there." His smile widened. "You're a born farmer, if ever I saw one. I've spoken to the owners, and they've agreed for you to spend the summer out there."

Two whole months! I felt my riches—all that candy, all those cigarettes, all that loose change—slip through my fingers like so much sand.

"Edward?" It was my mother speaking. "What do you say?"

I tried to conceal my disappointment, though I'm sure my face was etched with horror. "That's great, Dad. Thank you."

My father tousled my hair. "It's settled then."

I wonder if my father knew. A week later, breaking into the grocery up the street, Johnny Pete crashed through the skylight, thus ending the Bloody Shirts' great summer crime wave before it had really begun. Johnny wasn't badly hurt, but the sound of his yells and the breaking glass woke up half the block, and I imagine that when the cops showed up, he was more frightened than anything else. The other boys had fled but were quickly rounded up; it didn't take much thought to figure out who else was involved.

There was one kid, though, who obviously wasn't. He couldn't have been. Little Eddie Piszek was spending the summer in the country.

I don't know what became of those boys. No doubt many drifted into worse trouble, while others settled down into ordinary lives of work, marriage, and trying to keep their own kids out of mischief. They would be old men now.

The year after Johnny Pete fell through the skylight, we moved again, across Germantown Avenue into North Philadelphia. Though just a few blocks away (and technically still part of Nicetown), it was an altogether different kind of neighborhood. Bordering Stenton Park, it had a cleaner, greener feel to it, and parents kept a closer eye on their kids, who passed their afternoons in far more innocent pastimes: "Peggy" (a version of stickball) and "wireball" (an absurdly simple game: the only object was to bounce a Spaulding rubber ball off a telephone pole), as well as any other amusement we could concoct. The neighborhood was still working-class, mostly Irish and German with a smattering of Polish thrown in, and on summer evenings when the heat in our narrow row homes grew too close, all the parents would gather on their front stoops to drink lemonade and talk and watch us kids play. Under their gaze, my days as a junior hooligan were over, and it came as a great relief.

My father, too, had traded up in the world. Though the sweetshop had been profitable as such things went, it was a seasonal business, and in the winters he had been forced to take odd jobs of various kinds to make ends meet. (For a year or two, he had even traveled back to Scranton on weekends to work in the mines.) A methodical man, he had seen the limits to this enterprise and put enough money aside to purchase a small mom-and-pop store. It was a combined grocery and deli, no larger than a good-sized living room, and once again, we lived above it. (Quarters were still tight, though we had one less body to house: my sister Alice had married and moved out.) Our address was 1717 Wingohocking Street, a real tongue twister; in school, my teachers were always asking me to spell not only my name but my street as well.

I had been too young to be of much help with the sweetshop, but now that I was older, it was time to pitch in. Everyone brown-bagged it in those days; almost all the blue-collar workers in our neighborhood carried their lunch with them to work, and to get ready for them, my parents opened the store at 5:30 in the morning. Several days a week it was my job to help out with the morning shift before school—making sandwiches and selling coffee, sweetrolls, and doughnuts to the men on their way to the mills and factories—and again after school, stocking shelves and slicing meat and keeping the store clean. Shelf space was at a premium; canned goods came forty-eight to a case, but because we had room for only a dozen, we had to keep the overflow in the basement, and it was my job to keep the inventory flowing, scrambling down to the basement and then up again, my arms full of cans, flying up and down the ladder like Edmund Hillary on Mt. Everest. There were times when I ached to be out playing with my friends, but for the most part, I liked my first taste of work, the morning hours especially—the ritual of rising before dawn, setting the coffee on to brew, standing on the front stoop in the early stillness to watch as lights blinked on in all the houses. And then our first customer would appear—black coffee, a doughnut, a ham sandwich to go—and then another and another, and soon we were subsumed in the headlong chaos of the morning rush, and before I knew it, I would lift my head to see that it was 7:30 and time for school.

I was not always so industrious. On sunny afternoons after school, when the park seemed to call out to me and when my father had gone out to get his paper, I would sometimes sneak out of the store to play with my friends. Sooner or later my father would come looking for me, and I would spot him, a tall figure carrying the paper, coming over the rise; I can still hear his voice calling, "Ed! Ed!" As soon as I heard him I would take off like a shot, tearing through the maze of back alleys—left at Mrs. O'Leary's, a hard right at the Kurtzweillers', under the neighbor's laundry line, and across the avenue—and by the time my father returned, there I would be, damp and winded, innocently stacking cans of tomato soup on the shelves. I looked at him quizzically: *Yes? Were you looking for me?*

"Now," he might say, smoothing his mustache, "I could have *sworn* you weren't here a minute ago. And out of breath! How lucky I am to have a son who works so *very* hard. . . ."

I worked until 7:00, when the store closed. But there were always tasks left to do, and I raced through my final chores, waiting for that moment when my father would nod, releasing me. "Over here, Ed. This counter needs wiping," he might say, prolonging my agony. Or, "Those shelves over there don't look as neat as they should." But sooner or later he acquiesced, sending me on my way with a final admonishment not to stray too far. Then I was flying out the door, beating it up the street to 16th and Cortland to check out whatever was going on. All up and down the street radios were playing the *Amos 'n' Andy Show*, sponsored by Pepsodent ("You'll wonder where the yellow went, when you brush your teeth with Pepsodent"), and if I timed my trip just right, I could hear the entire fifteen-minute show as I passed building after building.

The lessons of the neighborhood streets and of working in my parents' store were far more valuable to me than anything in my formal education. In the classroom, first at J. Coop Jr. Junior High, then Simon Gratz High School, I was an average student at best. I would like to think I was bright enough to do better, but in those days, the system was quick to categorize you. At Simon Gratz, students were placed on one of three tracks: the academic track, for those students who seemed to possess the ability and background to go to college; the commercial track, which was mostly typing and clerical; and the industrial track, for students who needed to learn a trade. I was the son of a grocer from North Philadelphia; what possible good could college preparatory courses do for someone like me? I don't even remember being asked; someone in an office simply signed the forms, and I became an industrial student, learning automobile repair. I had little in the way of English or mathematics or foreign language; the assumption was that an industrial student was neither able nor inclined to pursue such things, a ludicrous belief on its face, because a blue-collar background says nothing about native talent or ambition, and many of us spoke a foreign language at home. (We frequently used Polish in my house, especially when family visited.) On the other hand, I cannot fault the system entirely, because for many students, it was far better to learn a trade than prepare for college courses they would never take.

One thing I did know: I hated automobile repair. My reason was simple. I hated dirty hands—a fastidiousness that I had acquired working in my parents' deli.

And somehow, I had also begun to see myself as different. I knew that automobile repair—and, for that matter, most of what I was learning in school—was largely irrelevant to what lay ahead for me. College, at least full-time, was obviously out of the question. My parents had nothing like the money needed for that, and I doubted they would have seen the sense to it anyway. But I knew that somehow I would find a way to continue my education. Like many fifteen-year-olds, I was an inward-looking boy, sunk down a great deal of the time in the adolescent quicksand of elaborate daydreams, and what I dreamed of was success. I couldn't imagine what form it might take, but I believed such a thing was possible.

My dirty fingernails and wounded pride notwithstanding, my freshman year began in celebration, for in the fall my father made a much-anticipated trip to Poland. Such a voyage was virtually unheard of for peasant immigrants. When a peasant left Poland, it was understood that he left it for good. It was unusual even to write home; to maintain a correspondence with family and friends in the Old Country would have been a poignant reminder of the permanence of separation, too painful to bear. (As a result, I never knew my grandparents, nor heard from them at all, not even a letter—an experience that is widespread among second-generation Polish Americans.) But my father returned, and like a pilgrim he returned alone, leaving my mother to run the store for the month he would be gone.

In some ways, the trip proved to be a disappointment to him. As he later confided, he was not warmly embraced as he had hoped to be, as the prodigal son returned. To the contrary, nearly everyone he spoke to assumed he had become rich (the belief that American streets were paved with gold was no metaphor to folks back home), and asked him for money. But even so, the voyage was for him a crowning achievement. Against the odds, he had mustered the resources to finance such a trip, to revisit the land of his birth. What carried him back was, finally, a pure nostalgia to see Poland again. I recall a photo of him, taken on the deck of the liner that carried him across the Atlantic, and like his wedding photo, it is the most articulate of images. He sits on a wooden deck chair, wearing a gray suit; at forty-nine he is still hale, trim, and handsomely mustachioed; he squints into the sun behind the camera, raising his hand in a gentle wave, though whether in greeting or in parting, it is impossible to say. My father had few interests outside of work and family, and a trip to Poland was, I believe, the only other thing he wanted out of life. So perhaps it is a wave of final victory.

It is over sixty years later, but even now when I drive past the spot on Route 309 where my father died, a twinge passes through me, an icy finger of longing. At fifteen, I was just beginning to know him; I was just old enough, finally, for the conversations that can pass between a father and his grown son. I was ready to hear all he had to tell me. But I never would. The May after he returned from Poland, my father drove out to Richlandtown, near Quakertown, to visit my uncle. On the return trip, his Nash was forced from the road. A car in the oncoming lane had lost control, and to avoid a head-on collision my father veered off to the right, rolling over and striking a tree. He died there in the car.

It happened on a Wednesday, while I was in school. At the end of the day, I came walking up the street, and one of the kids on the block yelled out to me: "Hey, your father died! Your father died!" I thought it was a cruel joke, but when I opened the door to our house and saw all the friends and relatives packed into the kitchen and heard my mother crying, I knew that it was true.

It was a thunderbolt, the abruptness of it all. I don't remember much of the days and weeks that immediately followed my father's death. As anyone who has lost a parent can attest, the feeling goes beyond loss, beyond bereavement. I was old enough to understand what had happened, but a part of me, a large part, rejected the information outright. I could get no traction on anything, and for a time, my mind simply spun, whizzing hopelessly like bald tires on snow. I passed the first few months in a kind of haze, a numbing fog of solitude that I thought would never lift. It was as if I had lost the only person who had ever really known me, ever really cared about me. I became a sullen and difficult boy, and I must recall that period of my life with shame. My mother certainly had enough to worry her, and considerable pain of her own. She was just forty-six and was now twice widowed, with two children still in school and a business to run. And though I helped out in the store, I did so sourly, and whenever my mother refused to accommodate my wishes, I would run upstairs and take my father's picture from the wall and start to cry—hot, manufactured tears, meant to tell her that I had always preferred him and always would. I used my father's ghost like a blackmailer. It was a wonder that she didn't throw me out of the house.

Only one thing could have lifted me from the surly waters of my grief.

The following fall, just before my sixteenth birthday—a somber occasion I did not look forward to without my father there to share it—a group of friends and I went to see a high school football game, at the old Baker Bowl on Broad Street in North Philadelphia, where the Phillies used to play. All my friends knew that my father had died, but they hardly treated me with kid gloves; their strategy for cheering me up was to be as "normal" as possible. Though I was hardly in the mood for a football game, I yielded to their urging to go along.

It was the first game of the year, and although I do not remember who was winning, I know that the game was quickly turning into a fiasco; either Simon Gratz was clobbering their opponents or being clobbered. In either case, the outcome seemed certain from the first ten minutes, and our attention drifted to a group of girls sitting in the row ahead of us. None of us was particularly smooth with women, and to get their attention we began pelting them with peanuts and popcorn.

"Hey!" One of the girls turned and leveled her gaze on me. She had blonde hair, a light spray of freckles across her nose, startling gray eyes. She shook a peanut from her long hair. "What do you think you're doing?"

I was speechless, too embarrassed to talk. She was the most beautiful girl I had ever seen. The light from her eyes seemed to shoot right through me.

"Well?" she demanded. "What gives?"

"Nothing," I stammered. "Just watching the game."

She gave a bright laugh. "Well, watch it then."

She returned to her friends, the group of them giggling, pretending to watch action on the field, all of us suddenly, brightly aware of one another.

One of my friends jostled me with his elbow. "I think she likes you, Piszek."

My face glowed. "Shut up, will you?"

Again his elbow punched my side. "Say something, you big dope."

I desperately wanted to. But what? "Hey," I managed.

She turned around again and gave a bored sigh. "What is it now?"

My voice caught in my throat; somehow, I managed to speak. "What's your name?"

Her name was Olga McFadden.

Chapter Three
Longer Learning

Q uick years; I had a sense that, somehow, the pieces had begun to snap into place. The most important piece was Olga, though from the day I walked her home from Baker Bowl, I never called her that. She was Oddie. Our parents never quite approved (custom dies hard: Oddie was Irish and Protestant, I was Polish and Catholic, and this was enough to make people think twice), but we somehow always found a way to be together. By senior year, it seemed certain that we would marry.

The chief obstacle to everything was money—and time. I was working long hours in the store now, both before and after school; my mother needed the help, with the girls grown and married. But more than that, I had calculated that I would need considerable savings if I was going to continue my education. The year after my father died, I asked her if I could receive a wage for working in the store and put this money aside for school. In the abstract, my mother supported the notion—how could she be opposed to her son getting an education?—but the idea was alien to her. I don't think that for a minute she had ever thought that any of her children would receive an education beyond high school; college was for the rich, not for working people like us. But in the end, she relented. I opened a bank account and watched the money add up—slowly, dime by dime—eyeing it with the intensity of a high-flying stockbroker tracking a ticker tape. Every cent I saved seemed to have the deepest importance; after our dates together, I would take Oddie home on the trolley, but walk the thirty-five blocks home just to save a nickel. My mother said it reminded her of the old days in Chicago before she had met my father, when she was too poor to afford carfare and would hike two miles and more in the snow and bitter wind to the houses she cleaned.

Like a soldier readying himself for battle, I prepared my body, too. A childhood spent dashing down the alleyways of Nicetown—chasing or being chased—had made me fast, and in the last two years of high school, I ran track for Simon Gratz. I was a poor miler, and not long-legged enough for sprints or hurdles, but at in-between distances I could open the throttle and run with the best of them. All those years avoiding Loki had turned me into a first-class quarter miler.

My final memory of high school follows suit; though I hardly recall our graduation ceremony, I remember my final track meet as if it were just hours ago.

Track season was officially over; at the end of the year, the school held a special cross-country race in which any varsity athlete could compete. The course went right through my neighborhood. It was a big event, and I wanted to do well in it, though the distance—two and a half miles—was not a natural one for me. I practiced by myself, running the course for weeks every night after my mother closed the store, until I knew by heart each rise and turn, every telephone pole and every tree. In those days, the sight of someone running was a curiosity, and my nightly workouts on the Nicetown streets were accompanied by a chorus of wisecracks—"Hey Piszek, where's the fire?" and "Hurry up, Piszek, they're gaining on you!" It was annoying, but I had no time to explain.

By the morning of the race, a Saturday in June, I had worked myself up to fever pitch. But when I saw the starting line, my heart sank. No fewer than fifty athletes had shown up for the race. None knew the course as well as I did, but surely I would be outclassed on raw talent alone. I threw all strategy to the wind and faced the line with one plan: run like hell.

At the gun, I sprang out as if I were running a quarter mile—not ten times that distance—jostled my way through the pack, and found myself, amazingly, in the lead. I passed the quarter-mile mark, then the half, then the mile. I was waiting for the lull, the hesitation in my stride that would signal the beginning of the end, but it never came. I ran on adrenaline alone, fueled by the surprising thrill that I still held the lead. With just a half mile to go I remained comfortably in front.

Then I heard, behind me, the sound of feet and breathing, and a rangy fellow I had never seen before, legs long as carnival stilts, huffed past me. I could hear that he was struggling, and I let him pace me till the last quarter mile. Certain that I could pass him, I cut to his left and drew even. The finish line came into view.

"Hey," he said, "why don't we run together? We'll cross at the same time. It'll be a tie."

I had never imagined such an offer. What did it mean? But then I thought: maybe he's not as tired as he seems. Maybe he *can* still beat me.

"Okay," I said, "let's do that."

We ran together to the last fifty yards. At the finish line a group of his friends were screaming, "Come on Luke! Pour it on!" Their urging was all it took. My opponent charged forward, catching me by surprise, and crossed the finish line just in front of me.

What a blunder! All those weeks of training, and I had tossed victory away. Perhaps Luke hadn't planned his move at all—I would like to think he was just pumped up by his friends—but the idea was scant consolation. Victory had been mine, fair and square, and I had bargained it away out of cowardice.

At the finish line, I was mobbed by my teammates, and Oddie threw her arms around me and kissed me.

"What's wrong?" she said, when she saw my face. "You came in second. That's great."

"That's what's wrong." I could hardly get my thoughts straight; and how would it have sounded to say, *I could have won*? "It's nothing," I said, and tried to smile. "That guy sure had a kick, didn't he?"

Graduation would be the next day. After the race, there was an award ceremony and a picnic, and then I took Oddie home. I had put the race out of my mind, but as I walked in twilight up Wingohocking Street, I felt my disappointment return and found myself thinking of my father. That moment of hesitation—would I have been so quick to agree to a tie if my father had been there, watching me? Then, almost without thinking, I spoke aloud, my voice carrying down the street:

"If the race is yours, Ed, win it. Don't cheat but don't get conned, either. If the race is yours to win, don't be afraid to let yourself come out on top."

I looked around, startled. Had anyone noticed or heard? Was it I who was speaking? It was. But those words—they might have been my father's.

After graduation I worked in my mother's deli, and on the advice of one of my teachers (who noticed I had no taste for automobile repair), I began a technical training course at Drexel University in air-conditioning and re-frigeration. It was a sensible choice, but it wasn't what I wanted; it felt like auto repair without the dirty hands. For a business degree, everybody said that the Wharton School at the University of Pennsylvania was the place to go, but I hardly dared imagine that such a place would want me, a Polish kid from Nicetown. Penn was Ivy League; all the blue bloods from the Main Line and Chestnut Hill went there. I thought it would be crawling with snobs.

One thing I did know. I couldn't work in my mother's store forever. I didn't see myself as a shopkeeper. And what would become of the deli if anything happened to my mother? It was a grim thought, but one I had to consider. With my mother gone, my sisters would feel as entitled to the store as I did, and I had heard more than one story of happy families falling apart over an inheritance. I didn't like imagining such a scene. To keep the peace, the store would have to be sold, and what good was a shopkeeper without a shop? It was time to move on.

I knew a good deal about food and even more about food retailing, and in those days, the biggest food company in the Philadelphia area was Campbell's Soup, headquartered across the Delaware River in Camden, New Jersey. The giant can of tomato soup that crowned the factory was a local landmark, the modern equivalent of the Liberty Bell or Independence Hall (and perhaps more fitting for an industrial city like mine). Getting a job there seemed the longest of long shots, but I shined my one pair of good shoes, climbed into my one good suit, and drove over to Camden for an interview.

As it turned out, I was exactly what Campbell's was looking for: young, gung ho, a little naive, and culturally acclimatized to the mom-and-pop retailers of Philadelphia's working-class neighborhoods. They hired me on the spot. I was officially a salesman but with a twist: I was one of a handful of fresh hires whose job it was to convince small stores, just like mother's, to take on new products. We called ourselves missionaries, and the description fit. Our job was to sell the gospel according to Campbell's.

I was also cheap. In the personnel manager's office I looked over my four-page contract. (*A contract!* I thought, utterly amazed; here was the real world at last.) I scanned the mumbo jumbo in search of a figure. At last, I spotted an amount: eighty dollars. Surely, I calculated, that was not my monthly salary. It had to be biweekly, or forty dollars per week. *Holy moly!* I thought. *Riches unimagined!* But then I took a closer look at the fine print and saw that the figure represented my monthly salary after all. Before taxes, I would be bringing home just $17.50 per week. Even in 1936, in the deepest trough of the Depression, these were sweatshop wages. But I was in no position to bargain; whatever Campbell's wanted to pay me, that is what I would get and be happy about it, too.

On my sales route, the working-class neighborhoods of Manayunk, Nicetown, Kensington, and Fishtown, Campbell's was having difficulty penetrating the market, and this baffled them. The problem was actually very complex. Across the board, Campbell's was in pretty dire straits. Once the 300-pound gorilla of the soup business, Campbell's was finally facing some real competition. A company on the Eastern Shore of Maryland, Phillips, had undercut Campbell's market by selling nickel soups, while

Heinz had come out with a superior, high-end soup—in effect, squeezing Campbell's from both above and below. Their counterattack strategy, in which we missionaries played a part, was to expand the line in the middle with new products. And it was a good strategy, as long as you could get these new soups to the shelves.

But there was also a human problem to consider. What most of the salesmen failed to understand was that folks in neighborhoods like Nicetown tended to be very suspicious of strangers and rejected newcomers out of hand. A slick sales pitch would never work. I had watched my father, then my mother, send more than one oily salesman packing in frustration. But the mistake these fellows made wasn't only their clubfooted approach. (Some actually called my mother "Mom"!) Once rejected, they never came back, or if they did, not soon. That meant that Campbell's was forever presenting its case with an unfamiliar face, a strategy doomed from the start. The best, most sincere salesman in the world would have to call at least twice before making a sale, and the first visit would have to be little more than a social call.

With six hundred fifty dollars I had saved, I put one-third down on a brand-new 1937 Ford and set out to put Campbell's Soup on store shelves across the city. The extent of my ambition was almost ludicrous; one-half wise-guy street kid, one-half wide-eyed farm boy, I actually believed I could talk my way into the annals of sales history.

The hardest beat to crack in the entire city was Manayunk (pronounced Manny-unk). Today, the Main Street of that old mill neighborhood has been redeveloped into a glittering row of upscale restaurants, boutiques, and shops. Even twenty years ago such a prosperous future would have been hard to imagine. But step a few blocks off Main Street, and the old Manayunk, the one I knew, still exists. One of the original industrial neighborhoods of the city, Manayunk occupies a slender wedge of land between the Schuylkill River and Wissahickon Creek, and its network of winding avenues, as narrow and vertiginous as goat paths, ascend a bluff as steep as anything in San Francisco. Tiny brick and stucco row homes—originally built to house the immigrant workers who kept Manayunk's fabric mills and breweries running a hundred years ago—file up the hill like dominoes. Some are barely a dozen feet wide and press their bare, porchless faces within inches of the street. Walking at night, a visitor can hardly help but see into the living room of every house he passes (though it is likely that his gaze would be met by a pair of watchful eyes). Cut off from the city like an island, Manayunk has always been a world unto itself—proud, suspicious, and blue-collar to the bone. If I could sell soup in Manayunk, I reasoned, I could sell it anywhere. Manayunk would be my symphony.

I had no philosophy of salesmanship but, rather, a sense of who my customers were. I would make two visits minimum, I calculated, before I would try to sell anyone a thing. On the first visit, I might introduce myself, tell the owner I was *his* Campbell's Soup representative (as if I worked for him!) and that I wanted to say hello. We might chat awhile, and just when it came time to make my pitch, I would look at my watch, plead another appointment, and excuse myself. The owner would be floored. A salesman, and no sales pitch! Perhaps a week later I would return, look over his inventory, and pronounce it first-rate—though perhaps, I would add, there were a few new products he might be interested in. "Let me check in with headquarters," I would say. "I'm sure if we all put our heads together, we can come up with something special for you." ("And by the way," I would add, "how's that little girl of yours doing? Won the spelling bee you say? Well how about that.") By then, of course, we would be old friends, and by the time I returned the following week, he would be ready to buy.

"You have an excellent array of Campbell's products," I would say, praise ringing in my voice. "Really, very, very excellent. But there are a few, just a few, missing. The boys back at headquarters agree. If you had these few, well, that would be an outstanding selection indeed." By this point he would be nodding. "Now, we have a very good asparagus soup, Mr. Polzack, but I don't see it here. What we could do to start off is take a case of forty-eight, perhaps a dozen asparagus, a dozen cream of celery, a dozen chicken gumbo, and maybe a dozen scotch broth. Don't get me wrong—" I would say, shaking my head vigorously. "I wouldn't recommend mock turtle or even bullion. But these four, they're very popular items. Very nutritious. And children love them. What do you say? Can I make up a case for you?"

"Well, if you think so. . . ."

"I really do. I really, really do."

Sold.

Before long, I was outdistancing all the other salesman by three- or four-to-one. The difference lay in simple arithmetic; they were trying to sell new products one at a time, whereas I was selling four. At weekly sales meetings, I smugly let my numbers speak for themselves. "Hey Ed," another salesman asked me, "how'd you get Polzack to roll over? I tried to sell him a year ago, and the crusty old codger wouldn't budge."

"Ah," I said. "You see, you're not *Polish*."

How long, I wondered, before the great Campbell's Soup Company of Camden, New Jersey, discovered it has a genius in its midst?

I like to say now that I was educated at Campbell's Soup college. But that is only half the story. Somehow, while holding down a full-time sales job and helping my mother at the store to boot, I managed to go back to school—to Wharton, no less.

Why Wharton would have a kid like me I can't say. Perhaps they needed students; it was still the Depression, after all. I don't remember taking an admissions test or filling out any long applications. Like my job interview at Campbell's, I simply showed up one day and asked to enroll.

I signed up for night school, which offered a general business curriculum: accounting, finance, business law, marketing, and a few slots for electives. Most of my fellow students were, like me, full-time employees. Most seemed to be in banking or insurance (cushy jobs, I thought), though a few, like me, worked for manufacturing companies. I paid by the course, about fifty dollars a throw; each course met one night a week for two or three hours. When I figured out how long it would take to finish at two courses per semester, I gulped: eight years. They shouldn't call it higher learning, I thought. They should call it longer learning.

For those first few years, it seemed I was going full blast every moment of the day, held aloft by momentum alone. After I finished my sales route, I would rush home to help my mother out at the store, then grab my schoolbooks, hop on the trolley, and ride downtown to Wharton. Classes finished at nine o'clock or later, and afterward, I always had studying to do and papers to write. Often, I would not place my head on a pillow until 2:00 A.M., only to rise again at 6:00 A.M. and start the process all over. Sometimes I felt I was on the verge of utter collapse and would fall asleep with a book in my lap or a pen poised on the paper; in the morning, I would find a thin trail of ink where my pen had slid off the page as I had lost consciousness.

The greatest hurdle I faced, though, wasn't time, energy, or even money. My greatest hurdle was cultural prejudice, the age-old peasant suspicion of education. It says a good deal about my background that almost no one I knew was in favor of my going to school at night. My friends from the neighborhood thought I was crazy for spending my evenings in class or in the library instead of drinking with them in the local bars and accused me of putting on airs. Did I think I was too good to drink with them? My sisters could only scratch their heads, dumbfounded by a person who would actually pay money to go to school. I longed for approval from my family but got none, not even from my mother, whose silence on the subject was deafening. My going to Wharton, she seemed to be saying, was a delusion that would pass. Only Oddie supported my decision, although she confessed she didn't quite understand it. Studying at night, my eyes bleary from reading, I sometimes paused to fantasize that I came from a different world—one that admired me for working all day and studying all night. But in the end I received only ridicule and hostility, silence and stares. What bitter irony: Wharton was my dirty secret.

Of all the courses I took, surely the one that left the greatest impression on me was not a business course at all but an English class I used to fill one of my elective slots. I have made hundreds of poor decisions in my life, but studying English was one I figured correctly. My command of the language was basic, even guttural. I had grown up speaking Polish a good portion of the time, and as an adult, I peppered my English with the rough-edged idioms I had heard all around me, the "dese, dose, and dems" that marked me as a street kid as sure as a tattoo. To succeed at Wharton, I needed to leave all that behind. But more than that, I had an intuition that a command of the language would help me to understand myself. If I could put my thoughts and feelings on the page, then I could make use of them. In language, I believed, I would find out who I was.

My professor was named Cunningham, and in my eyes, he was every inch the Ivy League English teacher—a gentleman of great refinement and dignity, bespectacled and gray templed, who favored elegantly frayed tweed suits and five-syllable words that I raced to look up during his lectures. He seemed to have read every book ever written, and when he spoke about "the ancients, the great ones," he lowered his voice to a register of reverential awe that made me shiver. I admired him tremendously, but like the fourth grader who punches a girl to announce his interest, I was forever trying to get his attention by acting like a clown. I was the class cutup, and looking back on those days, I can see why Professor Cunningham would have longed to give me a swift right hand. But alone, putting pen to paper in the silence of my own thoughts, I truly let loose, writing from the gut.

One March day, about midway through the semester, I was crossing Woodland Avenue when I saw him walking along with a pile of books under his arm. I had never seen him outside of the classroom before, and I was momentarily stunned. He was dressed as always in a tweed suit and had braced himself for the weather with an umbrella and galoshes. He didn't notice me but appeared lost in thought, in some internal communion with the ancients. I hustled to catch up with him.

"Hi, Prof! It's Edward Piszek."

"Edward." He stopped and examined me. He seemed a bit surprised, amused even, to find me standing there. "Well, how are you?"

"Great, Prof."

He paused, shifting the books under his arm to keep them from tumbling onto the damp street. "Edward, I'm glad you stopped me. I'm worried about you."

"Me? How's that?"

"Well, if I may speak frankly, it seems likely to me that you'll never be able to make a living. Your English is atrocious and you cover it up by acting like the class comedian."

I wanted to laugh. "I have a job, Prof. At Campbell's. A *sales* job, with good pay." (A small lie.) "So apparently somebody is conning somebody."

We reached the corner and he stopped. "That's just my point, Edward. You think it's all a con. And yet, your papers—I read them very carefully, you know, and I think you're trying to say something, something important. But, Edward, you know what happens when a clown tries to say something profound?" I could only shake my head. "We laugh at him. We all have a statement to make, you know. Every one of us. Someday you're going to try to make yours, but if you're the clown, no one will listen. And that won't feel very good, Edward. It won't feel very good at all. Are you following me?"

I shrugged. "I guess so."

"Don't guess, Edward." He lifted his gaze skyward, squinting into the light drizzle that had begun to fall. "Ah, here's the rain. Well, think about it, won't you?" He opened his umbrella and walked off.

His words haunted me. It had never occurred to me that I wanted to make a statement; I was just trying to understand myself. What could he mean? What did I have to say to the world? We never spoke again, and I somehow passed the class. I remember every word of our conversation on that drizzly March street but have no idea what grade I received.

Life is made of such messages, delivered when we least expect it.

Summers, when school was out, were my time with Oddie. The term over at last, we piled into my Ford one Saturday in June to drive out to Quakertown. We planned to meet my sisters and mother there, but along the way, I had planned a little stop. Because we both lived with our parents, it was always difficult to find time to be alone together, and on an earlier trip I had come across a rambling old estate in Fort Washington that I immediately identified as the perfect place to stop for a romantic picnic. The grounds were vast, far too large for a private residence. I guessed that it was a park or perhaps a hospital or school. A tiny millrace ran beside the long driveway, lined with stately pines; at the far end was some kind of house, though it was mostly hidden by trees.

No sooner had we stopped when a pickup truck came roaring down the drive toward us. The driver, an older man in a porkpie hat, pulled the truck alongside and rolled down his window.

"Hello there," I said.

He scowled. "Just what do you think you're doing?"

I was taken aback. "Having a picnic. That's okay, isn't it?"

"Of course it's not okay. You're trespassing. This is private property."

"Oh. Sorry, I didn't know." Despite his sour expression, I still thought I could talk him into letting us stay—always the salesman.

"I thought it was a park. I mean, it's so big."

"Didn't you see the signs?"

My eyes followed his gesture back to the main road. "I guess I didn't," I admitted.

"This is Emlen House. It's a private residence, not lover's lane. Now go on with you."

I saw there was no way to argue. Under his stern gaze, I put the picnic hamper and blanket back in the trunk.

"Well, I guess we'll be going," I said. "Sorry."

I was starting the car back up when Oddie stuck her head out the window and addressed the man. "Who lives here? It must be somebody famous, I'll bet."

He shook his head. "That's none of your concern, miss. You think someone who lived in a house like this wouldn't want their privacy?" Then he smiled. "But I'll tell you something, young lady. General George Washington himself had his headquarters here, just before he moved his troops to Valley Forge. This is a bona fide historic landmark."

We drove away, the old man still watching us. At the main road, I tooted the horn and waved before driving off.

"Bona fide historic landmark," I repeated, mockingly. "What a jerk."

"It sure was a beautiful place, though." Oddie opened her window wide to the spring air. "What did he say it was called?"

I tried to remember. "Mailer House? No, Emlen House."

"Emlen House, that's it." She released a long, dreamy sigh. "Imagine, having a place like that all to yourself."

I gave the idea some thought. In a way, I'd already had such a place: the farm in Quakertown. But that was long ago.

"That'd sure be something," I said.

Chapter Four
Dowry

In October 1937, on my twenty-first birthday, Oddie and I got into my little Ford and ran off to be married. At that time, Elkton, Maryland, and Niagara Falls were the two destinations for eloping couples, but Oddie and I had just enough gas money to drive five miles across the Delaware into New Jersey. We bought the license in Camden and were married in a little Lutheran church in Oaklyn, New Jersey. The only other people in attendance were the priest, a man who was sweeping up the vestibule, and our witness, a fellow salesman from Campbell's named Jules Farley. It was a crisp fall morning, and the three of us drove to a truck stop called the Oaklyn Diner for a wedding breakfast. Over bacon and eggs, Jules presented us with the one wedding present we would receive, a gift from all the salesmen on my team—a Sunbeam toaster.

"Well," Oddie joked, giving Jules a kiss, "there's my dowry!"

We had run away because our parents thought we were too young to be married; when we returned and told them our news, they accepted it cheerlessly. "Well," my father-in-law said, "I suppose it had to happen sooner or later." Oddie's mother said nothing, just sat in the kitchen and wept. We would have liked their support but lost no sleep over its absence. Eventually, we figured, everyone would get used to the idea.

We began our new life together at 1701 Ontario Street in Philadelphia, in a dingy, one-room apartment with a hotplate for a kitchen and a bathroom down the hall. The building was just a notch over skid row, a transient hotel that let rooms by the week. The other tenants were a lively lot to say the least. But the rent was what we could afford, just $7.50 a week.

Now that we were married, it seemed more important than ever to make my mark at work, and flushed with my success in English 101, I decided to write a booklet: *Tested Sentences That Sell*. For each product in the Campbell's line, I scripted a unique approach to get it to the shelves. Most of my ideas were just common sense, but there was nothing like my little book at Campbell's, and I hoped that it would get me noticed. Night after night, I banged away on my old Remington typewriter at the kitchen table, polishing every word to the finest grind. But each time I showed it to my sales manager, he would hand it back to me with some small complaint.

"I don't know, Piszek," he would say. "Some of this stuff just doesn't sound right for our customers." Each time I presented him with a new version, asking him to pass it up to management, he returned it with a new "suggestion." What I didn't realize was that there was absolutely no way he could pass it on; I was wasting my time. My job was to sell soup, not to change the company culture, and the last thing my boss wanted was an employee with more ambition than he possessed. In the end, my magnum opus, lovingly crafted at my kitchen table, chock-full of good advice, was never seen by anyone at all.

Our first child, Ann, was born just a year later. By then, we were living in our first real apartment, just a few blocks from my mother's store, at 1931 Wingohocking. The advertisement had described it as a basement apartment, but that was putting it mildly; the walls sweated with dampness, and from the apartment's three windows, you had to look up to watch the feet of passersby on the sidewalk outside. But it was cozy, and we had a nice little backyard for Ann to play in, shaded with trees. Work, school, a baby at home; we were a family at last.

Soon enough, Campbell's Soup threw a monkey wrench into things. I was transferred to Doylestown in Bucks County; my new sales route, ironically, took me along the same country lanes that I had traveled as a youth. The inconvenience of living so far out of the city was considerable, but my initial response was relief. What happiness to have again the feel of grass beneath my feet! We rented a small frame house just outside of Doylestown proper, a snug three-bedroom place that in every way reminded me of the farmhouse of my youth—there was even a stream that ran at the edge of the property. Happily, we had both electricity and indoor plumbing, but our meager rent of thirty-five dollars a month did not include a refrigerator, and we kept our perishables in a deep well in the backyard. When it came time to cook, instead of going to the kitchen, we went outside and hauled up, by rope and pulley, what we needed. My mother joked that it was as primitive as Poland.

And then I lost a full year at Wharton. My workhorse—my great '37 Ford, a car that had taken me all over Philadelphia and Bucks County without complaint, and in and out of town for school at night—suddenly gave out from under me. Later I learned that Ford was replacing the car's faulty transmissions for free. But I knew nothing about this, and it cost me over two hundred dollars to have a new gearbox installed. Two hundred dollars was a year's tuition almost exactly.

It was a crushing blow, and for a time I even considered giving up on Wharton entirely. For four years I had been going to school at night, and still, I had to explain what I was doing to nearly everyone. This new setback was terribly dispiriting. But I also felt, with a deadeyed certainty, that I wasn't meant to be a soup salesman for the rest of my life. There had to be something better out there, some calling more lucrative, more enriching, more interesting. Late at night, returning from the city down the dark country roads, I often found myself clenching the wheel until my knuckles were white, peering over the dashboard into the rushing darkness as if, just maybe, I might see beyond the reach of my headlights into some future that lay ahead. Always, though, the darkness was the same; it swallowed everything beyond the limits of my vision, beyond the immediate and pressing needs of the here and now. It was maddening, and the harder I looked, the more frustrated I became. When would I *know?* But then I would pull into the driveway and see the porch light that Oddie had left on for me, and I was instantly saved. Oddie would be waiting; upstairs, our baby, Ann, slept, a happy child safe in her bed. Whatever else might happen, *they* were my future.

But at Campbell's, I was slowly going nowhere.

I had done everything I could; I was selling well, breaking records even, but nothing I did seemed to get me noticed. Just the opposite: gradually, I had become aware of an unspoken resentment among my fellow salesmen, while my bosses seemed to take no more interest in what I was doing than if I had simply met my quotas and let it go at that. My enthusiasm began to wane.

Then in the summer of '41, the company transferred me back to Philadelphia. By then, Oddie and I were firmly ensconced in our small-town way of life (we had moved up to Chalfont, into a house with an icebox), and I resented having to move, because it accomplished nothing for us. Campbell's simply needed another salesman in the city, and at their whim, I was required to pick up with my family and march to my orders. It was a lateral move on its face; in my heart, I felt it was a demotion. We moved back to town, renting a small row house in the Overbrook section of West Philadelphia. For months, I dragged my feet to work. I might not have showed it, but the crisis was acute. Four years, and I was still doing essentially the same job as when I'd started.

It was 1941, and the talk was always of war. When would the United States get in? Could Hitler be stopped? And the Japanese—was the threat real? All through the summer and into the fall, the world held its breath.

But even in the midst of the crisis, ordinary life continued. There were meals to be made, a daughter to be clothed and dressed and taken to school, a mortgage to be paid. At Campbell's, the talk was of layoffs. If war came, any nonessential personnel would be let go, and salesmen would go first. But I paid this little mind. I was so overdue for a promotion I could practically taste it.

Finally, it happened. Almost five years to the day I had begun work, I was called in from the field for a special meeting with the northeast regional sales manager, Mr. Nixon. The instructions were specific: I was told to bring in all my equipment and samples and to report to his office at 11 A.M. I told Oddie the good news. Word of my sales manual must have finally reached the higher-ups, I explained, and I was certain to be promoted to an office job, probably a supervisory position; war meant consolidation, and Campbell's would want to keep only its very best employees. We went out for a cheap dinner to celebrate, and the next day I awoke as energized as a child at Christmas. I had canceled my daily sales calls, and the waiting was more than I could take; I could barely sit still all morning. Finally, Oddie could stand it no more.

"Just go," she said, shooing me out the door. "Let me get something done around here, and come back with your promotion."

I arrived at the sales manager's office in Camden twenty minutes early, sample bags in hand, to find I was not alone. Another salesman was waiting, too. Everybody knew him; he was one of the worst salesmen the company had. I wondered what he was doing there but tried not to dwell on the matter too much. The northeast regional sales manager no doubt had many items on his agenda besides me. We exchanged curt hellos and I took a seat.

Finally, he spoke. "So, you're getting canned, too, huh? It's a bitch, ain't it?"

I hardly knew what to say. "I don't think so. I'm here for a promotion."

He tipped his head toward my sample bag. It was then that I noticed he was carrying his, too. An icy kernel of fear formed in my chest. "Maybe you is," he said, laughing, "and maybe you ain't."

By the time my name was called, I had no more illusions. Once in the office, there were no pleasantries, no idle chitchat. Seated behind his big desk, the sales manager went about the business of firing me with a blunt swiftness that left no room for argument.

"Young man, as you know, it looks like there's a war coming, and though I wish it were otherwise, we've been instructed to cut back. . . ."

His voice droned on, explaining the intricacies of centralized economic planning and the war production board, all of it utterly reasonable and told with artful sympathy, but I barely heard a word of it. I slumped in my chair and tried to breathe. Fired! I'd been fired! I tried to listen but could not; beneath my calm exterior my anger rose and gathered like the trapped waters of a geyser. My thoughts raced: *The disloyalty! Five years and these are the thanks I get! Why, he never read my book at all!*

It was too much; I was going to blow. But just when I felt myself rise from the chair, ready to hurl myself across his desk and seize him by the lapels, something tipped inside me. It tipped, and then it fell over, shattering in pieces, and I burst into tears.

"Now, now, Piszek." The sales manager came around his desk and put his hand on my shoulder. "There's no reason to cry about it."

I'm sure he was as embarrassed as I was. But I hardly noticed. I blew my nose on a handkerchief and sobbed.

"Let me tell you something, young man. I know it may seem like scant consolation, but anybody who cares about his job as much as you do has nothing to fear. Your loyalty will always stand you in good stead, you mark my words."

I wiped my eyes. My face burned with humiliation. "If you'll excuse my saying so, that's easy for you to say. You *have* a job." I rose to go. "Just tell me one thing. Did you ever read my book?"

"You wrote a book?"

"A sales manual. *Tested Sentences That Sell*. My boss was supposed to send it along to you."

He put a finger to his lips, considering. "*Tested Sentences That Sell*. Now, I must say that doesn't ring a bell. Catchy title, though. You say you wrote it?"

"Forget it," I said.

There was nowhere to go but home. I drove down the street slowly, stalling for time. I had no idea what I would tell Oddie. I circled the block once, twice, three times, and finally parked the car. I was walking toward the house when I bumped into a neighbor; an insurance salesman, he had been laid off twice and knew immediately when he saw my face what had happened. I told him the story (though I didn't mention my tears), and when I was done, he gave me a jolly slap on the back.

"Well, hell, Ed, what were you working there for anyway? You were making peanuts, and for what? You're better off, believe me. Soup salesman, like hell. Now you're free to get a better job."

I knew he was just trying to cheer me up—his words might have come straight from my little sales manual—but I felt a smile come to my face. "You really think so?"

"Of course I do. Now you get in there and tell Oddie your good news. What luck!"

Oddie greeted me at the door. "Hon?"

I took off my coat. "Well, there are a lot of ways to put this, but the short version is, I got fired."

She nodded, a wan smile on her face. "Well, I had a feeling. I guess they'll never know now how lucky they were."

"I guess not. How much money do we have?"

She shrugged. "Some. Enough. Well, not really, but we'll be fine." She put her arms around me. "I have no doubts about you, Ed. Not one. You understand that, don't you?"

"I think so."

"Good. Now let's have dinner."

And that's just what we did.

Chapter Five
GE

Oddie was right, as she usually was. I memorized my social security number (still a relatively new concept, less than a decade old), set out to find work, and in a matter of weeks landed a job—a better job—as an expediter at a General Electric plant in Darby, a few miles outside Philadelphia. In all, I would work at GE for five years, the same time I worked at Campbell's and the same time it took me in later years to build a company from scratch to over a million dollars in annual sales.

My relief at finding a job so quickly was enormous, but in fact, I'd never really had much to worry about. It was the spring of '42, the war was on, and the American industrial machine was roaring to life on a scale the world had never seen. Almost instantly the anxieties of the Great Depression became a bad and distant memory; the question was not so much whether an able-bodied man or woman could find work but how much they were willing to do. Perhaps Oddie had understood this better than I had, or maybe she just had faith in me. The irony, of course, is that the war was in many ways a lucky break for me.

Like most Americans of my generation, I remember exactly where I was when I heard of the Japanese attack on Pearl Harbor. I was at a friend's house in the Mayfair section of Philadelphia, and when we heard the news, we nearly laughed. This strange, tiny country so far away—how could Japan, of all places, pose any threat? Surely the war would be over in a matter of months. We'd knock Japan, and then Germany, right off the map. History tells a different story though, and as days went by and the news of the destruction began to sink in, all of us realized that we were in for a long haul (and that this conflict would be like no other).

GE operated a huge switchgear plant at 59th and Elmwood, with over five thousand employees; the plant where I was hired was tiny by comparison, perhaps five hundred workers, and operated under the company's aeronautical division, making gun turret controls and ammunition boosters for the Army Air Corps. It was hard, difficult work, the hours were long, but all who worked there felt a closeness to the war effort. In the Polish neighborhoods of Philadelphia, everyone knew well that Poland had been first among European nations to fall and that our ethnic homeland had been under the heel of the Nazis for over two years.

I started at GE at seventy cents an hour; at the end of the six-day workweek I brought home a whopping $36.50. A pittance by today's standards, but it seemed like (and was) a gigantic leap from the twenty-five dollars I had been making at Campbell's. Besides the higher salary, the job at GE represented another important step for me. At Campbell's, I had been a salesman, a job in those days that was not quite white-collar and not quite blue. As an expediter, I was now *management*.

An expediter's job is just that—he expedites. I had a desk but rarely sat at it, and when I remember my days at GE, I see myself in almost constant motion, running here and there, using all my powers of persuasion to keep things moving on the line. In that sense, an expediter is like a boss, like a company president in miniature, but while he is responsible for everything, in reality, he has authority over nothing. Talk was my tool, time the stage on which I worked; I was the grease, the lubricant, of the line. I had to encourage, cajole, embarrass if necessary—anything to smoke out problems and make sure that the operation ran smoothly, from ordering raw materials to shipping finished goods on time. At Wharton, we learned about management, but it was always in the abstract. At the GE plant in Overbrook, I was receiving a crash course in the real thing. And if I was paid far less than some of the blue-collar workers I supervised, many of whom made two dollars an hour for knocking burrs off castings, I did not worry about it or told myself not to. My feet were on the managerial ladder at last.

My happiness was doubled when, in September 1941, Oddie gave birth to our second child—a boy, Edward Jr. I was overwhelmed with joy. For weeks I could only shake my head in wonder. I had heard it said that Martin Luther, when asked what a son meant to his father, replied: "Only such a man can look to heaven and declare, 'What do you mean I'm not immortal?' " Ann's birth had been a marvel to me; but a *son*. Here was an extension of myself, a boy to carry my name and heritage beyond the frail horizon of my own lifetime. At last I understood what my own father had felt, bringing me a gift from town or treating me to a ride in his Model T; I understood his patient amusement at my boyish theatrics, sneaking from the store to play with my friends, only to return at the sound of his voice calling my name. When Ed Jr. began to sleep through the night, we moved him to Ann's room, and returning late one night from class, I entered their room and stood at the doorway listening to the sound of their breathing. It was an awesome sound, utterly amazing to me. I hunched down on the floor and sat there for hours, drinking in their presence. It was possible, in those early days of the war, to imagine that civilization itself was ending, that the barbarians were finally crashing through the gate. Sitting on the floor outside my children's bedroom, I could nearly forget all of that—but of course, I also could not. I knew that around the world there were other parents—in Poland and Great Britain and Manchuria and everywhere else— parents who were keeping watch over their sleeping children just as I was doing, while in the near-distance boomed the guns and bombs of war.

At GE, my boss was a man named Kinsey, who was head of production for my division; but on a daily basis, I worked most closely with the controller in the machine shop cage, who oversaw payroll and synchronized jobs among the various shops in the plant. This was John Ritchie, a man who would later play an important role in the history of Mrs. Paul's Kitchens. He was a handsome gentleman, charismatic and popular (which I was not; no expediter is popular, because he is a professional nuisance), and we quickly became friends. And there was Faust: *Mr.* Faust, boss of bosses, who loomed over the operation like a divine being. I cannot say that I knew Mr. Faust, but as it turns out, he knew me—and would change my life in ways I could not then imagine.

Corporate culture is a funny thing. At one company, new ideas may seem threatening, and an ambitious young man might find himself quickly slapped down, told his ideas are no good, and sent packing. No matter that the idea is a sound one and might save the company thousands of dollars; in fact, the better the idea, the more resentment it causes, because anyone who didn't think of it first looks bad. This is what had happened to me at Campbell's, and at GE, I initially worried that my hotheaded enthusiasm might again mark me as a troublemaker, an enemy of the status quo. But I was too stubborn to change, and I am glad that I did not. In fact, I didn't let up for one moment. The minute I was in the door at GE, I began stuffing the suggestion box with memos on subjects ranging from the use of plastic instead of aluminum to improving the food in the cafeteria (the latter couched in a lengthy treatise on the connection between good nutrition and productivity). Some of my suggestions were implemented, others ignored. A few I forgot about the minute they burst into my brain. But at least, I figured, I wasn't getting into any trouble for *thinking.*

One thing bothered me in particular. In the Darby plant, strong acid was used in the manufacture of certain machine parts, and pure springwater was needed to rinse it off. This water—which was not cheap—poured twenty-four hours a day into a large tank, filling and refilling, whether it was needed or not. The waste was obvious, and to me, so was the solution: a water closet system. If a worker needed water to rinse a part, he could hit a switch, water would flow into the tank, and he could rinse to his heart's content. But in the meantime, if he didn't need it—for ten minutes or for three hours or for half-a-day—that expensive springwater wouldn't be going down the drain, taking the company's money with it. I wrote the memo, explaining in detail how much money would be saved, put it in the box, and waited to see what would happen. Months passed, and then one day I came into work and there it was: the very water closet system I had suggested, large as life. I asked around but no one seemed to know where the idea had come from. So it seemed the credit must have gone to someone else, and although I felt discouraged and grumbled my way through the next few weeks, I knew that sooner or later I would be noticed.

In fact, this had already happened, although I wouldn't put all the pieces together for a couple of years, until the war was nearly over. What tipped me off initially was my first promotion. At the end of business one Friday, John Ritchie pulled me aside and told me he had been transferred to the larger Elmwood plant. Losing the controller was no small matter; Kinsey had complained upstairs that there was no one who could take over so quickly. *Yes there is*, he'd been told. *Get that guy named Piszek*. So, Ritchie told me with a laugh that someone was looking out for me, and he wished me good luck, because I was going to start in the cage on Monday.

I hardly had time to think about who might have put my name forward for the job or even to be happy about it. All of a sudden, Ritchie was gone, and there I was, in a new job I knew nothing about. I didn't even know the names of half the people who reported to me, and without Ritchie to train me, I had to figure out my job the hard way—by pretending I knew what I was doing. "What should I do with this?" a worker would ask, and it was all I could do to mumble, "Whatever you did with it before." The first few days I felt like I was either drowning or fumbling my way through a darkened house I had never been in. Almost no one seemed interested in trying to help me out, except one: Sally Williams. Sally was in charge of payroll for the plant, a large and tricky job she did superbly. She was bright, sensitive—and beautiful. At the time we might have called her a "sweater girl," a statuesque woman with strawberry blonde hair and a luminous smile that drew men like a magnet. Bit by bit, Sally showed me the ropes, saving me from my own mistakes and gently turning me in the right directions.

One day I said to her, "You know, Sally, one day I'm going to be running something of my own. I don't know how, or when, or what it will be. But when it happens, I want you to know that you'll be my number one girl."

It was a preposterous, boastful thing to say (and of course, these days you wouldn't call her a *girl*). But I meant every word. Sally gave me one of her smiles, then thanked me in a tone of voice that said, "That's all well and good, I believe you just might, but for now, let's get back to work."

Sally was not the only woman working at GE by a long shot. Most people know about "Rosie the Riveter"—a name not for one woman but for the hundreds of thousands who went to work during the war. Fully half of the employees on the GE shop floor were women, and although there were occasional intrigues (Kinsey, for instance, fell in love with and married a woman who worked as a grinder), for the most part, the idea prevailed that we were all in this together, doing what needed to be done, and there was no monkey business. Most of the women had husbands or boyfriends or brothers who were overseas, a painful fact that all the men were aware of, and we treated them with respect. But I quickly saw that not everything was as fair as it could be.

One of the responsibilities of my job entailed doling out work vouchers—in effect, the orders for particular assignments on the shop floor. Back then, everything was done on piecework: some time-study expert had come in and decided how long a given job should take, and a worker would receive a flat rate for completing that task, no matter how long it actually took. (The time-study man was an almost mythical figure; no one ever knew who he was, yet his pronouncements were etched in stone, like the commandments on Moses' tablets.) I quickly figured out there were two types of assignments: those that took less time than was officially allotted and those that took much more. We called them gravy jobs and dog jobs. Building a torque tube, for instance, was the classic dog job: it took probably twice as long as it was supposed to. Someone received a voucher to build a torque tube, and their face fell to the floor; you might just as well have been giving them a prison sentence to hard labor. So there was, in effect, a built-in bonus system on the shop floor, overseen by the controller, who made the assignments however he saw fit.

It didn't take me long to realize that gravy jobs had always gone to white female employees, dog jobs to black female employees. Nothing was openly stated; that's just how things were done. But I found I could not, would not, do it. Preference of any kind ran deeply against my grain—I was a street kid, after all—and when I thought how some of these women, whose husbands were fighting just the same as anyone else's, weren't being given a fair shot to earn more money, it made me furious. The injustice was plain, and I vowed to correct it, but I also understood that the hardest thing to change was people's most deeply ingrained prejudices and that I would have to move carefully.

The next month I began by giving the gravy jobs to all the white women first. Then, the next week, I switched and gave the black women the better slots. Week by week I alternated, making sure that the balance was even or with the white women just slightly ahead—not by two or three gravy jobs, but just one. Who could say this was unfair? The white women were, after all, in the lead, just not by very much. It was a win-win position for me, so when the shop foreman approached me at the end of the month to tell me that he had received some complaints about the way I was doling out assignments, I was ready.

Carroll, the shop foreman, was a decent fellow with whom I got along well, and I believed I could pretty easily persuade him that I was being fair. But he had brought with him the union representative, a surly, old codger whom I barely knew, and I suspected he might be a harder sell. I escorted the two of them over to the books, which Sally had waiting.

I said, "Mr. Carroll. Gentlemen. Let me try to prove my case. I've given this matter some thought, and I'm all for being fair. Start at the beginning of the books. Look here. See? Miss White's got a gravy job. Then Miss Black's got it. Then Miss White. If you look through the month, you'll see that Miss White's had the cream-puff job three times, Miss Black only twice." I closed up the books. "Now, I suppose you could call that favoritism, because our black employees are a part of the union just the same as anyone else. But I think it's a reasonable way to do things."

Carroll looked at me, then back at the union rep. I thought I heard Carroll chuckle. "Okay, Piszek," he said, shaking his head.

"You're agreed then? That everything is fine?"

"Yes," he said. "I don't see a problem here."

The matter never came up again, and I realized something remarkable had happened. The change was small, but it was the right one, and I had made it work.

After a year or so at GE, I began to feel as if I was on pretty firm footing with the company, so I followed my instincts and decided it was time to buy a house. Oddie and I looked around and settled on Drexel Hill, a suburban town just outside Philadelphia, not far from the GE plant. For $3,995 (a lot in those days), we bought a brand-new, three-bedroom row house at 2206 Windsor Avenue, overlooking an empty parcel of land that reminded me, just a little, of the farm where I had grown up. The house was only a bit larger than the place we had rented in Overbrook, but in the most important way, it was completely different: we owned it. No more landlords; *I* was the landlord. And the extra room was promptly filled when Oddie gave birth to our third child and second son, George, in November of '44.

All this time, I was still at Wharton; I was a father of three and a full-time employee, but at night, I was still a college student, taking tests and writing papers and frantically scribbling notes during lectures. Two or three evenings a week I would come home for a quick dinner, then hop in the car to drive to Penn, where classes started at 7:30 and ran until 10:00 or even later. It was almost like having a secret life, for I had learned long ago not to tell people that I was going to Wharton. I had heard it too many times before: who did I think I was? Some things were better kept to myself.

Then miraculously, the day arrived when I finished my last course. I had been at GE for three years, at Wharton for seven. After all the years of sacrifice and the late nights after work, I was surprised by my own lack of emotion. Shouldn't I have felt *something?* Graduation represented, after all, the attainment of a major life goal. But because I had been so secretive about it all those years and believed that no one except Oddie really supported what I had been doing, I buried my own happiness so deeply that it never occurred to me even to go to the graduation ceremony. When Oddie asked me about it, I pooh-poohed the idea. I called Penn and asked them to mail me my diploma, and on the day my classmates ascended the stage to receive the handshake and sheepskin that would mark their entry into the world of educated people, I don't even remember where I was.

A few weeks later, Oddie and I took the children to my mother's house for dinner, and when I noticed my mother was rushing dessert, I asked her what was wrong. She said that she knew it was a school night and didn't want to make me late for class. I almost laughed. I told her to relax, that there was no school anymore; I had graduated at last.

And then I saw something I had rarely witnessed before. My mother, so strong and solid—a woman who never showed her pain when some-thing hurt her—began to weep. She stood at the table, her gaze fixed on me.

"It would have given me the greatest joy on earth to have seen you graduate," she said quietly. "I am so proud of you, iron horses could not have kept me away. Why didn't you tell me?"

Then there were two of us with tears in our eyes. All those years I had thought she didn't approve, and she had been silently rooting for me. It was the greatest gift imaginable to learn how she had felt. No march to the

Wharton stage could compare with that. I embraced her and thought: *Here is my graduation ceremony after all.*

In March 1945, I was transferred to GE's main plant at 69th and Elmwood—not quite a lateral move, not quite a promotion, because I was an expediter again, though this time for a larger department making electric switchgears. An Allied victory in Europe seemed near, and the plant was going day and night, churning out parts to make the final push; with over five thousand employees, it was like a city within a city, always humming with activity. The section where I worked manufactured parts for many different departments, making me the go-between that connected our division with other manufacturing operations throughout the plant. Most of my time was spent negotiating with their representatives, or "reps" as we called them, who would come to me with lists of parts they needed, or that were late, or to keep tabs on delivery dates—a learning experience that, without my knowing it, was preparing me for the complexities of running my own business. I got along well with most of the reps, and although I took their requests seriously, there was plenty of kidding around. A rep might come to me and say that he needed such and such a part right away, deliberately overstating the emergency to hustle me along, and I might say, "Oh, gee, I think we lost that shipment," and pretend to look for the work order, or tell him that he really did not need this particular nut to go with that particular bolt. "It's all in your head," I'd say. We might go back and forth like this for thirty minutes or so, but both of us knew we were horsing around, and in the end, the parts were always (or nearly always) delivered on time.

Although I counted most of the reps as friends, the one pointed exception was the rep from section eighty-three. He was an arrogant, humorless man, and he seemed to think that his orders always had priority. One afternoon he came rushing in and announced that he needed some part right away—not next week, or tomorrow, but that instant. He had caught me in a bad mood, and I decided to give him a hard time, even though I knew he couldn't take a joke at all.

"Sorry," I said. "We shipped all those parts to Germany. Didn't you know?"

Rep eighty-three would have none of it. He exploded in anger and stormed off to tell my section boss, who charged in a few minutes later.

"What did you do, Piszek?"

"Relax," I said. "I was just kidding him. Those guys in section eighty-three think they're God's gift."

"That's not for you to decide, Piszek."

So it was that an hour later I was being escorted upstairs by my boss to see Mr. Faust, my head filled with thoughts of being fired. I had never met Faust before—as an expediter, there was no reason I would—but I didn't see how, under the circumstances, he could do anything but can me. Faust was one of the plant's top four executives. He sat as far above me as the moon sits above the earth, and waiting in stony silence with my section boss in Faust's outer office, I could only think of that day at Campbell's Soup so long ago, the last time I had sat outside an office like this one. *Here we go again*, I thought, and as the minutes ticked by, my fears hardened into doom-filled certainty. I was a troublemaker, always sticking my nose where it didn't belong. Faust would excise me with the swiftness and thinly veiled distaste of someone flicking a fly from a bowl of soup. What would I tell Oddie?

But another part of me, the cleverer part, was thinking fast. How would I get out of this? What could I do to win Faust over, or at least save face? Probably my section boss had already painted a pretty unflattering portrait of me, so I would do my best to prove him wrong. And if I did—if I was able to make myself look altogether like the hardworking, helpful employee I knew myself to be—then it would be my section boss, not I, who would look like the source of the problem. By the time Faust buzzed his secretary and told her to let us in, I felt at least that I had a strategy. Even if I was going to be fired (still the likeliest outcome), I would not sink beneath the waves without a struggle.

I followed the section boss into the office. Faust was sitting behind a large mahogany desk, and although there were two chairs across from him, he did not ask us to sit. Before he could say anything, my boss picked up the thread; in an angry rush he told Faust what a wise guy I was, how none of the reps liked me (not true), and so on, not just griping about my run-in with rep eighty-three but enlarging his complaint to include every aspect of my work and personality. He went on for a minute or two while my face burned with anger, but then Faust cut him off.

"Tell you what," he said. "I think I can handle this myself. If you don't mind, why don't you go about your business, and I'll talk to Mr. Piszek."

"But—"

A terse nod silenced him. "Thank you," Faust said.

My section boss huffed out of the room. I was absolutely stunned. It looked like I had won the first round without even opening my mouth.

Faust gestured at the chairs across from his desk. "Have a seat, won't you?"

I sat. Faust took his pipe from off his desk, tamped it down, and looked at me again. "Would it be all right if I smoked?" he asked.

He was asking me if he could smoke—in his own office!

"Sure," I managed.

Faust lit the pipe and leaned back in his chair. "To tell you the truth, I don't see that you did anything all that wrong, Piszek, though we should probably talk about it. Let me put it this way. There are lots of guys you might like to tell off. Eighty-three probably deserved it." He leaned forward, holding me with his gaze, and lowered his voice to a whisper. "But you can't, you see. You can think it, think *the hell with so-and-so*, but if you say it, nothing gets done around here. For the continuity of the operation, you just can't always speak your mind. You understand that, don't you?"

I told him I did, and meant it—Faust was absolutely right.

He sat back and went on. "So, what do you say? Do you think you could maybe make it up to him somehow, even if you don't like him? I'd like you to."

"I will, Mr. Faust," I said. "That's more than fair."

"Fine." He nodded. "I'll consider the matter settled, then."

For a moment there was silence as Faust drew on his pipe. I had been too keyed up before to look around the room—the first real executive's office I had ever been in—and in the brief silence I let my eyes wander over the space. For an instant, I allowed myself to imagine that I was Faust, that this was my office.

"You know, Piszek, I've taken notice of you before." He waved a hand humorously in the air. "All those memos in the suggestion box. You seem interested in absolutely everything that goes on around here."

"I guess that's true," I said.

"It *is* true. And I think it means something. Have you given any thought to what you might want to do after the war?"

And then I understood. It had been Faust, all along, who had looked out for me, whose unseen hand had charted my course. It was Faust who had put me in the controller's cage, and later, had brought me over to the Elmwood plant; it was probably Faust who had ordered that the water closet be installed those three years ago.

"I was a salesman at Campbell's," I said. "I wouldn't mind being a salesman for GE."

"Wouldn't mind? Or is that what you want to do?"

I nodded firmly. "That's what I want to do."

"You're a college man, Piszek?"

"Yes, sir," I said. "I graduated from Wharton."

"How about engineering? Do you have an engineering degree?"

This I had not planned on. Why did you need to be an engineer to be a salesman?

"No," I admitted. "But I could do more than any engineer. I know how to sell."

Faust shook his head. "Unfortunately, that's not the point. This is a big company, and big companies have rules. To qualify as a salesman, you need to be an engineer. You're right"—and here he laughed—"it doesn't make a lot of sense. But that's the way it is."

I didn't know what to say, and my face probably showed my frustration, because Faust tried to cheer me up. "Don't let it get to you, Piszek. There are lots of other opportunities for a fellow like you. Give it some thought, all right? Because if you want to continue your career here, I think GE could be very interested in you."

"Thank you," I said. "I really appreciate your saying that."

"Like I said, give it some thought." He smiled. "Now if you'll excuse me, we both have things to do."

I think it would be fair to say that when I left Faust's office I was a different person. I was twenty-six years old and had been working all my life, but until that day, I had never heard anyone in a position of real authority tell me that I was going about things in the right way—that there was more to success in business than being popular and well liked. I had believed in my own talents but didn't think that anyone else had noticed except Oddie. Faust's words were more than encouraging; they were a kind of blessing. I went back to work and patched things up with rep eighty-three, and when I saw my section boss, I told him that Faust had chewed me out and that I was a reformed man, which I knew was the answer he needed to hear. The funny thing is, I don't remember seeing him again after that day. Perhaps the company transferred him to another division. He might have been fired. Either way, I had a new boss by the end of the week.

As the months went by, something else began to grow in me, an idea that Faust had planted without meaning to do so. *Big companies have rules*, he had said. I wasn't an engineer and didn't plan to be one; this meant I couldn't do what I wanted to do at GE. In fact, as long as I worked for other people, I would encounter such obstructions, arbitrary distinctions that didn't make any sense and had nothing to do with merit. A big company like GE, I saw, was full of *systems:* not just the obvious day-to-day things, like who reported to whom, but a whole web of influences, habits, and perceptions—deeply entrenched ideas about everything from the efficiency expert's pronouncements to who was blue-collar and who was white. Together they constituted an unwritten rule book or a kind of web. And once you were inside such a web, you were stuck like a fly in a spider's glue. So GE might be "interested" in me, as Faust had said, but if I stayed with the company, my fate would always be ruled by others. Only the entrepreneur, I realized, was truly free. Only the independent businessman could take an idea and really run with it, explore the value of creativity in the marketplace, hazard the risks, and reap the rewards. Gradually, I was coming to the realization that I needed, someday, to start a company of my own, and I would not be satisfied until I did.

And what did I know how to do? Knowledge is like a house with many rooms, and mine had four. All those years in my mother's store had taught me about retail, especially food retailing. From Campbell's I had taken away a solid experience with managing a territory, pitching new products, and selling a line—everything that goes on between the distributor and the customer. At Wharton, I had learned the basics of marketing, accounting, management, and finance. Then there was GE, my real-world baptism into the intricacies of plant management, with daily crash courses in everything from dealing with unions to making payroll.

As the end of the war approached, I had begun to think in concrete terms about what I wanted to do next. It was like an itch I couldn't quite scratch or the sound of a voice from behind a closed door. I listened for it on the shop floor at GE, and later, driving my car home from work; at night, after we put our children to bed, Oddie and I would sit in the kitchen to talk, and I would say, "I can tell there's something out there, something I'm supposed to do, I just can't see it yet."

Something else was bothering me, too, because I had gotten myself into a terrible mess. These days a psychologist would probably say that I had simply channeled my appetite for risk into the most readily available form. I had become a gambler, and alas, not a very good one. Things had gotten so bad that I'd had to take a night job as a riveter just to cover my losses and keep our household running. It was hardly what I had hoped for when I first got involved with Mark Potter, who had introduced me to the glamour of the gambling life.

Potter had taken a shop job at GE to beat the draft. He was a nervous, high-strung man whose hands and body were constantly in motion, and he always seemed to know where the action was. On anything and everything, Potter had the angle; he was a true operator, a gambler's gambler, and though he was not more than a year or two older than I was, I looked up to him and thought him quite sophisticated.

One day we were walking together past a jewelry store, and Potter stopped me to point out an expensive lady's watch in the window. It was a Bulova, a real top-of-the-line item, with two little diamonds on the face.

"Tell you what," he said. "I've got a hot bet, but I need fifty bucks. You advance me the money, and I'll give it back to you tomorrow, and I'll buy you that watch to give to your wife."

It was a lot of money, but Potter always seemed to be winning. And I had never given Oddie anything like that watch before. "Tomorrow?"

"Maybe the day after," he said. He shuffled his feet. "C'mon, what have you got to lose?"

The answer was obvious: fifty bucks. But I decided to take a chance. I gave him the money.

"You won't regret it," he said.

That night I told Oddie what I'd done. She shook her head disparagingly. "You don't have the sense you were born with. You'll never see that money. Who is this Potter?"

But a couple of days later Potter pulled me aside at work. "We came in," he said, peeling off two twenties and a ten and putting the watch in my hand. "See? I told you you wouldn't regret it."

I was hooked, and before long, I had become a kind of gopher for him, accompanying him on trips to New York to spend his winnings at the Brass Rail or some other swanky nightspot, then to the fights at Madison Square Garden. No money changed hands between us, but he paid for my train fare, the cab rides, dinner—everything. My duties were vague; I was one part secretary, one part hired friend. I know now that in New York, Potter was pretty far out of his league, and having me around was part of his act. I was a gambler's prop, placing his phone calls and carrying his cigars so he could look more like a big shot. And in return, I got a tantalizing peak at how the "swell people" lived. Sitting in a restaurant like Luchow's, with the music playing and the crowds flowing around us, I felt like I had stepped into a movie. I kept a weather eye out for the smallest detail—how people greeted one another or ordered their food or spoke to someone on the telephone—all with the idea that I was learning something I needed to know.

It wasn't long before I had graduated from gambler's sidekick to a gambler in my own right. Such easy money, I thought—which is, of course, exactly what the bookies want you to think. And I was a bookie's dream, a man who didn't know anything in particular about gambling or horses but who thought he had a "system."

According to my calculations, all very scientific, a surefire way to win at the track was to bet on a single postposition. It didn't matter what horse was running there, whether a favorite or a long shot or somewhere in between; I would pick a post for a day's races, then bet on whoever was running in that lane, doubling my bet each time, until a horse came in. (The hazard, of course, was that a long dry streak could clean you out, and you wouldn't be able to cover your next bet, but I didn't give this a lot of thought.) As long as I stuck to my system, I believed, I would be okay.

And for a while I was. Then one Saturday afternoon, I lost the first four races on post number three, putting myself eighty dollars in the hole. I felt discouraged and decided to sit the next race out, because the horse at post three was an odds-on favorite at 4 to 5 to win and wouldn't pay enough to cover my earlier losses. Perhaps I just lost my nerve. Either way, number three came in, and there I was with no bet down. I was furious at myself—the point of having a system is to follow it to the letter, and I had flinched—and my fury made me reckless. Instead of going home and chalking the day up to bad luck, I placed another bet. And another, and another, until by the eighth race, I had no money left. None. I had lost almost five hundred dollars, all the money that Oddie and I had saved over eight years. It was absurd, crazy, beyond belief. A day's foolishness, and we were totally cleaned out.

That night, wracked with remorse, I waited until our children were asleep before I told Oddie. I didn't know what to expect; certainly she would be angry. I finished my story and waited for her reaction. Then she told me something I'll never forget. She looked across our kitchen table at me and said, simply, "Well. You'll get it back."

"But it's all we had—"

"No. It's nothing. What's five hundred dollars?" She waved a hand. "The money's nothing. And you know what Ed? You don't think it's anything, either."

And sitting there with her, as strange as it sounds, I suddenly knew with shining clarity that I *would* get it back, and a lot more besides. Say what you will, but I felt at that moment as if I knew something, that my future was nearby. *What's next?* I thought. *What's next?*

Chapter Six
Third and Cambria

In 1946, with the war over at last, millions of servicemen began to stream home. The whole country sighed with relief; it was a happy time, one of homecoming and reunion, as so many families welcomed the return of a son or brother or husband. But the good news of our victory was tempered by a gnawing sense of the human cost. There had been radio, of course, and photos in the papers, but it was not until the war was over that Americans got a full look at the devastation. The destruction was mind-boggling. Much of Europe had been reduced to rubble, the great cities and small towns laid waste, their churches and homes and city halls swept aside as if by a mighty hand. Most disturbing of all were reports from Poland of the discovery of the death camps, places with names like Auschwitz and Treblinka, and of the skeletal men and women found there, staring blankly from behind the wires. The soldiers who found them were said to weep; some had even gone mad. For everyone, but especially for Poles, the stories of these places confirmed our worst fears. At least, we thought, it is over.

For GE—and the rest of American industry—the end of the war posed some complicated questions. For nearly five years manufacturing had been running full tilt, with the armed forces as the single, biggest customer. The shift to a war footing had been total: it was, for instance, nearly impossible to buy a civilian automobile during the war, because virtually none were made. In 1946, nearly every major industry in the country lost its best customer virtually overnight and had to retool itself for civilian markets. (The good news was that demand for consumer goods was high. Half a decade of wartime deprivation and rationing had starved the American consumer for nearly every kind of product, from cars to radios to sugar and clothing.)

The end of the war also caused great turmoil among workers. Thousands of soldiers, sailors, and marines were being mustered out each day and expected to return to their civilian jobs, only to find that they had been filled (by women, no less) or no longer existed. Many GIs had gotten married just before enlisting or else married when they returned. Jobs and housing for these new, young families were in critically short supply, and although we did not know it yet, the baby boom was under way. For the unions, too, there was a five-year backlog of unaddressed grievances. Since 1941, the need to sacrifice on behalf of the war effort had kept labor quiet. With the nation now victorious, it was natural that the American worker, so important to that victory, should want to share in the rewards.

At GE, we could smell a strike coming, and when it did, it was long and fierce. At 69th and Elmwood, thousands of workers lined the pickets (many of whom did not even work for GE), and management soon called in the police. I was part of the crowd outside that cold February day, and when police on horseback tried to disperse us, we mounted what I thought was the most clever rearguard action since the Battle of the Bulge. One of the union leaders had passed paper sacks of marbles among the strikers, and as the police came within striking range, the picketers dumped their bags and strewed bouncing marbles all over the place. It was a sight I will never forget—the frantic horses scrambling and stumbling as they tried to maneuver across our impromptu minefield of marbles. We laughed with crazy joy, all of us thinking: *Score one for the little guys. Try to push us around, and see what it gets you.*

It was a glorious victory, but it would take more than a playground stunt to upstage company management. Days dragged into weeks with no end in sight, and many of us began to feel desperate. No one knew when the plant would open again or, more importantly, if we would be there when it did. As strikers, we received union unemployment insurance, but it was a fraction of the usual salary. And in the meantime, with three kids and no paycheck coming in, I watched the rest of our money dribble away.

Then I heard from Mark Potter. Potter had left GE near the very end of the war—he had seen the end coming—and seemed to have settled down some. With winnings from a gambling hot streak, he had bought a taproom in the Kensington neighborhood of Philadelphia, on the corner of Third and Cambria. Kensington was an old mill district, blue-collar to the teeth, and there were bars just like Mark's on two of the other three corners where he had set up shop. But he was making a nice run of it, he said; those were hard-drinking days, before television kept people home at night, and working men and women flocked to the corner tavern the way people would later gravitate to the TV set. And, meanwhile, GIs were still pouring off the troop ships, their pockets fattened with mustering-out pay, looking for a place to wet their thirsts.

I might never have heard from Mark again, because after my disaster at the track, I had sworn off gambling and off Mark Potter, too. But then the Commonwealth, in order to make taprooms more "responsible," had passed a law requiring bars to serve food. Mark did not know anything about food; he was a gambler turned bar owner, pure and simple. He said he had heard about the GE strike and had a proposition for me. Was I interested?

I told him I was and the next day went down to Third and Cambria to visit him. The area seemed pretty run-down, and Mark's bar fit right in— it was just one notch above a dive. The inside was cramped and dimly lit, with a sticky floor and old paneling on the walls. Like most mill taprooms, it had a separate "ladies' entrance" that led to a back room that was, in theory, a more respectable venue where wives and girlfriends could drink out of earshot of all the rough talk at the bar. Mark had bought the whole building and was living in the three-room apartment upstairs.

"So, what do you think?" he said. "I know it ain't the Brass Rail, but it's all mine."

I told him I thought it was nice, doing my best to sound sincere. I was still wondering what he was up to; this was Mark, after all, the man with all the angles. I didn't think for a moment that he had changed, bar or no. "So, what's the proposition?"

We sat at the bar, and he poured me a beer. "Ed, the state's after me. I have to serve food if I want to keep my license. I can manage maybe some little cheese sandwiches or liverwurst, but that's about all. What would you say to running a food concession out of here?"

"You mean work for you?"

"No. Not exactly. We'll work together. The money you make from the food is yours, and in return for keeping the state off my back, I'll pay all the utilities. Heat, electric, everything. No rent on the kitchen, either. You just pay for your own supplies." He stopped, and gave me a hard look. "You know, if you can cook as well as you can criticize, you could make some good money here."

True enough. All those years working for my mother and at Campbell's had made me pretty particular about food. I thought I was a pretty fair cook, and whenever Mark and I would eat together in New York and he would remark how good the food was, I would say, "The crab meat, it's not back fin," or, "You know, that beef isn't prime cut," or, "Well, it's all right, but a little overdone in my opinion." It used to drive him crazy—I was supposed to be the gopher, the yes-man—and my criticism had become a joke between us. But I also cared about food. It galled me when a hoity-toity restaurant like the Brass Rail tried to pass off something as good when it obviously was not.

And from a purely practical point of view, Mark had a point. Who knew how long the strike would go on? I was restless and quickly running out of money. I was going to have to stop the hemorrhage soon, and something about going into the food business, even if it meant working in the back of a mill district bar, seemed right to me.

"You'll cover all the utilities?"

"That's what I said. It's a win-win deal, Ed."

That was all it took. "OK, Mark," I said. I put out my hand, and we shook. "You're on."

Some years later, I would become friends with baseball Hall of Famer Robin Roberts, the winningest right-hander ever to pitch a fastball for the Philadelphia Phillies, and the franchise's first twenty-game winner since the great Grover Alexander. One time he said to me, "You know, Ed, I remember when I was a kid the very first time I held a baseball in my hand. And holding it, I knew. I just *knew*."

It was exactly that feeling—an unshakable recognition that the key to my life was in my hand—that came over me a few days after visiting Mark's taproom, when I stood in Philadelphia's Reading Terminal Farmer's Market. Not a baseball, but butter. I had just bought a one-pound brick, and as I clutched it in my hand, then lifted its solid shape above my face so the light streaming in from the market's high, gritty windows caught and held its soft yellow color, I *knew*. The feeling came upon me in a flooding rush the likes of which I had never felt before. For a long moment I stood in the midst of that teeming market, with restaurant and food buyers rushing around me, their voices bouncing through the room's high, echoing spaces, and understood, almost without thinking, that my aimlessness had ended. I would not go back to General Electric when the strike ended. I would never work for anyone else again. In a flash, I had become my own boss, and the change was like a rearrangement of every atom of my body. It sounds absurd, but I was so moved that I could not continue my errands; and when I walked to the market's exit, I paused in the doorway, casting my eyes carefully up and down the busy street, and then, with great deliberateness, placed one foot beyond the threshold.

Mark and I had agreed that my concession would open in a week. I needed to quickly get my business up and running. For several nights Oddie and I stayed up late together, hashing out strategies, until she practically fell asleep at the kitchen table. (In later years, I would conduct planning sessions for Mrs. Paul's in much the same way, talking over a kitchen table.) One thing I had learned at Wharton: never reproduce a business that already exists. Find a niche, something new. I quickly figured out what mine would be.

Every taproom in Kensington was already serving food to meet the Liquor Control Board's mandate. Virtually all of it was bar food, nothing you could call a meal, and none of it was cooked with care. Liquor was the real moneymaker, and food was just an afterthought. I decided I would try to make the best taproom food in the mill district, better even than the food people ate at home. Deep down, I knew I did not want to sell my food only to the barflies; I wanted to sell the wives as well as the husbands. No liverwurst or five-cent clams for me. I would serve hot roast beef and steak sandwiches, hamburgers made with prime beef, lamb chops, pork chops, fried oysters, shrimp—and one item the workingman had never before laid eyes on in a mill taproom—deviled crabs. Although I had never made them before, I didn't think it could be that hard. In those days, there was a takeout restaurant on Roosevelt Boulevard, called Koch's; Oddie and the kids and I would often drive out there on the weekends for an order of deviled crabs. They were delicious and wonderful with beer. I thought with a little know-how I could reproduce them, and at the Acme Market, I bought a cookbook with a basic recipe for twenty-five cents. For several nights running I jimmied around with the ingredients until I hit just the right mix of spices—nothing too overwhelming, but just enough to complement the crabmeat's flavors and bring them to the surface. Deviled crabs would be my flagship item.

My strategy also touched one of my most deeply ingrained beliefs: that the "little people" had powers of discernment that restaurants and grocers always underestimated. I knew what good food was; given the chance to taste the difference, Mark's bar patrons would, too. Of course, I would have to charge a little more to cover the cost of my ingredients, but if the price was fair and the food was good, customers would come back for more. So, while the bar across the street was charging a dime for a hamburger, I would charge fifteen cents—but mine would be twice as good, making it a bargain. For deviled crabs, I decided to charge a quarter, but they would be as good as any in a real restaurant.

At that time, right after the war, food was actually quite difficult to come by, but in this matter, I had two advantages. The first was my own pious stubbornness. Food rationing stamps were still in use, but I vowed from the get-go that I would never pay a nickel on the black market. This meant that I would pay less for good ingredients in the long run, though I would have to look a little harder and negotiate a little more carefully. The second advantage was that I knew exactly how to do both. All those years in my mother's deli and later working for Campbell's gave me ingress to a host of small, local suppliers—and more importantly, an understanding of the ways they liked to do business. Give a little, take a little, that was the rule, the transaction rooted not in suspicion but in mutual respect.

"*Tak*" (meaning "yes"), an old Polish supplier said to me, "you want fifty pounds of butter a week? See this lard over here that I can't sell? You buy twenty-five pounds of the lard, I sell you fifty pounds of the best creamery butter. OK? Tak?" And I said, "Tak."

The day I opened the concession was the most frantic since my first day in the controller's cage at GE. The kitchen was a tiny room, less than fifty square feet tucked in an alcove behind the bar, with a three-burner gas stove, a small icebox, and a pint-sized oven no bigger than a child's toy. With all the appliances going, the space was hot as any sweatshop. I was always bumping into something, dropping something. The time went by in a hurried haze of popping butter, clattering pans, and Mark's urgent voice barking orders back to me from the bar. Somehow, I kept up.

Within just a few days, I was a hit. Everybody in the bar was talking about the food, especially the deviled crabs. "Who's the Polack kid you got working back there?" people asked. "Where'd you get the gourmet cook?" The only person who wasn't happy was Mark (because customers were spending money on food they might otherwise have spent on drinks), but he was hardly complaining; the food was a drawing card. In Kensington, taprooms like Mark's relied heavily on their regulars, and suddenly we were bringing in people from all over the neighborhood. "That's Ed Piszek," he would say, poking a thumb over his shoulder in my direction. "My chef."

But Mark was still Mark, and he couldn't let a good deal go by without operating a fresh angle. Just a week after I had opened the concession, he reneged on our deal.

"From now on," he said, as I was setting up for the night, "no more free utilities. You want to stay here, you're going to have to foot the whole bill." It was simply outrageous, and I told him so; not only did he want me to pay the gas and electric to run the kitchen and cool his beer, he wanted me to pay for the utilities in the upstairs apartment as well, because there was only one meter. We haggled back and forth, and in the end I settled for half. It was still a raw deal, but I didn't see that I had much choice. At least he hadn't asked for a percentage of sales.

It was along about this time, too, that I realized I needed an extra hand. For the most part, I cooked by instinct, and there was a great deal I simply didn't know how to do. And just when I realized I needed it, help arrived. John Paul was the husband of one of my wife's girlfriends, someone we had both known for years. He was from the old neighborhood and worked as a retail bakery wagon driver, driving house to house in his horse-drawn wagon (this in 1946!) selling bread and pastries for Freihoffer Bakeries. But as a younger man he had worked as a diner short-order cook, and when I told him about the concession, he was intrigued. We were standing in his backyard on a Saturday afternoon, and before long, I was peppering him with questions.

"The secret to oyster stew," he told me, "is not to throw the oysters into the hot milk when they're still cold. The milk will curdle that way. What you should do is heat the oysters up first, sort of sauté them, and just when the edges begin to curl, pour the milk in. You're onto it, you just have to do it the other way around."

I told him it sounded like he missed the kitchen.

"Yeah, Ed, I really do. A wagon's a hard grind. All those cars don't make it safe for a horse these days. Maybe I could come over and show you a few tricks. You know, shortcuts."

I jumped at the offer. John began to stop by the bar after he was done with his rounds, and the two of us would cook together until closing. The kitchen was much too cramped for two people, but the work made him happy, and I was relieved to have the help and the company. The kitchen had one tiny window above the stove, facing a glass-strewn alleyway where billowing laundry hung against a dark rectangle of sky. Sometimes, even in the midst of a rush, I would pause at the stove to look out and wonder: *Could a real business be coming out of this? Could it?* And then Mark would yell an order back to us, or John would bump against me on his way from the oven to the icebox, and I would return to work.

Just as I had predicted, the deviled crabs were my most popular item. I went through a couple of dozen in the first week, six dozen the week after that. They were a lot of trouble, though, because I had to make them ahead of time; if I didn't guess right, customers would go without, or I would be throwing extra crabs—and profits—into the trash. Saturday night was the toughest, because the bar was closed on Sundays; any leftovers on a Saturday night had to be tossed out.

One Saturday night, just when I had sold my last deviled crabs, into the bar walked one of Mark's big-spending regulars, a tough, old drunk with a handlebar mustache. I never learned his name, but he reminded me of stories I had heard of Big John, the man whose drunken rage had made my father sell his saloon in Chicago. The big spender asked Mark for half a dozen to go, and when Mark told him we were out, he went into a nasty sulk.

"You tell that Polack kid to make enough of 'em next time!" he yelled, storming out.

Mark came back into the kitchen. He was hopping mad. "For God sake, make more of those damn crabs, will you?"

"What am I supposed to do?" I barked back. "They're no good if they're not fresh. I try to make just enough so I don't have any leftovers."

"I don't care," he said. "Just make enough next time."

So the next week, I made a huge batch: not six dozen, but twelve. And sold them all. By ten o'clock Saturday night, there was not a deviled crab in the house. Around midnight, the big-spender lurched back into the bar, even drunker than usual, and again I had to tell Mark we were out.

"You think I want to have that guy on my hands?" he yelled. "I don't need this trouble. Make more to shut him up!"

It was a stupid thing to do, but I felt like a gauntlet had been thrown down. "All right," I said. "Next week I'll make twenty dozen. Will that keep you happy?"

"Six dozen, twenty dozen. I don't care. Just make enough."

I made the twenty dozen—240 deviled crabs—and the next Saturday, the big spender did not show. I had sold eight dozen.

After closing, I sat in the little kitchen, shaking my head. On top of the stove sat my leftovers, twelve dozen unsold deviled crabs. How could I have been so dumb? I packed up a dozen to take home to Oddie, and felt an almost physical pain at the thought of throwing away the rest. They represented the entirety of my week's profits, and they were headed for the trash. I looked out the tiny window, then suddenly, I had an idea.

I would freeze them.

I said it aloud. "Freeze them. Why don't I *freeze* them?"

My mind spun. Why couldn't I? Frozen vegetables had recently been introduced in supermarkets; I had had them many times. But deviled crabs—*cooked* deviled crabs. Could you freeze cooked seafood? If you could, wouldn't somebody have tried it already?

But I had nothing to lose; a week's profits were as good as gone. All I had to use was the small ice-cube tray compartment in the kitchen fridge. I took out the ice trays and jammed it with crabs, so many I had to lean on the latch. I jacked up the cold knob all the way, took a deep breath, and sealed the refrigerator door. I cleaned up, washed off the stove, closed and locked my little window, and as I reached up to turn out the lights, took one last look at the refrigerator. I shook my head hopelessly. Probably I was kidding myself. *It won't work*, I thought, and glumly drove home, certain I would be returning on Monday to throw the crabs out.

I awoke the next morning with my head still full of frozen crabs. But because it was Sunday and the bar was closed, all I could do was wait. That day Oddie and I had planned to drive out with the kids to the old farm in Quakertown, where we would meet my sisters' families and my mother for a picnic. I was happy to go; I thought it would take my mind off things, and nothing but the old farm made me feel quite as restored. The old family friend who had bought it from my mother and father had gotten too old to manage it, and soon that land—hallowed ground to me—would pass into a stranger's hands.

It was a beautiful April day, like something in a poem. The air was warm and sweet with the smell of sunlight and new grass, and it seemed as if no time had passed since my childhood. Oddie and the kids and I arrived first, and soon the scene was just like the old days, as more cars pulled up to the pond and Piszek kids flew out the doors to run across the fields. My mother arrived, and we spread a blanket for her on a small hill overlooking the farm and the pond below. I thought she looked like Queen Victoria sitting there, and Oddie and I joked about it.

I eventually found my way to the old millstream, that great source of flowing strength. Oddie came with me, and we sat on a familiar rock that poked out into the bubbling waters. From the woods, I could hear the laughter and shouts of my children as they tore through the brush, playing some game of their imaginations. It seemed only a moment ago that one of the voices had been mine. But I was the father now, the provider. For a while we sat without speaking, listening to our children's happy voices ricocheting through the trees.

"Oddie," I said at last, "I'm worried."

"What about?"

"I calculated wrong and blew the whole week's profits by making too many deviled crabs."

"Oh," she said. Then she shrugged. "So you made a mistake. It happens. You threw them out?"

"Well, no. They're sitting in the ice compartment of the bar fridge."

She looked at me. "I don't get it."

"I had this notion. I'm trying to freeze them."

"I still don't get it."

"They were going to go to waste, you see. I couldn't just throw them out. Tomorrow I'll thaw them out, and if they're still good, I'm back in business."

Oddie laughed softly. "So much worry over some deviled crabs."

"But that's not all. I can't help thinking that I'm onto something." I picked up a stone and tossed it into the water; the ripples expanded and disappeared, swallowed by the currents of the slow-moving stream. "Let me ask you something. Have you ever heard of frozen cooked seafood? Seen it for sale, I mean?"

Oddie thought for a moment. "No," she declared. "I don't think so."

"Neither have I. So I'll be the first. *If* it works."

"Ed, why don't you just tell me what's on your mind."

"Can you believe—a business? My own business. Frozen cooked seafood. It might just work."

Oddie looked out over the creek. Then she stood up. Her voice was full of certainty. "Yes," she said.

"Yes, what?"

"Just yes." She was smiling. "You'll do it."

"What will I do, Miss McFadden?"

"Whatever you figure out. You'll succeed at whatever you figure out."

The next morning I rushed in my shiny Dodge to Third and Cambria, ran into the little kitchen, and flung open the refrigerator door. There they were, frozen hard as ice pebbles. I took out two of the crabs and put them in a pan to heat them. They looked fine, and as they thawed in the hot butter, their sweet, meaty smell filled the kitchen. I pulled them off the heat, put them on a plate, took a deep breath, and bit into one.

Deviled crab.

Nothing but deviled crab.

I could barely stand. It tasted exactly the same as if I had made it fresh that very morning, better even, at least to me. My week's profits were saved, but I barely thought about that now. At Wharton, I had created one mythical business after another. But this was no fiction, no class exercise. Frozen food was the coming thing—anyone could see that—and I had just cornered the market on frozen deviled crabs.

I made myself a cup of coffee and took it out to the empty bar. It was just 6:30 in the morning, and outside, the streets and mills were silent. For a while I sat at the bar and sipped the coffee, and before long my mind drifted to a picture I had once seen in a classroom textbook of the great H. J. Heinz. The photo was taken when he was just starting out, a young man like myself, and he was standing on the street in front of his first place of business, a dumpy little storefront. The photo was unremarkable except for the smile he wore—confident, as if he knew something no one else did. Then I shook my head to dislodge the image. I was getting way ahead of myself, I thought. But still. . . .

I needed another set of taste buds to tell me I was not hallucinating. That night when John Paul came into the bar, I sat him down on a stool in the kitchen.

"Here, John. Take a taste of this deviled crab and tell me what you think."

"What's up?"

I took the crab off the stove, put it on a plate, and placed it on the counter before him. "I tried something new. An experiment. Tell me what you think."

He took a few bites, chewing thoughtfully. Then his face fell.

"Ed, it doesn't taste any different. Whatever you added doesn't show up. It tastes just the same." He took another bite. "Nothing beats fresh, though, I'll say that. I'd keep it just the way it is."

I wanted to dance and even tried to, shuffling around the tiny kitchen. "Ed, what's gotten into you?"

"You know what you just ate? Do you know?" I slapped the countertop, and John jumped. "A *frozen* deviled crab, that's what. That crab was cooked last Saturday night."

"What are you talking about? I saw you take it off the stove just now."

"Sure. All I did was reheat it. And you couldn't tell the difference."

John looked at me. "Well, I'll be damned." He took another bite. "Frozen. Who woulda thought?"

"John, it's better than that. All day long and all day yesterday I've been thinking this could be a business. Frozen deviled crabs, in a nice box with a price tag. Not some dinky operation in the back of a bar. A *business*, John."

"You mean like Bird's Eye? Those big companies?"

"That's just what I mean."

"You're crazy, Ed. Who are you to compete with those guys? I mean, you may be right about this, but they've got millions."

"That's no reason, John. Who are we *not* to think like those guys? How did they start out?" I slapped the counter again. "Like this, John. Just like this. Somebody had a good idea, and they ran with it."

"But we're nobodies."

"Every somebody started out as a nobody." It sounded absurd; I was talking in gibberish. But I was on fire. "Eight years at Wharton, John. I know what I'm talking about."

"You and your ideas. Always spinning in your head."

"Sure, but this time I've got a product." I pointed at the half-eaten crab on his plate. "That's real, John. You tasted it yourself."

John took another bite, as if to make certain. "Amazing." He shook his head and chuckled. "I swear it tastes fresh." Then he looked up. "Okay, so how *do* you start a business, Mr. Bird's Eye?"

I had already considered this. "We'll need some money. Probably a lot. But we can borrow it. We'll figure it out."

"How much money you got now?"

"Well, not a lot," I admitted. "Fifty bucks in the bank."

He rolled his eyes. "Broth-*er*. Those guys at Bird's Eye are going to lose a lot of sleep."

"Someday they just might." I poked a thumb toward the door. "I've also got my Dodge out there. It's worth a good six or seven hundred. I can sell it and get something cheaper. That will leave me with about three hundred. You got any money?"

He scratched his head and thought. "I guess I've got about three, maybe three hundred fifty, saved up."

"Well, how about it?"

"You mean together?"

"That's exactly what I mean. A fifty-fifty partnership. You want to spend the rest of your life driving a bread wagon? Be serious. And with your three fifty and the three fifty I can scrape together, we'd go in as equals. What do you say?"

The question hung in the air. Then John smiled. "Jeez, a business. I can't believe I'm saying this. OK, Ed. Yes. Yes it is."

We reached out over the stove and shook hands in that tiny kitchen in the back of a bar at Third and Cambria.

The next weeks were a whirlwind. Delivering my little speech in the kitchen behind Mark Potter's taproom, I had won a partner and sold my first customer—but I had also sold myself. To fail now—or worse, not to act—was inconceivable.

Even so, I was plagued by silent doubt. What were we doing? Ann was seven, Ed Jr. was three, little George was still in diapers, a chatty eighteen-month-old interested in everything. There were bicycles to buy and shoes for school and gallons of milk and a hundred other things besides. It was all very trite, but it was true: people depended on me. What did my children need from me but a stable, sensible, and happy life? I had heard it so many times—*Hey Piszek, who do you think you are?*—that part of me wondered, too. It was not so long ago that Loki was pinning me to a wall and shaking me down for nickels; that I had run through the Nicetown streets, closing my ears to wise-guy remarks, dreaming of victory; that I had taken a roundabout way home from school to avoid my friends, tired of explaining that an education was something I wanted and needed to pursue. And I had an easy out, if I wanted it. The GE strike had about run its course; after all the showmanship and posturing, each side had about exhausted its rhetoric, and a settlement was in the air. How easy it would be to simply step back into the life I had left behind.

Deviled crabs. H. J. Heinz. I shook my head. It was all craziness.

But I did what I had always done before—what anyone must do when he realizes he has cast himself into deep and unfamiliar waters. I picked a point and swam toward it.

I needed a plan, a clear heading for the compass, and common sense said that if we were going into the frozen food business, we needed four things right off the bat. We needed money (I wondered how much; despite what I had told John Paul, I doubted the seven hundred dollars would go very far); we needed a freezer (this from a man who had recently stored his milk and butter down a backyard well); we needed a "factory" (a space something about as large as my mother's store would do; in any event, that was all we could afford); and we needed customers—*lots* of customers.

But the first thing I had to do was get out from under my arrangement with Mark Potter. Because John knew his way around the kitchen as well as I did, we agreed that he would oversee the day-to-day workings of the concession until we had the basic elements of our new enterprise in place. It would have been more efficient, of course, to close the concession right away, but I didn't think it right to leave Mark flat, and besides, we had a powerful motivator not to: every dime was suddenly more precious than ever before. (How many new businesses have died at birth because someone could not quit his job?) It was a small detail, but without John Paul to keep things going at the bar, I think my life might have turned out very differently.

In the meantime I set about gathering as much information as I could about how to market a frozen food product. I understood, generally, how the food business worked, but most of my experience was at the retail level. A majority of the larger stores and even the smaller ones—those that could afford a freezer case—were carrying some kind of frozen food by '46, but my knowledge was all anecdotal. Nowadays, a start-up company like ours would probably hire a marketing research firm with high-paid consultants and number-crunching software. We suffered no such distractions; the only way to find out what was on the market, and where, was to go have a look. The two of us divvied up the city and got to work.

Money was the second item to consider. I loved my Dodge, but it had to go. I drove it to the dealer, finagled six hundred fifty dollars for it, and drove away in a ten-year-old Chevy with rust on the quarter panels and a fresh set of wiper blades. Not beautiful, but it ran—and I had cleared three hundred fifty dollars on the deal to match John Paul's stake. In a stroke, we were capitalized. Pulling out of the lot, I glanced in the rearview mirror and saw the salesman positioning my beloved Dodge on the lot, ready for a buyer. He is certainly wasting no time, I groused. But my pocket bulged with cash. Well, I thought, when I woke up this morning I only had a car; now I have a car *and* a business.

We had a lawyer friend draw up a partnership agreement, designating us as equals in the company, and flush with our newfound legitimacy, John Paul and I made our first capital investment: a freezer. It was nothing fancy, just a big chest, twelve feet long by about four feet high by a yard deep. The price was four hundred dollars, a titanic sum that, thankfully, I was able to finance, paying it off at twenty dollars per month.

But where to put the thing? Just a week in business, and already I had put the cart before the horse. I gave the delivery company my mother's address and arranged to be at her house the morning the freezer would arrive. She had given me permission to use her garage for storage, but on the appointed day, I found my sister Cecilia's husband, Bill, standing in front of the garage, arms crossed resolutely over his chest. I climbed out of the Chevy and approached him.

"Hello, Bill." I was willing to give him the benefit of the doubt, but it didn't seem likely he was there to help. "What gives?"

My mother came out of the house. "Talk to him," she said to me.

Bill held his patch of ground before the door. "How long have I been using this garage as a workshop, Ed? Hmm? You tell me."

Somehow, I had forgotten all about this. Some months earlier, he had asked our mother if he could use it as a woodshop. It was nothing professional—just a hobby.

"I guess I'm asking for a favor," I said.

At that moment the delivery truck appeared in the alleyway. On its bed, draped with a tarp, lay my freezer, looking like an enormous casket. For a few seconds we both looked at it.

"Listen, I'll need the space for just a few days, Bill. Maybe a couple of weeks. I'm sorry I didn't tell you about this. I guess I just forgot."

"You and your ideas." He shook his head bitterly and pointed a bony finger toward the truck. "I hear you're going to freeze crabs in that thing. Crabs!"

The driver got out of the cab and lumbered up to me, carrying a clipboard under his arm. "Which one is Piszek?"

I nodded and scribbled my name on the delivery form. The driver went back to the truck and loaded the freezer on a dolly. He had an assistant to help him, a teenage boy who might have been his son.

"Don't think he's going to put that thing in there," Bill said. "Because you're not."

My mother joined us at the garage door. I could tell the whole thing had upset her badly. "I want this settled," she said.

"Tell him," Bill said to her.

The driver clambered down off the back of the truck and looked us all over. He was perspiring heavily in the surprising, early spring heat. "I have other deliveries, folks. What's it going to be?"

"Just a minute." I turned to my mother. "Mom, it's your garage. Whatever you say is okay with me."

"You're damn right it is," Bill cut in. "Because I was here first."

I shot him a withering glance. "Will you listen to yourself?" I said. "Mom, you're going to have to decide."

She paused a moment, wiping her hands on her apron. Then she poked her thumb at the garage door. "Sorry, Bill. My son's going into business. In it goes."

Thus, with a poke of the thumb, our space problem was temporarily solved. But a permanent solution had to be found. Until that day I had delayed looking for a place to open our "factory" (again, I hesitate to use the word, because our needs were little more than four walls and a roof, and that as cheap as possible), but in the days that followed, I placed this priority at the top of my list. I scoured the classifieds but found nothing. How could I have been so dumb! The postwar housing crunch was in full swing. For nearly five years, there had been virtually no new construction (our little house in Drexel Park Gardens was a rare exception), and now GIs by the hundreds of thousands were looking for a place to put their homes and businesses. Many had amassed tidy little nest eggs during the war and could easily outbid me if it came to that. Somehow, I had missed all of this. Against such forces, my search for a vacant storefront seemed like a straw in the wind. Why wasn't anything ever easy?

But the big picture—that was my strong point. That Sunday night, not two weeks after I had dished up my first frozen deviled crab to John Paul, the two of us met for dinner at my house in Drexel Park, and we sat down over coffee for a strategy session. Sunday night was his only night off, when the bar was closed; because of this, we hadn't spoken as often as I would have liked, and circumstances had left much of the early planning to me. At last, I thought, John could hear all the schemes I had cooked up on my own. Finding a location for the plant was at the top of the list, but before long, I drifted on to other things: how we would capitalize, which bank we would approach for financing and when, which stores would get our products first, how we would market and advertise, and so on. I worked myself up into quite a lather. What had started as a conversation had become a sermon, until I paused a moment to catch my breath and saw John Paul's face. Salesmen are great readers of faces, and I had been a salesman long enough to know what I was looking at. I was bungling the sale. I was steamrolling my partner, bossing him right out of the company before we had even begun. It was true that John Paul was no businessman and knew little about marketing or packaging or finance, but that was no excuse. He was risking his entire life savings on this venture. (What was I risking? The price of a car.) And I was treating him as if he did not matter at all.

Oddie sat at the kitchen table with us, and I glanced at her to see if I was right, and I was. Her eyes said: *Ed, do something.* But an apology would not be enough. I had to make amends. Then an idea hit me, a beautiful, wonderful idea, and I rose from my chair and addressed the room as if I were speaking to a marbled hall of shareholders, company heads, whole divisions of salesmen and accountants and advertisers.

"Ladies and gentlemen," I said—and here I got a small laugh from Oddie—"we've spoken of many things here tonight. But what is the one thing we haven't addressed? How does a company, any company, announce itself to the world?" I let the question hover. "Ladies and gentlemen, I am speaking, of course, about a name. We absolutely don't exist without a name. And it must be the perfect name." I leveled my gaze on John Paul, as if to single him out from a packed room. "We're selling a food product, but it's not any food product. It has no starches or fillers. It's absolutely pure, and every bit as good as homemade. No phony junk from a factory. Food that the fussiest, most persnickety little old lady would make herself. I'm telling you, we must name our company after that woman. How about . . . Mrs. Paul?"

John met my gaze, and I saw the light come back into his eyes. "Well, no harm in that," he chuckled.

With that one stroke, I had my partner back. I turned to Oddie. "And you, madam?"

"Mrs. Paul." Squinting, she spoke the words as if tasting them. "No, Mrs. Paul's. With an *S*. Like it's hers." She cast her eyes around the room. "Like it comes out of her kitchen."

"Mrs. Paul's Kitchen," John repeated. He gave a tight, happy nod. "I like it, Ed. I like it a lot."

"Then it's settled." I lifted my coffee cup. "Ladies and gentlemen of the board, I give you Mrs. Paul's. Mrs. Paul's, our little old lady."

Then, a stroke of luck. The next day, driving through the neighborhoods of Manayunk near my old sales route, I saw a For Rent sign hanging in an empty storefront, with a phone number to call. The windows were smeared with white soap; I could still discern, hanging over the doorway, the ghost-like shape of the sign that had once hung there, advertising some business long gone. The door was locked, but I cupped my hands around my face and peered through the windows to have a look. I saw cracked plaster walls, a single lightbulb hanging from a chain, an old plank floor so scuffed that it looked like horses must have trampled it; in the middle of the room was a pile of plaster dust and, lying beside it on the floor, a lonely-looking broom. The room could not have been more than six hundred square feet. I called the number and spoke to a man who seemed, curiously, not to care one way or the other if I rented it. I had forgotten to write down the address; he gave it to me over the phone—179 East Street, the southwest corner of East and Terrace—and we met that afternoon at the store to sign the lease. The cost was forty dollars a month, a little more than I had hoped to pay but now was happy to spend.

At the doorway, we shook hands. He was an older man, wearing coveralls with the name "Archie" stitched on the breast pocket. I guessed he worked nearby and owned a few rental properties in the neighborhood.

"What did you say you wanted this place for anyway?" he asked.

"Manufacturing." The word felt enormous in my mouth. "We're going to make and market frozen deviled crabs."

"Crabs, huh." He shook his head, rocking back on his heels and jingling the loose change in his pockets. "How about that. There's money in a thing like that?"

I laughed. It was a perfectly straightforward question, and strangely, I had never asked it that way. Everything else aside, was there money in it, yes or no?

"I think there is," I said. I shrugged. "Maybe a lot."

"Well, for your sake, I hope that's true."

We shook hands again, and he turned to go. As he descended the cement steps to the curb, I called out after him.

"Say, what was in here before? If you don't mind my asking."

"In here?"

"Yeah." I poked a finger upward at the ghost sign above my head. "What business."

He shook his head sadly. "You don't want to know," he said. "Gone with the wind. Pray for better luck, Mr. Piszek."

He left me in the store. It was early evening, and lamps were coming on up and down the narrow street. I tried the light switch, but to no avail; the electricity hadn't been turned on yet. In the back of the room someone had left a pile of empty cardboard boxes, and I tore off a piece and checked my pockets for something to write with. The landlord had taken my only pen with him, so I went out to the Chevy and rooted around until I found one of my kids' crayons tucked between the rear seat and the door. Back inside I printed on the cardboard the words "Mrs. Paul's Kitchens," and underneath it, "Seafood Specialities," and propped it in the window.

In a little while, the front windows were flooded with light, and I heard John Paul's car. The door swung open.

"Ed?"

I was sitting on the floor, my back propped against the wall. I climbed to my feet. "What do you think?"

John Paul looked around. "So this is the place." The empty room, small as it was, made his voice echo. "Well it's dark, I'll say that. No lights yet, huh?" He tipped his head toward the front window. "I saw the sign. What did you use? Crayon?"

"I know it's dark. The electricity hasn't been turned on. What do you *think?*"

"Well, it's not the Taj Mahal, I'll say that." He smiled. "Okay? It's a dump. It's perfect. How about we get a beer, Ed?"

"Don't you have to get back to Mark's?"

John shook his head. "Nah. Potter can handle things. What's he going to do? Fire us?" He clapped his hands together happily. "So what do you say? One night of goof-off before we get to work."

I agreed, and we locked up the store together. On the sidewalk outside, John paused and turned back to look at the sign, propped in the darkened window.

"You know, sometimes all of this seems totally nuts. I can't believe we're really doing it."

I nodded. "I know what you mean."

"Mrs. Paul's Kitchens." John clapped my shoulder. "It's quite a name. Hell, it's *my* name. I hope this works, Ed."

"Me, too," I said.

One thread connected me to my old life, and it was time to sever it. The next afternoon I drove down to Third and Cambria to see Mark Potter. By now, Potter suspected something was going on—I had not been to the bar for at least a week, except to drop off supplies for John—so I assumed my break with him was just a formality. Probably he would be just as glad to see us go.

I found him reading a paper at the bar. It was just two o'clock, and the room was empty save for a couple of regulars who worked night shifts at a bakery nearby. I said hello to them and then sat down next to Mark.

"Well look who's here." He turned the pages of his paper without looking up. "Says here that business everywhere is in a slide, though you wouldn't know it around here. Lots of people in the bar last night looking for something to eat. Many, many unhappy people."

"Sorry about that, Mark. Something came up."

"Something came up." He exhaled sharply through his nose. I had about had it with Mark Potter. I had planned to give him two weeks' notice, even find him another cook to run the concession, but now I hardly cared.

"You can tell John Paul I don't want to see his face around here anymore. And that's just for starters."

"Well, you won't see him, Mark. That's why I'm here. John and I are going into business together. It's all set up."

"What are you talking about? You are in business." He folded up his paper. "Or at least you were. You and me are gonna have to get a few things straight here."

"I'm talking about something else, Mark. Something bigger. We're going into the manufacturing business. Frozen food."

"Is that right?" He gave a little, mocking laugh. "Be serious. Like Bird's Eye and them other guys? Sure you are, Eddie boy."

"That's the gist of it. It's already done. I would've told you sooner, but it took a while to get things in place. So you can consider this my notice. I hope there's no hard feelings."

For a moment, Potter said nothing. Then his eyes did a slow turn around the room. "Cripes, Ed." (So now it was Ed, not Eddie boy.) "You come in here and tell me you're leaving me flat? Just what am I supposed to do now?"

"I don't know, Mark. I'm sure you can handle it."

"Jesus. You know I can't cook like you do." His initial arrogance was utterly gone; he had begun to sweat, and for a moment I felt sorry for him. He spun on his stool to face me and fixed me with his gaze. "Listen Ed, I'm telling you, don't do it. That's the real world out there. Those big companies, they're not like you and me. They'll skin you alive. You'll lose your shirt, I'm telling you."

"It's already done. My mind's made up, Mark."

"Ed, I know you. I know what you can handle. Remember the watch, the fifty bucks? This is me talking to you, Ed. Don't do this to Oddie. You've got a sweet deal here. Don't blow it."

I stood and put out my hand to shake. "Take care, Mark."

He didn't reply, just looked at my hand with a vague disgust. I might have been offering him a loaf of moldy bread.

"Aw, get outta here," he said finally. He waved in the general direction of the door. "The hell with you, Piszek."

I put my hand in my pocket. "If that's how you want it."

"Oh, you'll see, my friend. Those guys will chew you up and spit you out like the little pit you are. In a month you'll be back here begging."

"Goodbye, Mark."

I moved toward the door, then stopped. Mark had already gone back to reading his paper. It would be my last vision of Mark Potter sitting on a barstool in a dingy taproom in Kensington, angry at everything.

"Hey, Mark."

He turned around slowly, as if he'd already forgotten I'd ever worked for him.

"You know that watch?"

He narrowed his eyes and shrugged. "What about it?"

"It keeps lousy time."

Two weeks since I had frozen my first crabs, and we were in business. John and I rolled up our sleeves and cleaned up the Manayunk plant. With mouthfuls of nails we built an assembly line, hammering together cutting tables, a packing area, and plywood shelves around the stove. John had a friend in the paint business and managed to get a few cans cheap, and we painted everything a uniform white. John joked that it reminded him of a hospital or a lunatic asylum. To save money, we did all the work ourselves, except for the plumbing and electric, which, thankfully, were rather simple matters; we needed only a gas hookup for the stove (a used four burner I had bought for twenty-five dollars), a sink and drain line, and a separate heavy-duty electric line for the freezer. Instead of a refrigerator, which we couldn't afford, we picked up an old-fashioned icebox and arranged to have blocks delivered twice a week. I tried to get a phone installed but couldn't; the woman at the phone company explained that there was some deficiency of wire capacity in the area, and full service wouldn't be available for at least a year. For the time being, my only connection to the outside world was a pay phone across the street; my "executive office" was our front windowsill, enlarged with a piece of scrap lumber.

Already, we had burned through a third of our start-up funds, and we had yet to cook a crab. John and I had agreed to pay ourselves only a bare minimum salary of thirty-five dollars a week once we got started, so we could plow any profits back into the company. But even so, I knew we were going to have to borrow money soon, and to qualify, we would need to show some kind of profit.

But how much was enough? At Penn I had learned about an organization called the Alexander Hamilton Business Institute that provided basic services to small businesses like ours for the price of a subscription to their newsletter. Their name was, of course, laughably grand; I have no doubt now that the great Alexander Hamilton Business Institute was probably little more than a half-dozen people operating over a doughnut shop or garage. But at the time I was suitably impressed. The day I had traded in my Dodge I had written them a letter, carefully worded to give them a general idea about my plans without tipping my hand. *Gentlemen*, I wrote, *I would like to go into business, manufacturing and marketing a frozen food item. In your professional judgment, what is the absolute minimum amount of money that is needed?*

Three weeks later, John and I were painting the ceiling at the plant when Oddie drove up. Our youngest, George, was with her; the other children, Ann and Edward, were in school. I stopped working and met her at the door.

"What's up?"

She handed me a thick envelope, and I knew at once what it was. "I thought this might be important," she said.

John climbed down off his ladder. "Let's hope it's good news," he said, crossing his fingers.

I will not say that my heart was pounding in my chest, but I opened the letter with a sense of its deep importance, as if our future were contained within. I had yet to hear a single word of encouragement about what we were trying to do, and I badly needed it.

"Well," I said, "here goes."

"Five thousand at least," John Paul said. "I just know it."

Dear Mr. Piszek, it read,

We are in receipt of your inquiry about going into the frozen food manufacturing business. After careful deliberation, it is the opinion of our expert staff that such a venture would require an absolute minimum of fifty thousand dollars in capitalization during the first year.

There was more, but I did not bother to read on. Fifty thousand dollars! It was not just too much; it was all the money in the world. I began to laugh at the sheer craziness of it.

Little George tugged at my shirt hem. "Why are you laughing, Daddy?"

I tousled his hair. "Because someone's playing a joke on us, kiddo. A silly little joke."

"Some joke," Oddie said. "You're only . . . what? Forty-nine thousand dollars short."

"I think I better sit down," John said. He perched himself on a lower rung of the ladder and mournfully rubbed the back of his head. His face had gone ash gray. "Geez, Ed. Are they serious?"

"I'd say they are." I was still laughing, and I had begun to know why: a great weight had suddenly lifted from my shoulders. "They're the great Alexander Hamilton Business Institute. I'd say that makes them infallible."

"So what do we do?"

"Do? We do nothing. Don't you see, John? This is great news."

"Great? What's gotten into you? It's a disaster."

"Not in the least. Let me ask you something. What would we do if they said five thousand? Or even ten?"

"I don't know." He shrugged. "Try to get it, I guess."

"Exactly. And you know what? We'd fail. We'd take this letter to the bank, and they'd throw us into the street. But this way—" I crumpled the letter and tossed it in the waste can—"this way, we don't even have to try. So the great Alexander Hamilton Business Institute says it takes fifty grand to start up a business. Well, I've got news. It doesn't. I've never done this, but neither have they. Here's a new law, Piszek's law. To freeze deviled crabs in Manayunk, it takes exactly what we have. Seven hundred bucks."

Just then, there was a rap on the window. I saw that it was a woman with dark hair, holding a small child on her hip. She pointed at the sign, and mouthed, "Are you open?"

John rose and opened the door for her. "Excuse me," she said, "but I saw the sign."

"We're not open yet," John said. "Sorry."

"Oh. Well, too bad."

The woman shrugged and went on her way. I watched her go, wondered what she had wanted, and then it hit me all at once. She was not talking about the name on the sign, but what I had written underneath: Seafood Specialities.

"Somebody tell me. What day is it?"

John looked at me quizzically. "You mean what day? I dunno. The eighteenth."

"No, no. What day of the week."

"It's Friday." John paused and looked at me. A smile broke over his face like a spotlight blazing on a stage. "My God, it's *Friday*."

Oddie put her hands on her hips. "What's going on?"

I wanted to explain, but I was running calculations in my head as fast as I could. St. John the Baptist Church was just five blocks away, St. Josaphat's three blocks beyond. Holy Family, St. Lucy, St. Mary of the Assumption; if I had stood on the roof, I could have seen them all. The houses were spaced close, maybe a hundred to a block; the neighborhood was solid working-class Polish Catholic for ten blocks in each direction.

A hundred blocks. Ten thousand Catholic families. And they all ate fish on Fridays.

John narrowed his eyes at me. "Are you thinking what I'm thinking?"

"A takeout business."

He nodded. "It should tide us over."

"What woman wants to cook every Friday?"

"Exactly. A man comes home, he's tired, the wife's been stuck in the house with the kids all week. . . ."

"But going out? Too expensive."

"So she says, 'Honey, how about some deviled crabs from that joint down the block?'"

"Or fishcakes. Scallops, maybe. She had the deviled crabs last week. We'll have to expand the line."

"*Nobody* knows how to cook fish."

"And if ours is just as good as she can make it. . . ."

"Better even." John slapped his knee happily. "Hell, it's a natural, Ed."

We stopped, breathless. Oddie was looking at us as if we had lost our minds. "Would one of you geniuses *please* let me in on the big secret?"

"I think we just found our financing." I went to the wastebasket and pulled out the crumpled letter. "Memo to Alexander Hamilton Business Institute," I said, "from John Paul and Ed Piszek. Thanks for the advice. We open on Thursday."

And so we did. Six days later, with absolutely no fanfare at all, John Paul drove into the Manayunk plant at five in the morning, turned on the lights, and propped a new sign on the windowsill: "Now Open, Take-out Available." By the time I got there an hour later, I walked into a sweet haze of sizzling grease, sputtering cream sauce, and plump crab freshly plucked from the Chesapeake and delivered that morning in a barrel by railway express. I was twenty-nine years old, but I felt as if my life was just beginning.

We had figured correctly; our Friday night takeout was an instant hit. From the start we considered it just a sideline, something to be discarded once we got our product into stores, but in the meantime, it would let us operate in the black. There were no precedents for what we were attempting, no models for success or failure, no proven methods for assembly or packaging. A baker has centuries of tradition to tell him what pans or whisks to use, but we could only improvise. In a single twenty-quart pot, we cooked the cream sauce, butter, and crab; we then cooled the mixture in the icebox, stiffening it so we could divide it into three-ounce portions with an ice cream scooper. Once the crab cakes were formed, they were rolled in bread crumbs and deep-fried, then frozen immediately. We packaged them two to a box, affixed a simple label, and wrapped them in cellophane. The price: fifty-nine cents.

From the start, John ran the line—making him, in essence, our entire workforce—whereas I took our product on the road. Our market research had showed us more or less what we had expected to find. Frozen vegetables and French fries were abundant—the giants, Seabrook and Bird's Eye, dominated—and pastries, cakes, and pies were beginning to appear, but frozen *prepared* food was virtually nonexistent. (The lone exception could be found, ironically, in our own backyard. Henry Martin, a tiny company based in Philadelphia, was marketing some frozen seafood, including deviled crabs. We discovered this too late to do anything about it, and happily, the problem took care of itself; within a year or two, Henry Martin was out of the frozen food business.) This meant that we had virtually no competition but no proven markets, either.

One thing I had learned at Wharton: you could get killed entering a market that the consumer did not know, or worse, did not care about. Thus, from the outset, my strategy had to be one of creating a market and filling it simultaneously. If a housewife didn't trust frozen seafood, then I had to create that trust. One thing I could rely on was the intense quality of neighborhood life in Philadelphia. My little corner of Manayunk was a case in point—we were not in business three weeks before the lines were forming on Friday afternoons. If our product was good—and I believed it was—then word of mouth would be our best, cheapest advertising.

Still, our Friday takeout concession was one thing; getting the frozen product into stores was another. It was the classic catch-22 proposition: a grocer wouldn't carry a product if there wasn't a demand, and demand couldn't be created unless people knew the product. As a salesman for Campbell's, I had had it easy; everyone knew the Campbell's name and knew what to expect from a can of Campbell's Soup. But Mrs. Paul's Frozen Deviled Crabs were a mystery to everyone.

I scratched my head for a couple of weeks until it hit me: grocers were consumers, too. How simple! Who was a grocer but a consumer on a grand scale? And didn't a grocer carry those products in his store that he would buy for his own table, put on his own table? I had seen the principle in action before, right under my nose. For several years, a salesman from Heinz, a fellow named Charlie, had called on my mother, trying to persuade her to carry Heinz Ketchup. Heinz was the premium brand; it sold for twenty-five cents a bottle, more than twice its major competitor, a brand called Ritter's. My mother wouldn't budge, refusing to believe that one brand of ketchup could be worth so much more than another. Then one day Charlie came into the store, made his customary pitch extolling the virtues of Heinz Ketchup, and concluded by asking my mother for a piece of blotter paper. To amuse him, she obliged; Charlie then proceeded to pour half of the ketchup from a bottle of Heinz and half from one of Ritter's onto the paper. In no time at all, the Ritter's was gone, leaving only a moist, red ring and a puddle on the counter. Then, Charlie swung into his pitch. "See?" he said. "With Ritter's, you're paying for water! Mr. Heinz, he's selling real quality!"

It was a perfect selling angle, and it worked its magic on thousands of storeowners just like my mother. That red ring—by the time Charlie was through, Ritter's Catsup did not even seem like food. Despite the high price, Heinz came to dominate the ketchup market, because the consumer—who was, in this case, also the grocer—could see that the product was demonstrably better. (So successful was the blotter test that a version of the same pitch was a television advertising staple for the company well into the 1970s.)

In this fashion, I formulated my basic sales strategy, one that would last many years. Of course, no blotter would do the trick for me; my appeal was taste, pure and simple. If anyone was going to buy my product, they were going to have to try it first. With scraps of plywood, I constructed a box to fit inside the trunk of my Chevy, a makeshift, portable refrigerator insulated with stacks of newspapers, and filled it with boxes of our deviled crabs. Then I took a one-gallon thermos jug, with a wide mouth, and filled that with hot-cooked crabs each morning—my samples, which I would serve in soufflé cups.

Initially, I built my sales route from my old Campbell's route, focusing on the small mom-and-pop stores in the working-class neighborhoods north of Center City. The real money, I knew, was with the big chain stores—Acme (number one, the absolute muscle of the market), Food Fair, Penn Fruit, Frankfurt-Unity, and Baltimore Markets—but these would be impossible to crack without a sales history and would have to wait. Besides, if word of mouth was my sole means of advertising for now, the smaller, neighborhood stores were a better choice.

In each store—whether or not I knew the proprietor—my approach was the same. I timed my visit as best I could so that several shoppers were in the store (housewives were ideal: they were the prime consumers for a product like mine), then approached the owner.

"Mr. Jones, perhaps you remember me. I'm Ed Piszek, and a few years back I represented Campbell's Soup in this area." (Whether or not I had actually sold him Campbell's was beside the point, and invariably, most claimed to remember, even if we had never met.) "I have something new today that I would like you to try. Mrs. Paul's Deviled Crabs. They're absolutely pure, made with only the freshest crabmeat, butter, and milk."

At this moment I turned to a customer shopping nearby. "Madam, would you be so kind? Perhaps I could persuade you to try a new product."

I served them both a sample from the thermos. Although the owner invariably gave a noncommittal shrug, the woman promptly raved: "My, they're delicious! What do you call these?" A few more ladies gathered round, and soon I had developed a coterie of enthusiasts. "Where in the store are they?" a woman asked, and that was my breakthrough.

I turned to the owner. "Mr. Jones, I happen to have several boxes out in the car. Let me put some in your freezer over there. A pure Philadelphia product, fresh and pure as that woman's baby."

From the owner, a nod: capitulation. "Frozen, you say? And they taste like this? All right, give me a dozen."

I would load up his freezer, stacking my boxes next to the Bird's Eye Broccoli and Seabrook French Fries, and be on my way. Out in the car, Oddie, fresh from her appearance as the randomly selected taste-testing housewife, turned to me.

"Well? How'd I do?"

"Darling, you should be on Broadway."

By early summer, Mrs. Paul's was in close to thirty neighborhood stores, and we were on our way. We were so busy that we were running two shifts at the plant; for the time being, Oddie and John's wife, Katherine, were taking over the second shift until we could hire some employees. Most significantly, the profits from our Friday night takeout concession covered our basic operating expenses handily. This meant that John and I could put aside any profit from the frozen end of the business to grow the business. (I called this the "Johnny Grant Theory of Capitalization" after a kid I had known back in my Wingohocking Street days. We used to gather after school to shoot craps for pennies, and Johnny was the acknowledged master, always ready to play. He used to brag that he never lost a cent, and this was true; if he won, he always let his profits ride, sometimes amassing a small fortune in the process. If he lost, he took his original stake and went home. I had marveled at the intelligence of this strategy and never forgot it. The moral was clear: never touch your start-up stake until there is enough to pocket some and keep playing at the same time.)

So we were in the black, for now. In the back of my mind, I was already calculating an advertising strategy—word of mouth and in-store taste tests would only go so far—but this, I knew, would take plenty of money, which we did not yet have. At Wharton, I had learned that the basic rule of thumb for an advertising budget was 5 percent of gross sales. But this seemed anemic to me, especially for a start-up company in an industry that did not then exist. With the takeout end of the business running full tilt, I figured that we could take the plunge with 15 percent. But even so, that amounted to a paltry seventy dollars a week.

I was mulling the problem over one night when I got a phone call from my old boss at GE. The strike was over, he told me. So much had happened that I had practically forgotten that I was still, technically, an employee of General Electric. Before I could tell him I was no longer available, he cut me off.

"Mr. Faust wants to have a word with you. Could you come down to the plant tomorrow?"

It was almost as if I had become a different person, and any temptation to return had long since left me. But Faust had been kind to me—more than kind. I said nothing except that I would come.

I met him at his office at 4:00 the next afternoon. The plant was busy again, whirring with activity as if the strike had never happened. How long had it been since I had laughed in the cold at horses flailing around on a carpet of marbles? It seemed like years. The secretary led me into Faust's office, and I sat across from him, the wide desk separating us. Faust was looking over some papers.

"Ah." At last he looked up and pushed his papers aside. "Mr. Piszek, thank you for coming. Now that the recent labor difficulties have concluded, I was hoping that we could discuss your future here at General Electric. I have an offer that I think might interest you."

I was deeply moved. Once again, Faust was looking out for me. And I knew at once that I would be betraying his generosity if I did not speak immediately.

"Mr. Faust, I appreciate that, but I'm afraid I won't be returning. You see, another opportunity has come up, and I've decided to go in that direction."

"Oh?" His tone was not irritated or even especially surprised, merely interested.

"Yes sir." I took out one of our new business cards, printed that very week, and reached across his desk to hand it to him.

"Mrs. Paul's Kitchens," he read aloud. He tapped the edge of the card on his desk. "I don't believe I'm familiar with them. What have they offered you?"

I'd never said it before, and a shiver of satisfaction snaked the length of my spine. "I'm the CEO."

Faust raised an eyebrow and studied me for a long moment. No doubt, he wondered if I was playing a joke. "Mr. Piszek, forgive me. Do you know what CEO stands for? But of course you do."

"Yes sir. It's my company. I started it three months ago."

"And what does Mrs. Paul's make?"

"Frozen precooked deviled crabs." I shrugged. "It's a long story. I'd be happy to send you a sample."

Faust leaned back in his chair and lit his pipe. "Mr. Piszek. I've had a busy afternoon, so allow me a moment of cornball sentiment. Do you know why we bothered to fight and win this last war?"

"Sir?"

He smiled, smoke drifting around his face. "We won it," he explained, "so that a man like you could walk out of a control cage and come back a few months later as a CEO." Faust rose, offering me his hand to shake. "Now, I must return to work. I would be glad to try your product. I would be honored. And the very, very best of luck to you, Mr. Piszek."

He was a good man, and remembering this moment, I am sad only that it was the last time we ever spoke. I have no idea whatever became of him—though, in my experience, a man like Faust could only do well. Whatever else is true of the business world, ruthless men are a dime a dozen. It is the decent man who rises highest. It is a lesson I learned that day.

Leaving the plant to get my car, I crossed Elmwood Avenue and saw, above me, a large sign advertising Camel cigarettes. With the war over, cigarettes were in supply again, and the big tobacco companies were engaged in an all-out advertising blitz, trying to cut a slice out of the civilian market. I stood for a moment, studying it. The ad itself was ordinary, no different, really, than a hundred others: there was a catchy slogan, a picture of the package, some nonsense about the relaxing health benefits of smoking Camels after eating. (How long ago 1946 seems now!) It was unextraordinary in every way. What struck me was its clever positioning. Someone had thought to place the billboard so that, for workers coming off a shift, it would be the very first thing they saw. How many hundreds would, at that moment, reach unconsciously for a cigarette, a *Camel* cigarette? It was masterful marketing, elegantly simple and effective, and I didn't need to wonder that there were a thousand billboards just like it, hovering by the exits of a thousand factories all across the country.

Who were my customers? I knew the answer well: housewives. Billboards would be no good for them; I had to reach them in their own homes, in their own kitchens. But how? My mind drifted, alighting on a memory of boyhood days—hurrying through my final chores at my parents' store to steal one sweet hour of evening play in the park with my friends, hurrying to the corner and hearing, from each window I passed, the familiar voices and canned studio laughter of *Amos 'n' Andy*, punctuating the summer dusk.

In a flash, the answer came to me.

What did every housewife in America have sitting right there in her kitchen, playing all day long?

The radio.

All day long, she listened to the radio.

That night, I met with John Paul at my house for our weekly strategy session. The business was expanding rapidly. We needed two, maybe three, new employees just to keep up, and we decided we would hire women from the neighborhood, thinking this would be both fairly inexpensive and good for business. (It was both.) But when I mentioned my notion to get Mrs. Paul's on the radio, he balked.

"The radio?" He shook his head. "That'd cost a fortune."

"Maybe so. But we won't know unless we ask. Think of it, John. Just one spot—thirty lousy seconds. How many women would that reach? I spend half an hour at least on just one taste test. Someone hears about us on the radio and asks for us at the store up the corner, she's doing our work for us."

He scratched his head. "It makes sense. Well, sure. We might as well try. How do you go about it?"

I had given this some thought. "We'll need an ad agency, first of all. Someone who knows the radio. I've heard of one, N. W. Ayer. They're a big outfit, supposed to be good."

"N. W. Ayer, huh." John laughed. "Sounds pretty fancy for a couple of guys slinging fish."

"Fancy is just what we need."

I called to make an appointment ("Yes? Hello? Ed Piszek here, CEO of Mrs. Paul's Kitchens up in Manayunk. Wondering if there's someone down there that might like to talk about a new ad campaign for us . . ."), and the next week, I put on my best suit and drove down to their office. My appointment was with a Mr. Cooper, and after a brief wait in the receptionist's area, a woman appeared and introduced herself as Mr. Cooper's assistant. She led me down a long hallway of offices to her desk, where she took a yellow legal pad from her drawer and invited me to sit.

"I hope you don't mind, but I'll need to ask you a few preliminary questions about the campaign you had in mind." She gave me a warm smile. "It's just how we do things around here."

"Of course," I said.

"Now, the full name of your company is Mrs. Paul's Kitchens? And you're here as the principal of that company?"

"That's right."

She scribbled something on her pad. "And what business are you in, exactly?"

"Frozen food." I cleared my throat. "We're manufacturing a line of frozen seafood." She continued writing, though I could not see what. "Frozen deviled crabs. The finest quality."

"I see. And were you thinking about print advertising?"

"Actually, I thought the radio might be the best for us."

"I see." She smiled at me, then returned to her writing. "Interested . . . in . . . radio . . . advertising." At last she looked up. "Very good. Now, Mr. Piszek, it would help us to know the extent of the campaign you envision."

"I'm sorry?"

She smiled. "Forgive me. I mean what your annual advertising budget will be. Approximately."

She's certainly wasting no time, I thought. "Well, we're not exactly sure."

"That's quite understandable. A rough estimate is fine, Mr. Piszek. Just to give us some idea where we're headed."

John and I had discussed a figure: thirty-five hundred dollars. I decided to go high, because I could bargain down from there. She had returned to her legal pad, her pen poised.

"We're thinking about five thousand dollars."

For an instant, she froze. "I beg your pardon?"

I felt a cold sweat of embarrassment poke out along my hairline. "Well, we could go higher. Seven?" (Of course, we could do no such thing.)

With a brusque finality, she capped her pen and rose. "Just a moment, please."

She left me alone, and I had a few moments alone to curse myself. What was I doing here? I had always known my figure was low, but in the back of my mind, I had hoped that somehow my big ideas might interest someone enough to take us on. I could see now how stupid that was.

I waited a few minutes, and just when I was about ready to leave, a tall man appeared at her desk. He seemed a little out of breath, as if he had just jogged down the hallway.

"Mr. Piszek. I'm Frank Cooper." We shook hands. "I'll come right to the point, because you seem like a serious man. Your figure is just too low for us. I wish it was different, but that's just the way things are. So, no hard feelings, all right?"

"Well, sure," I said. "None taken."

He pulled out a notepad from his jacket pocket and began to write something. "Listen, here's a name for you. I don't want you leaving here thinking we were no help at all." He tore off the page and handed it to me. "Shepp Knapp is a friend of mine. He used to work here, until the rat race got to him. He's a freelancer now, and I bet he'd be glad to talk to you."

I thanked him, put the note in my jacket pocket, and gathered my things to go.

"Frozen food," he said, looking at his assistant's pad on the desk. "What are you freezing? Vegetables?"

I shook my head. "Deviled crabs," I said. "We used to serve them out of a bar in Kensington."

He touched his chin, mulling this over. "Not a bad idea. I've heard a lot worse."

He walked me out, and at the door we shook again.

"Give Shepp a call, all right? And mention my name."

"Thanks, I will." I was halfway out the door when I stopped. I had to know. I turned and caught his eye. "If you don't mind my asking, how close were we?"

He laughed. "Not very. You were short a zero, Mr. Piszek."

What could I do? I laughed, too. I laughed all the way home.

Shepp Knapp's office was a tiny table in the corner of his living room. He was older than I expected, close to retirement probably, and I liked him immediately. How many meetings had John and I conducted over the table in my tiny kitchen? We were both freelancers, really.

The first thing Shepp looked into was our packaging. I had brought him a sample box, and he eyed it with disapproval.

"Well. That certainly is a box," he said.

In fact, I had given our packaging some consideration. I knew we had to update our look, to make it distinct. I envisioned a silver label with crimson trim, crisp and modern-looking.

"Silver is not a color," Shepp proclaimed. For another minute he said nothing, just studied the box as if there were some secret panel he might locate if he concentrated long and hard enough.

"Green," he said at last.

I was aghast. The one thing I knew about packaging was that green was verboten, especially for seafood. It was the color of rot, garbage, decay. Green was the color a person turned when he had poisoned himself. I was trying to get people to eat something they had never tried before. Green was the last thing I wanted.

"Perhaps with a little red on a white background," he continued. He nodded to himself. "A warm green, like the colors of a kitchen."

I explained my objections, and he listened patiently. Then when I was through, he took our plain little box and held it up in his hand. "Correct me if I'm wrong. There's no product like yours on the market?"

"As far as I know."

"And frozen food is the coming thing. A whole new industry, waiting to be born."

I saw his point. "I hope so."

Without missing a beat, he continued. "What color is your kitchen?"

I had to think. "Yellow, I guess. The cabinets are white. You don't think the package should be yellow, do you?"

"And what color is the floor?"

He had me. "Green linoleum. Green and white, actually."

"We must never be afraid of something new, Mr. Piszek." He returned the box to the table between us. "That's the message your package will convey. As for the radio—" He shook his head. "I'd say it's out of our range, for now."

It depressed me to hear him say it, but I liked the way he had spoken: *our* range. So Shepp was on board.

"Let me give it some thought," he said. "We'll come up with something."

The plan he concocted was a good one, not least of all because it was cheap. If we could not reach the housewife in her kitchen, we would get to her husband as he rode home, hungry, on the subway. We printed up some simple cards and bought space on the El trains in North Philadelphia. "Try Mrs. Paul's Deviled Crabs," the ads read, with a picture of a smiling chef holding one of our boxes. Positioned right at eye level, and reaching its audience just when dinner was on his mind, they possessed the same shrewdly effective simplicity as the Camel billboard I had seen outside GE's Elmwood Plant. Not a bull's eye, I thought, but at least headed for the target.

Still, I did not abandon my radio dreams. More than ever, I believed that advertising was the key to our business, to any business. If all we could afford so far was print cards on the El, so be it; but if our business was going to grow, we had to reach audiences far larger.

In fact, by autumn, I had begun to think that it was time to take on the big chains. Mom-and-pop groceries were important to our business and always would be, but anyone could tell that the era of the neighborhood store was drawing to a close. The chain supermarkets, with their high volumes and deep discounts, already commanded a huge slice of the business; the age of the automobile guaranteed their market share would only grow larger. By early '47, it was clear to anyone who paid attention that a new era of economic prosperity was approaching, quite different from anything the nation had ever experienced; you could feel it, hear it, like the first rumblings of an avalanche in the hills above. The statistics were everywhere. Businesses had begun to expand, the birth rate had soared, and new housing starts were flying through the roof. GI benefits flooded the market with cheap loans, and colleges were bursting with new students, men and women who might never before have been able to afford an education but now could, courtesy of Uncle Sam. They would become engineers, doctors, lawyers—in other words, consumers with money to spend. The atomic flash that had ended the war in the Pacific had stunned us all with its awesome power, but it had also proven something that most Americans had long believed true: the future belonged to American technology.

It was a big leap, in some ways, from the Manhattan Project to our pint-sized operation in a Manayunk storefront, but I had begun to understand how everything was part of a system, a zeitgeist, and that the system was a kind of story. I imagined it this way:

A GI, the son of a union pipe fitter, returns from the war and goes to college; he studies law or business or engineering; he graduates, and with his young wife and two small children, he buys a house (a new one, because only new homes are available for sale; it stands in a field where cows once grazed and is surrounded by fifty other houses exactly like it, where an identical story unfolds); with a paycheck fatter than his father ever could have dreamed of, he buys a car, a glossy new Chevy with space-age lines and chrome that gleams like ice, and fills his kitchen with appliances to match; he drives to the supermarket (which, like his house, is also new, with freezer compartments the size of railroad cars) to fill up the trunk with a week's load of groceries at a time. And along the way—from Omaha Beach to college lecture hall to suburban subdivision—he leaves a wake of prosperity, a bread crumb trail of cash that magnifies his story a thousand, thousand fold. He leaves his green mark everywhere he goes, from the carpenter who builds his house to the hardware dealer who sells him his lawn mower to the investor who takes a chance on a shopping center in a potato field that used to be the middle of noplace; *everywhere.*

It was a story in which everybody seemed to win, so it made me instantly suspicious. (What would happen, for instance, to the cities left behind? What would happen when the corner grocery went out of business? Someone had to lose, and the social cost was no abstraction to me. I shuddered to realize that it was small merchants like my mother who would watch the coming prosperity float by.) Such a rosy vision of the future could not be the whole truth. But it was a compelling truth. Quite by accident, I had chosen the perfect moment to go into business—even, as I now believed, to invent a whole new industry.

Someone once asked the gangster Willie Sutton why he robbed banks. His answer: "Because that's where the money is." For us, the money was in the chains. But cracking the chains would take more than clever salesmanship. For six months, I had avoided the problem, because it seemed insurmountable. The corner grocery was an easy sell; the owner was the buyer, and he could stock his shelves with whatever he liked. But the big stores bought through middlemen—food brokers or distributors—who worked specifically with certain stores and manufacturers. In effect, the brokers controlled the retail end of the industry; if I wanted a broker to deal my product, I had to give him exclusive rights to distribute it, an arrangement that would be negotiated as a "discount" that really amounted to a legal kickback. These were the big boys that Mark Potter had warned me about. (Though how he knew about such things I could not say; probably, he was guessing.) Even giant companies like Seabrook and Bird's Eye had knuckled under, allowing themselves to be sold only in certain stores.

I saw that once I let a broker into my tent, there was no going back; I might get Mrs. Paul's into one chain store or the other, but only one. That might be fine for Seabrook, with as many as thirty or forty products to stock the shelves. For them, an exclusive arrangement guaranteed them a predictable market share without competition. But with only three products to sell (by now we were freezing scallops and fishcakes in addition to the deviled crabs), our business would wither without the widest possible exposure to the market.

John and I discussed the problem and concluded there was only one thing to do. We would ignore the "exclusive" system entirely. Our company policy would be that we would sell to everyone—directly to store buyers or through distributors if it came to that—at one price. It was a gamble; we would certainly make no friends for it, neither among the Seabrooks and Bird's Eyes of the world (who were only too happy to sell their products without competition) nor their distributors (who grew fat and happy on their "discounts"). Neither did we see ourselves as champions of the free market. To the contrary—we could barely afford such principles. If the existing system of exclusive distribution rights, crooked as it was, would have worked for us, we would have cheerfully waded in. We found ourselves in the oddest circumstance: that rare occasion when ethical courage and sheer practicality coincided.

I took my pitch to the buyer for Food Fair, Philadelphia's largest chain. By this time, we had been in business half a year, and I had my pitch down pat. I met with the buyer in his office, and I laid it on thick—the freshest ingredients, only ninety-three score pure creamery butter, the finest Maryland crabmeat, and so on. I told him how many cases a week we were selling in the small mom-and-pop stores (exaggerating the number only slightly). I showed him letters we had received from happy customers (a great many of them from Oddie's friends) and served him hot samples right on his desk.

"So what do you say?"

He wiped his mouth on a napkin. It was clear from his face that he liked what he had eaten. "Well," he said, "we don't have much freezer space in our stores. You're coming in here with a brand nobody ever heard of before. How can I be so sure it'll sell?"

I was ready for this. "I'll tell you what. I know the freezer you've got at 56th and City Line." (It was among their largest stores, and the one where Oddie shopped.) "There's room for an additional product. Let me put Mrs. Paul's in that one store and I'll show you."

He shrugged noncommittally, though I could see he was tempted. "Well . . . I don't know. If it doesn't sell, I'm still stuck with it. I'm not sure about this nonexclusive policy thing, either. Aren't you getting a little ahead of yourself?"

"Okay. Here's what I'll do. Give me the order and don't pay the invoice until you know the crabs have sold. I'll *give* you five cases. They're yours. Don't pay until the last one is gone."

"You mean that?"

"Absolutely I do. And you've got nothing to lose."

"What the hell?" he said. "Sure, Mr. Piszek. Five cases for City Line."

He agreed to call his manager to let him know I would be delivering the order, and the next morning, John and I loaded up five cases in the trunk of the Chevy—at twenty-four boxes a case, and fifty-nine cents a box, a little over seventy dollars' worth of product. It was not much, but I felt as if I was delivering the most precious cargo of my life. John stayed behind to mind the plant, and I drove across the Belmont Avenue Bridge and up the hill to City Line. It was a clear day in late fall, the sky an icy blue, and I drove with the windows open. The good weather seemed auspicious, a happy sign. We were on our way.

Then behind me I heard, then saw, an eighteen-wheeler, filling my mirror. I pulled into the right lane, and as he passed me, I saw the word *Seabrook* emblazoned on its side. My whole car seemed to shudder as he blew past me.

I thought then of the little paper-lined, insulated box in my trunk, and a cavern opened inside me, a black abyss of doubt. How many tons did that one truck carry? And how many more trucks like it did Seabrook have? What was I thinking? Compete with *them?*

I was so shaken that I slowed the Chevy to a crawl and found a place to pull over. For a long moment I just sat there, lulled into a kind of trance by the whoosh of passing traffic and the bright sunlight dancing on my hood.

But then, as suddenly as it had arrived, my black mood lifted. "Trust yourself," I said. "Drive."

I delivered my five cases to the store manager and watched as he put them in the freezer case. Shepp had been right after all: the green *did* look sharp. I thanked the manager and went on my way.

An hour later—though I was not there to see it—Oddie stepped up to the case, removed a box, and turned to the woman standing next to her.

"Why, I've been looking for these everywhere," she exclaimed. "Have you ever tried these?"

The woman eyed the package. "My Gregory loves deviled crabs. But frozen?"

"Best I've ever eaten," Oddie said. She winked. "You mark my words."

For the rest of the day, the store was deluged by Mrs. Paul's enthusiasts, virtually every friend and relative I could talk into going. Perhaps some strangers bought a box or two. I really do not know.

At noon the next day I called the buyer to inquire how we were doing.

"For Christ sakes, that stuff flew outta here! We're cleaned out already. Send me an invoice and get your fanny over here with ten more cases."

"You got it!" I fairly yelled into the phone. I called Oddie with the news and hustled down to City Line with the new order. Once again, Piszeks of every shape and size descended on the store, though this time with instructions to buy only half of the store's inventory.

Then a quarter. Then an eighth. A month later, I had an order for the whole chain.

My parents' wedding photo, 1914.

My father, Peter Piszek, with customers at his Chicago Heights saloon, about 1916.

A Sunday gathering at the Quakertown farm, 1922. Top (left to right): my sisters Alice (12), Irene (14), and Amelia (4); my mother, family friend Mrs. Shelski and her two children; bottom: my father, my sister Cecilia (8), the author (6), and Mr. Shelski. The Shelskis owned a local hosiery factory.

The author at age sixteen on the banks of Tohickon Creek.

With Oddie on a Sunday visit to Quakertown, 1936. A year later we would marry.

A Mrs. Paul's sales meeting in Miami Beach, 1957, yields a lighter moment. Pictured here are many key people from the early days of the company, including Hal Montgomery, our ad man (far left); Frank Moore, our assistant director of sales (in back); my brother-in-law Joe Mott (in front); and Jack Kelly, our director of sales (second from right). Courtesy, Doris Barnes.

In the fifties, Mrs. Paul's tried a number of unusual advertising venues, such as this bus-shelter sign in New York State. With a captive audience, these ads proved surprisingly effective.

"The Fishcake King" in our new Henry Avenue offices, late 1950s. Courtesy, Snyder's Studio.

Philadelphia radio personality Jack Pyle of WRCV was one of many broadcasters who helped put Mrs. Paul's on the map in the late fifties and early sixties. To this day I credit radio with the company's success. Courtesy, Jules Schick.

Where seafood is concerned... everyone wants the best!

Try Mrs. Paul's *Premium Quality* Fish Sticks!

These are *extra special* fish sticks . . . made entirely from the finest, freshest, best-tasting fish that ever came out of the deep, icy waters of the North Atlantic. They're breaded in "custom ground" bread crumbs and then cooked to a crisp, delicious golden-brown perfection in Mrs. Paul's special, exclusive cooking medium.

Sure, they cost a few pennies more. But once you've tried 'em, you'll never settle for less.

One of a continuing series of advertisements telling millions of housewives about the Premium Quality of Mrs. Paul's products—the most widely-advertised frozen seafood line in America.
Mrs. Paul's Kitchens, Phila. 27, Pa.

For a complete fish stick dinner, try Mrs. Paul's Fish Stick Dinner Deluxe

Try Mrs. Paul's economical Family-size package of Fish Sticks

A typical newspaper advertisement for Mrs. Paul's, circa 1960.

One of the mobile X-ray units we took to Poland in 1967. Fanning out across the country, they were the workhorses on our two-year program to eradicate tuberculosis. The words on the truck read "Provincial Outpatient Clinic for Tuberculosis." The gentlemen beside me are health ministry officials and representatives from CARE.

Project POLE kicks off in 1971 on NBC's Today show. Such appearances gave our endeavors instant national exposure. Pictured with me are Father Walter Ziemba of the Center for Polish Studies and Culture of Orchard Lake, Michigan (center), and the show's host, Frank McGee (right). Courtesy, Bill Ray/TimePix.

With Oddie at Emlen House in the heyday of Mrs. Paul's Kitchens. Courtesy, Bill Ray/TimePix.

Negotiating in Poland in the early 1970s.

With Jim Michener on a trip to Reims, France, in 1972. From the moment we met, Jim and I became the closest of companions and traveled the world together.

With the Holy Father and Cardinal John Krol in Rome's St. Peter's Square, 1982. The man to Krol's left is his secretary, Father Joseph McFadden. Courtesy, Arturo Mari.

The greatest day: Lech Walesa comes to Emlen House on a cold November morning, 1989, to ring Liberty Bell II. The man behind him is his interpreter. Courtesy, Eric Mitchell.

Congratulating President Carter on his receipt of the Rotary Award for World Understanding, 1994. I received the same honor two years earlier, one of my proudest accomplishments. The photo was taken at the Carter Center in Atlanta, Georgia.

A private moment with the Holy Father in Vatican City. One of the great statesmen and religious leaders of the modern era, his friendship and counsel have been a guiding influence in my life. Courtesy, Arturo Mari.

With baseball great Stan Musial at Emlen House on my eightieth birthday.

Receiving the Commander's Cross with Star of Polania Restituta, one of Poland's highest civilian honors, March 1998. Courtesy, Damazy Kwiatowski.

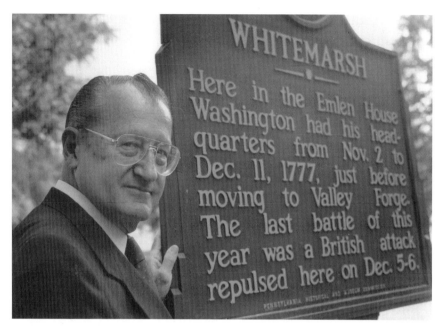

By Emlen House's roadside historic marker. Oddie and I first saw Emlen House in 1934, when we tried to picnic there and a groundskeeper chased us away. Twenty-two years later we bought it. Courtesy, Susan Rankin.

With my son Bill at the dedication of the Edward J. Piszek Stadium in Kutno, Poland, August 2000. It was a stirring tribute—and a complete surprise.

Chapter Eight
Radio Days

Mrs. Paul's Kitchens was just nine months old when a momentous day came. I arrived at the plant on a fine winter morning and saw, outside, a brand-new telephone pole. I cast my eyes upward along its length; suspended from the top was a lone man in a hard hat, his waist wrapped by a tool belt that must have weighed fifteen pounds.

He called down to me. "You Piszek?"

"That's right."

He descended the pole with surprising aerial grace and went into his truck. After a moment of digging around, he reappeared, carrying a chunky black telephone.

"Where you want it?"

I had by this time memorized every nick, crack, and profane etching in the phone booth across the street. It seemed to be a kind of clearinghouse for off-color speculation on the virtue of every unmarried woman in the neighborhood. For a moment, I was actually speechless with joy.

"Listen, Mac," the repairman said, not bothering to conceal his impatience. "It's just a telephone. I haven't got all day."

"I don't know. The windowsill?"

He shrugged carelessly. "The windowsill, the wall, upstairs, downstairs. I'll hang it from the ceiling if that's what you want. It's all wires to me."

"Put it on the sill," I said.

He pulled a crumpled work order from the pocket of his jacket. "Sign here, Mac."

The telephone was not our only improvement. A few months before, we had taken on our first employees, three older women from the neighborhood whose kids were all grown and gone. Now we were up to a half-dozen workers. The small room was getting so crowded it was difficult to move, and the workday was a muttered chorus of "I beg your pardon" and "excuse me" as employees shuttled sidestep to negotiate the thin lanes between the worktables. The joke was that the only way to get fired was to walk straight forward.

By the end of that first year, we had cracked three chains. After Food Fair, I had taken my pitch to the buyer for Penn Fruit. "Our company has a nonexclusive policy," I had told him. "It's the same everywhere. One test store is all I'm asking for. Just one store. I'm telling you, we'll fly off the shelves." What I did not tell him, of course, was that, except for Food Fair, everywhere was nowhere. It didn't matter. He dismissed me quickly, telling me to come back and see him in a week. For six straight weeks we jousted back and forth, until, out of sheer exhaustion, he let us into one store, on Market Street in downtown Philadelphia. ("I admire your grit, I'll say that," was all he said.) And once again, a battalion of Piszeks appeared from the woodwork and cleaned him out.

Acme proved even tougher. No "come back and see me" this time; their buyer told me, with a wave of his meaty hand, to get lost. We launched a preemptive strike: for eight weeks running, my friends and relatives stopped by three targeted stores in Northeast Philadelphia and pestered the managers for Mrs. Paul's Deviled Crabs. I wondered when they would catch on, but they never did; in the end, we sold them, too.

With all my attentions pointed at the chains—that required constant courtship—I could no longer concentrate on the small, one-owner stores. Our print ads were now all over town, and we had to be, too. How would it look if a man coming home from work saw our placard on the El but could not find us in any stores nearby? I saw that it was time to hire another salesman.

In those days, we dealt strictly in cash—or green, as we called it. From buying supplies to paying workers, everything was in real money. This included the salesman's bond. The standard arrangement—the same one I had lived with as a salesman for Campbell's—was that a salesman put up five hundred dollars in exchange for samples and a route. He would eventually get it all back, but in the meantime, the company had the five hundred dollars just in case he skipped.

As a salesman I had groused against the injustice of this system, but as an employer, I began to see the benefits, especially for a small company like ours. Five hundred dollars was a great deal of money, nearly our total initial capitalization; paid in advance by a new employee, it amounted to an interest-free loan. At forty dollars a week plus commissions, anyone we hired would, in essence, be bankrolling his own salary for an entire year.

The man we found for the job was a ringer, too—an old friend from my Campbell's days, Paul Fanning. A strapping, handsome fellow with an Irishman's gift for gab, he took over our small store operation with gusto and was quickly matching me sale for sale. I went on a couple of sales calls with him to watch him operate, and it was like watching Fred Astaire dance. Each move he made had a grace that belied all calculation, all sense of a thing rehearsed. Finding Paul had been a major stroke of luck.

At the end of the first year, we ran our books and saw how we had done. We were astounded. Mrs. Paul's Kitchens was ten thousand dollars in the black. Not a fortune but more than we had ever imagined; just to be operating out of the red was a miracle. By that time, we were running two eight-hour shifts a day, and at the close of business on a Friday, John, his wife Katherine, Oddie, and I cracked open a bottle of champagne and toasted our success. Paul was there, too, and a few of the women who had just come off their shift.

There would be no raises for a while—every extra dime was going back into the business, as Johnny Grant had taught me. But it was wonderful to pause a moment and reflect on our success.

John Paul raised his glass in a toast. "So, Ed, what next?"

I had a long list. We still needed an ad campaign, something that would take Mrs. Paul's and turn it into a bona fide brand name. We needed to expand the plant; our freezer was already busting at the rivets, and a walk-in unit would not fit in the space we had. We needed money, certainly; it was time to go to the banks. But we needed one thing even more than all of these.

"What we need," I said, "is to take this show on the road."

There were at that time two retail stores on the East Coast that specialized in frozen foods. (Today such a concept would be laughable, like a hardware store that sold only hammers, but frozen food was still new enough, still strange enough, to most consumers to qualify as a specialty item.) One was virtually in our backyard, in Ardmore, Pennsylvania, on Philadelphia's Main Line. The other, and by far the larger of the two, was in White Plains, New York, about forty minutes north of Manhattan. Thinking about it, I realized Ardmore could wait. The way things were going, I would sell to them eventually. But White Plains—that was a whole different state. I called the manager on the phone, described the product, and asked if I could schedule an appointment.

"What appointment?" he said. "If it's frozen and it's edible, I'll take ten cases."

So it was that easy. Ten cases was more than I could keep cool in the trunk of the Chevy, so I rigged up some asbestos blankets for the backseat and said a quick prayer that I wouldn't run into any traffic. There was no Tappan Zee Bridge in those days, no shortcut; I drove north through New Jersey, took the Holland Tunnel under the Hudson, and promptly got lost in the middle of Manhattan.

Perhaps lost is not the word: turned around, maybe. All of a sudden, I was headed downtown instead of up, soaring down Sixth Avenue on a warm spring day with a Chevy-load of rapidly thawing deviled crabs. I began to panic, then steadied myself. At last I got my bearings and fought my way north again.

I followed the manager's directions to the store and found, to my relief, that he had gone to lunch. But the crabs looked all right. I handed them to the stock boy at the back door, then drove around and parked. I couldn't come all this way and *not* look.

In later years I would spend a great deal of time going to frozen food conventions, meeting with suppliers in gigantic warehouses crammed with every manner of frozen dinner, macaroni (before people called it pasta), vegetable, pie, and cake. It would be no exaggeration to say that I spent most of my adult life literally surrounded by frozen food.

But the White Plains store—modest as it was, it was a revelation to me. In the freezers that lined its walls, and in its giant walk-in display area, was virtually every frozen food available at that time. Seabrook, Bird's Eye, Dulaney—all the big names were there, and a hundred little ones. An entire industry was spread before me like the contents of a vault. How many other stores were there like this one? All I had done was pick up the phone, and now Mrs. Paul's was in two states. How could I reach the others?

I stepped outside into the pale summer sun. It was lunchtime, and I walked across the street to a little diner to get a bite to eat before heading home. My mind was racing. We *had* to advertise. But without distribution, there was no point. We would have to take it one step at a time, market by market, city by city.

I ordered my lunch and bought a copy of the New York *Daily News* to check the box scores while I waited for my meal. The Phillies were having a good season, though nothing to brag about; they had lost to Pittsburgh the night before, both games of a twilight doubleheader. The paper said they were leaving the next day for a two-week road trip to Boston, Chicago, and St. Louis.

Pittsburgh. Boston. Chicago. St. Louis.

And I thought: *Of course.*

Here it was, all neatly laid out. On the page in front of me, on the counter of a greasy spoon in White Plains, New York, were the names of all the major league baseball teams of 1947: the Phillies and Athletics in Philadelphia; the Pirates in Pittsburgh; the Red Sox and Braves in Boston; the Giants, Yankees, and Dodgers in New York; the Cleveland Indians; the Washington Senators; the St. Louis Browns and Cardinals; the Cincinnati Reds; the Chicago Cubs and White Sox; and the Detroit Tigers. A city could not support a team unless it was a major population center, but more importantly, it had to have enough newspapers and radio stations to reach the fans. Baseball was a business—a smart, well-run business for the most part—and its franchises were located in the cities where news traveled easily. I needed no consultants, no marketing researchers, to tell me what I was seeing. It was all perfectly, fantastically obvious.

The waitress brought my food, but I was no longer hungry. I tore out the sports page, took out a pen, and while my lunch grew cold beside me, I numbered each city in the order in which I had to enter its market—my marketing plan for the next two decades.

It would take nearly as long for that scrap of paper, taped to the wall above my desk, to crumble into yellow dust.

Back in Philadelphia, I moved up my advertising timeline. I didn't care what it cost—we had to get on the radio and establish Mrs. Paul's as a brand name in Philadelphia if we were going to approach the banks for financing to take our operation into other urban markets.

I liked Shepp, but I felt strongly that we needed someone else, someone with vision for the company. Then one July day, help arrived as if from nowhere.

His name was Hal Montgomery, and he called me out of the blue, explaining that he was a junior copywriter at an agency in town and had some ideas he hoped would interest me. We met on the steps of the plant on East Street, and he made his pitch. He had seen one of our placards on the El, bought a box of deviled crabs and tried them with his wife, and knew at once (or so he said; to this day he swears it is all true) that he was just the man to help me.

"Hang on a minute," I said. I left him on the curb, went into the plant, and returned with my torn-out page from the *Daily News*.

"This is what I want. City by city."

Hal looked at the clipping and nodded. "Well, I think you can do it. And I know that advertising is the *way* to do it."

"You mean print advertising."

"Actually, no." He tipped a shoulder. "To a certain extent, sure, but it's not the only choice. Have you ever thought about radio advertising,

Mr. Piszek? I know you're concerned about cost, but I think there's a way."

I took out my pen and wrote down my address in Drexel Hill. "Come for dinner," I said.

And so began a relationship that was more than just business; in the truest sense, Hal became a third partner in Mrs. Paul's, the man with whom I built and shared a vision of the company. He came for dinner on Sunday, and the next night, and the next; in our tiny kitchen, the main "conference room" of Mrs. Paul's, we talked until well after midnight. Hal did not own a car; he was struggling as hard as I was. But he lived just a couple of miles away, and for many years, such evenings would conclude with Oddie and I flipping a coin to see who would drive Hal home.

Hal was more than big talk; to get us on the radio, he had a concrete plan in mind. Working on an earlier account, he had struck up an acquaintance with a local radio personality named Stu Wayne, the morning DJ on KYW. Stu was especially popular with housewives—he had a low, throaty voice that was pure radio—and between spinning records and delivering the news and weather, he did local ad spots. Hal supposed he could get us into the studio to meet him, and if we hit it off, Stu Wayne might make a pitch for us on the air.

We drove down to the station a couple of weeks later. Aside from a receptionist and an engineer, Stu was all alone, and he moved with the fluidity of a high-wire acrobat—dashing down the hall to tear news sheets off the wires, cueing up 45s, logging everything into the station book, all in the three minutes or so between singles by the Andrews Sisters or Frank Sinatra. Busy as he was, he still seemed glad to see us. I had brought along some samples and a five-pound box of chocolates (in case he did not like fish), and he munched away on a little of each while we talked.

"Hey," he said, "you know, these are pretty good. You'd never know they were frozen. Mrs. Paul's is the name?"

"That's right," I said.

Just then the record ended. Without missing a beat Stu lifted the needle; swung down the microphone; rattled off the news, weather, and time ("Nine thirty-two on a beeee-YOU-tiful Tuesday morning in the City of Brotherly Love . . ."); then flicked his eyes up at the two of us. "Well guess who's here?" he said on air. "I've got a visitor today, a fellow named Ed Piszek, who's got a little company down in Manayunk, and I do mean a *little* company. They're making some of the best deviled crabs I ever had, and he calls it Mrs. Paul's. Ed is worried I'm gonna starve to death up here, so he drops in now and then to feed me some of his delicious deviled crabs. Boy, you should hear him, folks. He's *all* excited about the dairy-fresh milk and creamery butter they use. And let me tell you, if you like deviled crabs, Mrs. Paul's is A-number-one. Now, here's a little something I know you'll like almost as much, the Ink Spots doing 'If I Didn't Care.' "

The needle dropped and the song began, the Ink Spots' crooning voices squeezing like honey out of the tiny studio speaker. Stu swung around from the mike. "How's that?"

It was ten times better than any prepared ad could ever have been, a hundred times. "God, that's terrific," I managed.

Stu smiled. "Anything for a five-pound box of chocolates. The crabs ain't bad either." He winked. "Come back anytime."

Outside, Hal and I walked to the car. I was still trembling with excitement.

"How many people do you suppose heard that?"

Hal looked at his watch. "Nine o'clock, a Tuesday . . . hmmm." He smiled. "I'd say, anywhere between twenty and thirty thousand. Could be more."

"You're a genius," I said.

Hal negotiated with KYW for regular spots on the Stu Wayne show, half a dozen a day, for seventy dollars a week. Almost instantly, demand went up 30 percent. We were rapidly outgrowing our plant, and I could see that a day would soon come that we had to move. But in the meantime, a more critical need loomed: we had to have a walk-in freezer. Unless we could keep our product cold, we would collapse under the flood of new orders and soon be out of business.

I found part of the solution right away. The dairy where we bought our milk, just three blocks away, had an extra loading platform and an unused space in back. The owner agreed to let me put a new freezer there, and, at night, use his platform to load and unload. It was perfect—as long as I could come up with the cash to buy a freezer.

A good-sized walk-in model would cost several thousand dollars. It was a gigantic sum. But perhaps, I thought, we were finally good enough on paper for a bank to finance it for us. I took my books downtown to the office of the Pennsylvania Company and applied for a loan.

At his desk, the commercial loan officer looked my ledger over. From time to time he nodded his head or clucked his tongue or made a mark in pencil, but otherwise, he was as inscrutable as the Buddha. Finally, after about fifteen minutes, he put it aside.

"How much are you worth now, Mr. Piszek?"

"About the same as a freezer," I said. "It's right there. About five thousand, net."

"And you believe that frozen foods is a viable business? With long-term prospects?"

"Absolutely I do. As sure as I'm sitting here."

He looked over the balance sheet again and patted it with his palm. "Well, everything seems to be in order here. But I'll have to say no."

I was dumbfounded. Hadn't he just said everything was in order? How could we be in order and not get a loan?

"How can that be?" I moaned. "We can barely keep up with our orders *now*."

"I understand that. But you see, Mr. Piszek, there are simply too many questionable projections here. Take this line item, for instance—five thousand dollars for advertising in the next fiscal year?" He gave a little chuckle at the absurdity of the figure. "Well, suffice it to say, it's simply too much. We can't risk it. It's these kinds of things I'm talking about, you see."

"Frozen food is a new industry. Without advertising we'll die. Hell, advertising is the reason we're growing so fast we need to borrow money."

He folded his hands on his desk. "Yes. Well, as I said, the bank isn't in a position right now to take such a chance." He gave me a patronizing smile. "I'll tell you what. You seem like a serious young fellow. Perhaps, maybe, if you cut this item from your budget, we could be prevailed upon to loan you a few thousand."

"And cut my own throat?" I took my books and put them in my briefcase. "No, thanks."

The same story was replayed at bank after bank. It was maddening. Without a fresh infusion of capital we couldn't keep up with demand, let alone expand; without advertising, there was no reason, as far as I could tell, to be in business in the first place. Why couldn't I make anyone understand that?

For several months I was practically obsessed by the problem. In my mind, the world's bankers became a virtual conspiracy of shortsighted, antibusiness, glad-handing obstructionists. Even Oddie tired of my ranting, saying, "For God sake, Ed, if they don't want to give you the money, stop asking!" I railed on about the problem to virtually anyone who would listen.

One day I stopped in to chat with one of my suppliers—a big bear of a guy who dealt cooking oils and shortenings for Capital Cities—whose name was Paul Newsome. He had grown up more or less in the same neighborhood as I had, and he had worked his way up to regional sales representative for the company. I was one of his smallest customers, but we had always gotten along well, and he had watched with interest as our business grew. Just a few days before, I had been turned down by yet another bank, and the sting of it was still fresh. In his office—a chaotic hole-in-the-wall of ringing phones and fat ledger books—Paul listened while I let off my usual head of steam: the narrowness of vision, the stupid-ity, the whole ball of wax.

When I was done, Paul rocked back in his chair and gave a little laugh. "Well what did you expect? They're bankers, Ed." He waved a thick hand at the air above his head, as if brushing away a bee. "All they care about is the numbers."

"They're morons," I said. "They can't see what's right in front of them."

"Maybe not. But they don't know you like I do." Paul leaned forward and folded his hands on his desk. He leveled his gaze at me. "Let me ask you something, Ed. How many hours have we sat in this office talking about your business?"

"I don't know. A lot."

"Dozens. Maybe a hundred. And how long did you spend with that guy . . . what's his name?"

"Twenty minutes." I shook my head. "I see what you're getting at. But I don't know any bankers, Paul. Not personally. Guys like us don't travel in their circles."

"Maybe you do know one, Ed."

"Yeah? Like who?"

He shot me a broad grin. "Well, like me, for instance. Why don't I loan you the scratch?"

I couldn't have been more amazed. "Five thousand bucks? You're kid-ding me."

"Why the big surprise? You're good for it, aren't you?"

"Well, sure I am. You know I am."

"That's my point. I know you are. They don't. It's their mistake, but no use crying over it. There's a problem to fix." He rapped his desk with his knuckles. "I say, let's fix it."

So it was as simple as that. The terms we negotiated were more than fair for both of us: I would pay Paul 6 percent, plus 5 percent of our net profits, until the loan was paid off. At that time, the banks were paying just 3 percent, so it was a good deal all around—especially because he was loaning us a sum that matched the entire net worth of the business.

Paul said that he would come by the house that night to finish the deal, and at a little after nine, just as we had finished putting the kids to bed, we heard Paul's car pull up in front of the house. In lumbered Paul, cradling a brown paper grocery sack under his arms. He plunked down at our kitchen table, and Oddie brought him a cup of coffee. I guessed the bag contained a couple of beers for us to share.

Paul sipped his coffee and looked up at us. "Here you go."

He lifted the paper bag, turned it upside down, and out tumbled a cascade of wadded bills onto the kitchen table. I saw fives and tens, and intermixed, a few twenties. Nothing folded or stacked; the bills were crumpled and stained, as if they had been stuffed into a pants pocket and then transferred to the bag. He might have been delivering a load of laundry tickets. All told, they formed a pyramidal mound that buried the salt and pepper shakers.

Oddie gasped, and so did I. It was the most money either one of us had ever seen in one place, let alone on our kitchen table. I knew immediately that I was looking at a good portion of Paul's life savings. Paul, like me, was a Depression baby. He didn't trust banks and bankers any more than I did. Where had he been keeping all this? In his mattress? Behind a picture on the wall?

"So." Paul laughed and hit the table. "You want to count it? You should see your faces."

"Count it?" I said. "I want to kiss it. That's my freezer right there." I put my hand on his broad shoulder. "I won't forget this. You mark my words."

"Just make it work," he said. "Hell, Ed. Make a fortune with it."

And that is just what we did. With a new freezer, we could keep up with demand; with our production up to speed, and distribution in place, we could expand locally and begin to approach other markets; with fat orders on the books, we could borrow the money to advertise. Paul's five thousand was a small sum, but for Mrs. Paul's it was a bonanza.

The chain reaction began almost immediately. With our equipment logjam broken, our balance sheet looked instantly better, and I found a banker who agreed. His name was Nelson Jones, and he was at the time a commercial loan officer with the National Bank of Germantown, later to become part of Girard (and still later, Mellon Bank). Nelson was no number cruncher; he believed that the frozen food industry would not go the way of the straw hat or spats, and he understood that advertising would be central to any business success in the postwar economy. He also was the first banker I had met who took seriously all my years at Campbell's as part of my claim to running a food company of my own. He loaned me another three thousand on the spot, so I could continue advertising on KYW; within five years, his bank would be writing Mrs. Paul's an unsecured line of credit for one hundred thousand dollars.

I think of those first years, 1946 to 1950, as our radio days. Without our radio campaigns, I have no doubt that Mrs. Paul's would have vanished altogether, been blindsided into nonexistence by one arbitrary reversal or another or, at least, been a smaller company, entirely local. The radio (and later, television) became our lifeline, our voice in countless American kitchens, and it didn't matter if we were still, technically, a small company. Early on, I had discovered that the great beauty of advertising was in its ability to sell a product rather than a company. Beamed into a kitchen or living room, the messages of a multimillion-dollar international conglomerate and a tiny outfit in a Manayunk storefront are indistinguishable. On the air, a small company is as large as its sales pitch. Quite by accident, Mrs. Paul's was on its way to becoming one of the first success stories of the modern advertising age.

By early 1947, I could see that Mrs. Paul's had begun to break out. It would not be long before we would outgrow the storefront once and for all; already we were running twenty-four hours a day to maintain production in our tiny plant with its narrow alleyways and ancient stove. Still, John Paul kept things running smoothly. By now it was clear, too, that we had fallen into a division of labor that was natural for both of us, with John acting as head of production and myself overseeing all other aspects of the business. (There were no titles involved, no contracts, not even a handshake—it was simply how things shook out.) Soon we were joined by Frank W. Moore, my old friend and a colleague at GE, who took over as our sales manager. We were, in other words, fast acquiring the structures and demands of a real company.

Curiously, Mrs. Paul's might have grown twice as fast had I not refused to buy into the existing system of "exclusive" distributors. Initially, this was mere exigency, rather than any structured position, and by selling directly to the chains, I had managed to avoid a showdown. But as we grew, I understood that distributors would have to be involved, and that my "one-price" policy would meet with opposition if not open warfare. Only one food company I knew about had managed to break the distribution headlock: my own former employer, Campbell's Soup. But Campbell's was so large and threw so much weight that it could act with virtual impunity. Unless I could convince distributors that carrying my line would simply make them more money than not carrying it—a difficult proposition, because most would not even engage you in conversation unless you promised them a 3 percent discount at the outset—any insistence on an open selling policy would come across as monumental arrogance. Functioning as a kind of cartel, the distributors had a vested interest in quashing upstarts. It was not beyond imagining that they could cut me out of certain markets and, in the end, drive me out of business entirely.

My first experience with an out-of-town distributor did not give me reasons for optimism. Ever since my drive up to White Plains, I had kept my sights on New York, the largest market in the country, where the dominant chain was A&P—the largest, oldest, and most established grocery chain in the nation. In a sense, every supermarket in the country was a stepchild of the Great Atlantic and Pacific Tea Company, which had virtually invented the modern discount grocery and ushered out the age of the "general store." It was the granddaddy of the industry, and to put Mrs. Paul's on its hallowed shelves was tantamount to an instant pedigree.

I called on A&P and was quickly directed to their distributor. "No problem," he said. "We know your product. Give us an exclusive in New York, and you're in. A 4 percent discount should do it." I explained our one-price policy, and that was all it took; before I could finish, I was ushered out so quickly there might just as well have been a trapdoor under my chair. (In the end, we would call on the A&P almost monthly for nine years—by which time we were a major brand elsewhere in the state—before they let us on their sacrosanct shelves.)

As I had feared, word got around; though I found a couple of small distributors to get us into a few New York stores, the big boys lined up against me, as unshakable as a monolith. At food convention after food convention, I was dismissed with a wave of the hand. No exclusive—no deal. Did I think maybe I was Campbell's Soup? It was dispiriting, and I began to doubt the wisdom of expanding beyond Philadelphia.

What I needed was one distributor, just one, to come around and see things my way. If I could do this and prove that a one-price policy could be profitable anyway, then the headlock would be broken.

In the meantime, in my own backyard, a showdown loomed. Early in '47, I had in fact violated my own policy and allowed a distributor into the tent—the Gaudio Brothers of Camden, New Jersey. Gaudio was not the most powerful distributor in the region, but it pulled considerable weight, and I had negotiated a small discount with it to get into several of the chains. As long as it was the only distributor I dealt with in Philadelphia, Joe Gaudio more or less had agreed to overlook the fact that I was selling directly to other stores he did not handle.

Then in the spring of '48, the industry experienced a sudden downturn—a frozen food "depression" if you like. Overproduction by several of the largest manufacturers had flooded the market with cheap frozen food, especially frozen fruit. (Ironically, for a small company like ours, such downturns meant little; we rarely stockpiled more than a few weeks' worth of product and so could adjust accordingly. And besides, no one else was making frozen deviled crabs yet.) Hardest hit were the distributors, who frequently maintained huge inventories. And Joe Gaudio was sitting on a warehouse full of frozen bing cherries he couldn't move for more than two cents a pound.

So, he was vulnerable. He was also desperate and could be fierce. It was precisely at such a moment that I had long expected him to call in all of his markers, including mine. I could almost hear him: "You want to sell to Acme direct? Well, you go right ahead, Piszek. But if you want to get in anywhere else, you're going to have to negotiate a new discount with me—say, 6 percent?"

I decided to strike first, to make the moment mine. Joe and I got along well, but our relationship was not personal. He was all business, a powerhouse of a man, and I was a little intimidated by him. At his waterfront Camden office, I laid out my pitch.

"Joe, I have something here that I think might interest you. My hunch is that, if all goes well, we can triple your sales, maybe more." Joe leaned back in his chair and said nothing. From my satchel I removed a stack of new ads. I was gambling that no other customer ever involved him in their planning, much less in an advertising campaign. He would feel flattered. And the data were persuasive. I had carefully prepared my presentation to show how his sales would grow under our new campaign.

"Joe, I know that you're sitting on a large inventory you can't move. But I'm telling you, with these new ads, you're going to be selling Mrs. Paul's three times what you're handling for me now."

Joe looked the ads over, nodding thoughtfully. "Well, these seem good to me." He looked at me carefully, as if studying me. "But why are you telling me this? Hell, Ed, if you want to advertise, that's your business. What's the hitch?"

"The hitch is money, Joe. This is going to be expensive. If I'm going to get my advertising investment back, I need to charge you more. I'm sorry."

Joe's face fell. "But you just said—"

"I know. But I'm simply going to have to pass the cost along for a while. I wanted to tell you personally. That's why I'm here. We've been friends too long for me to send somebody else over."

"I don't get it." He shook his head. "You're telling me you're going to have to charge me more, but it will all work out in the end? How about I drop you like a hot brick, Ed?" He shot me a crooked grin. "How would that be?"

It was a gamble, but I had prepared for this possibility and believed it was a bluff. Joe was on his knees—all those cherries in his warehouse were like an open artery bleeding cash.

"Joe, I wouldn't like that at all. I'll be honest with you. I need you, but you need me, too." I paused. "So maybe there's another way."

"Yeah? What's that?"

"You let me take this to a couple of other distributors. Drop your exclusive. It won't cut into your sales substantially, and I'll get Mrs. Paul's on more store shelves. That way, I can recoup my cost just as fast."

I was asking him to commit a crime that, in the frozen food industry, was the equivalent of heresy. And in retrospect, this one moment may have been the single most important in the history of our business, a moment in which everything we would do for two decades was defined.

"All right," he said finally. "You're breaking my back, but all right."

To this day I wonder if tough old Joe Gaudio knew what he had done. But of course he did; he had to know. I drove back to Manayunk that afternoon practically singing out loud; my new contract with the Gaudio Brothers was the key to the distribution lock. In Philadelphia at least, Mrs. Paul's was free and clear of the exclusive distribution agreements that had doomed us to slow growth. No other brand in the industry, including the mighty Bird's Eye, enjoyed that kind of availability. And as long as Joe Gaudio still made money—which he would—I had the proof to take to other distributors in other cities. It would not be easy, I knew. It would be a battle, city by city. But once we were in, a consumer who saw our ads in the paper or heard them on the radio could buy our product in virtually any store.

What were Paul Newsome's words exactly? *Make it work*, he had said. *Make a fortune with it.*

Chapter Nine
Riding a Rocket

nd that's just what we did. The most surprising thing was how little time it took.

By 1951, Mrs. Paul's was a firmly established company in the Philadelphia market and had begun to appear on shelves from Boston to Miami. We were selling well in Pittsburgh, doing nearly as well there as we were at home, and in Baltimore, too. From the cramped confines of our one-room plant on East and Terrace, we commanded a business that was worth some three-quarters of a million dollars. As crazy as it seemed, we were poised to take our product nationally.

In early spring of that year, I flew out to San Francisco for a frozen food convention, leaving John Paul to look after things. Such conventions were a major source of new business for us, and San Francisco was the largest of the year, attracting vendors from all over the country; for nearly a week I hustled buyers and distributors, landing several contracts in the process, including one for a small chain of stores in Ohio, our first in that state. It was a tremendous amount of work, and I barely slept or ate, racing from one meeting to the next. But it was also a convention; there were parties, dinners, and nights out on the town, and at the end of the week, I was invited by a group of buyers to join them for a couple of days in Reno. I could hardly refuse; if business was going to be conducted at a craps table, then that is where I had to be. I telephoned Oddie to tell her I would be a couple of extra days (promising not to gamble too extravagantly; my Mark Potter days had taught me that much) and left a message at the plant for John, with a number in Reno where he could reach me if an emergency came up.

The truth was, though—and I felt it even as I hung up the phone— that my working partnership with John had begun to strain, and a trip to

Reno was sure to sting. Personally, we still got along as well as any two men ever could. We had prospered beyond our wildest imaginings, but it hadn't been so long ago that he had driven a bread wagon while I was slinging crab cakes over a Kensington bar. When, at the end of the day, he and I might sit on the front stoop of the plant and have a beer in the fading light, it was just as likely that we would talk about the Phillies or our children as about the business. In the purest sense, John and I were pals, just two kids from Nicetown who had gotten very, very lucky.

But as Mrs. Paul's had grown, I could tell that John had begun to feel adrift, uncertain about his role in the company and a little jealous of the way I spent my time. While I traveled all over the country, John was, essentially, a working cook, chained to the stove. He had little interest in the kinds of decisions required to manage a large operation. I tried to involve him as best I could, but I knew, and I knew John knew, who was really running Mrs. Paul's. We were both drawing a hundred dollars a week in salary, but we could have hired someone to do what he was doing for less than forty. Nothing was said; the problem, unstated, was like an itch neither one of us could quite scratch. Probably, we were both waiting for things to work out by themselves.

I flew back from the West Coast on an early Thursday morning, scheduling my arrival in Philadelphia around 5:00 P.M. so I could go straight to the plant and tell John about the convention. But when I got there, John had already left for the day—strange, because he never left before six o'clock. I asked Bill Wehmeyer, the foreman on the shift, if John had left any message for me, and he told me no. But of course he had. The message, though unwritten, was plain as day.

When I went into the plant the next morning, I saw immediately that my initial impression had been correct. John was not a man to complain, but I could tell that his pride was wounded. We spoke briefly about the convention, and I waited for him to say something about Reno, but he didn't. He listened while I told him about the new contracts, nodding and saying "uh-huh" as if he hardly cared.

For a week we barely spoke. What words passed between us were strictly business, formal and cold. It saddened me more than I might have imagined, as if I was losing more than a friend, which I was; I was losing my partner. John's wounded silence was like a skin of ice over my heart. At last I could bear it no longer, and I invited him over to the house for dinner. He accepted the offer with a resigned nod. He could not have doubted what I had in mind.

I had arranged for Oddie to take the kids over to her mother's, so we could have the house to ourselves. It was a warm night, and we grilled a couple of steaks in the backyard, sipping cans of beer and chatting about nothing, really—how warm the evening was, how the Phillies were doing, what our kids were up to in school. We ate our dinner at the picnic table in the backyard and afterward sat on a pair of lawn chairs to watch the last of the light go.

"Well, we might as well get it over with," John finally said. "It's not working out, is it?"

I sipped my beer. "I don't know, John. I suppose it depends on how you feel."

"C'mon, Ed. I know you too well." He was surprisingly cheerful. "I forgot to ask you. How was Reno? I bet you had a swell time."

"I guess I did. You could go out there, if you wanted."

"No, I couldn't." He smiled, though sadly, I thought. "I mean sure, I could take a vacation. But the conventions?" He lifted his shoulders in a shrug. "You know, I really don't think I'd know what to do with myself. Being the big CEO, hustling everybody in sight—that's *your* job. Don't take this the wrong way, Ed. But it really suits you. You were born to do this."

"Maybe so." I didn't know what else to say. "I hope that's true."

"No maybes. But I'd be lying if I didn't say it didn't put me in something of a spot. You want to know the truth, Ed? I don't have the foggiest idea about this stuff—advertising, the banks, all of that. Sure, I know the basics, but sometimes . . ." His voice trailed off. "What I know is, I'm the cook. I may be a full partner, but I'm just the cook. Anybody who can read a recipe could do my job."

For a while we sat without speaking. It was terrible what we were going through, as sad as a divorce.

"You could be a silent partner," I offered.

At this, John laughed. "And what? Take half the profits just because I staked you . . . what, three hundred and fifty bucks? Not my style. I work for my keep, Ed, you know that. And sooner or later, you know, you'd resent me for it. Maybe not now, maybe not next year. But if things keep going the way they're going, it'll happen eventually, because handing over half the profits would hold the company back, would hold *you* back. I may not be a Wharton grad, but I know people, and I know you."

"I really wouldn't, John. What's fair is fair."

He sighed resignedly and rubbed a big hand over his face. "Fair is lots of things, Ed. Fair is the reason we're having this conversation. But there's also *smart*."

And this of course was true; whatever we did, however things turned out, we had to think about the company, too. But I also didn't want anyone ever to say that I had taken advantage. When John and I had first drawn up our partnership agreement, we had included a clause that allowed either party to buy the other out at net worth. I had gone over the books the night before and come up with a figure that seemed right: about one hundred fifty thousand dollars. I knew in my heart that the company was mine—I had poured my heart into it—but I also knew that I had to let John have first crack at it.

"Take a week, ten days if you like, to see if you can raise the seventy-five grand," I said. "I want you to have first go. The company is yours, if you want it."

"And if I don't?"

"Then I'll try to raise it to buy you out. Hell, maybe neither one of us will be able to put the dough together. Maybe we're just stuck with one another."

"There you go again, being fair." John laughed and then fell silent, leveling his gaze on the table between us. "You know how this is going to work out."

I looked at the ground. "Yes," I admitted. "I think I do."

"Just so you know." He rose to go. "Ten days. I'll use every one. No one will ever say I didn't have a chance." Passing me, he stopped and put a hand on my shoulder, speaking to the air, the dark sky above. "Know something else. You're a decent fellow, Ed. And as for me, no regrets. It's been a great run." He squeezed my shoulder once, and I felt my eyes fill with tears. Then he left me sitting in the dark yard.

I spent most of the next week on the road. In part I was relieved not to have to face John again, at least not right away. Like a couple breaking up, things would be awkward between us for a while, until the deal was final and some time had passed. But I was also nervous that he might change his mind. All he had to do was say, "I've raised the money," and the company was his; I had given my word. It was a prospect, however unlikely, that I simply did not want to think about.

The other problem was the money itself. John would have a hard time putting it together; but if he let my offer slide, I was not sure I could come up with the figure, either. And if I couldn't, there we would be, just where we started, only with too much already said to turn back.

The days passed with still no sign from John. Finally, on the tenth day, I came into the plant to pick up some samples, and John looked up from the stove and met my eyes. He wiped his hands on a dishtowel and tipped his head toward the front door. "Let's go to the private conference room," he said.

We went outside and sat on the stoop across the street. It was a cool day, the air still damp from the night's long rain, but the pavement had dried, leaving everything clean and bright. John lit up a little cigar and blew a plume of bitter smoke down the street. "Ed, I promised you an answer, so here it is. I can't raise the money, and I don't really want to. Hell, I'd probably bankrupt us in a year without you to tell me what to do. But we can't go on like we are. It's just not right, and I'm thinking as much of myself as I am of you. I've been training Bill all week, and I think he can take over the production end of things. He knows pretty much everything, and I think everyone gets on with him."

For an instant, my heart soared with relief. He was right about Bill, too; John had picked his successor wisely. "All right, John. I'll see what I can do about the money."

He took another long puff and smiled. "Well, that's another thing, Ed. I've spent most of this week figuring out how to help you buy me out. The way I see it, I really don't think the banks are going to be loaning you the rest of the dough. It's just too much, even for you, and the last thing you need to do is mortgage the whole operation. You don't need to be strapped with that kind of debt, anyway. So, I've talked things over with Katherine, and we're agreed. Give me twenty-five grand, and we'll take your note for the other fifty. Your word is good with us."

It was more than I could have hoped for, and I was so moved I couldn't speak. Not even a brother would have done this. How could I ever repay such kindness?

"John, do you know what kind of favor you're doing?"

He tipped one shoulder and smiled. "Sure I know. But listen, Ed. I know that if I ever needed the money, you'd do anything to come up with it, right? So it's better than any bank. I'm a Depression baby too, remember? And besides, I'd rather watch the company succeed than hang around like this. I feel like dead weight."

And then I had a marvelous idea. "John, I'll tell you what. You're drawing a hundred dollars a week in salary, right? Well, as long as Mrs. Paul's is in business, I'll pay that salary. A hundred dollars a week for life."

"Hmm." He drew on his cigar and thought. "A hundred bucks for doing nothing? I don't know, Ed."

I shook my head. I was determined to do this, to make him understand why. "I won't take no for an answer. And it's not for nothing. You made this company with me, John. Goddamnit, I'll pay you out of my own pocket if I have to. If you say no, I'm going straight to Katherine."

He laughed and rolled his eyes; I'd made a sale. "Well if that's how you feel about it. . . ."

"It is, John. It really, really is."

John stuck out his hand to shake. "Okay, Ed. A hundred bucks a week for life. Who am I to say no?"

We shook, and John looked up at the sky, squinting into the sun. His voice, when he spoke, was far away. "You know, I've been laid off a couple times, fired once, quit. . . ." He shrugged, remembering. "Well, I don't know how many times. This isn't like that. Remember that night when I met you here, the first night?" He returned his look to me, and I saw a melancholy shadow float over his face. I was about to speak when he shook his head to quiet me. "It's okay, Ed. I'm glad I got the chance. Hell, I'm rich now, sort of. You owe me seventy-five grand, which is as good as money in the bank." His face trembled, and I thought he might cry; I thought *I* might cry. There was no bitterness, only a sense that our lives had changed, we were no longer Ed and John, and we would miss one another. But then he gathered himself, took a final puff, and crushed his cigar out on the pavement, and I knew no tears would be shed. He pointed a thumb over his shoulder, toward the plant. "Well," he said, clearing his throat. "I guess I'd better get back to work."

I was about to tell him to take the rest of the day off but stopped myself. Let it be a day for him just like any other, I thought. In the end, I would come up with all the money—not just the seventy-five to buy out his share of the company but another hundred thousand on top of it to place in an irrevocable fund that would pay John the interest. He would draw a hundred dollars a week from it, just as I had promised, until sometime in the mid-seventies. We had lost track of one another by then; I didn't even know where John was or what had become of him, when one day he telephoned me out of the blue from California, asking if I would be willing to pay him the remaining money from the buyout, in cash, for an oil investment he wanted to make. I agreed, and we talked for a while; strangely, it was the last time we ever would speak.

"Me, too," I said.

Two weeks later John stopped coming in to work; Mary took over production, and Mrs. Paul's was mine. The change was slight, as I thought it would be. Bill took to the job quickly, there were no complaints or confusions, and we kept up with demand, churning out the crab cakes and breaded cod fillets (a new product for us) from our tiny plant.

For five years I had been working twelve to fourteen hours a day, barely pausing to taste my success. We were still crammed into our tiny house in Drexel Park, a house that had begun to seem smaller with each passing year as the kids grew. Oddie had her hands full: Ann was thirteen, Ed nine, George seven. I helped as best I could, but in my heart I knew that building the business was the best gift I could give my family, and Oddie never complained about the long nights or weekends of work. It was as if we were on some kind of wild carnival ride, a roller coaster that never slowed down, took each turn more sharply than the last, though somehow we held on. I was thirty-five years old, and could not have been more surprised by how happy I was. John was right: I had found my life.

One thing was certain: we couldn't stay in Drexel Park much longer. Oddie and I had been talking about moving for a while, but there never seemed to be enough time to follow through on the idea. Then, the following fall, I came home late one night to find on the kitchen table a photograph of a house, a handsome little colonial I had never seen before, with shutters, a sloping lawn, and an attached garage, everything bright and tidy and new. Attached to it with a paperclip was the realtor's business card. While Oddie finished putting the kids to bed, I examined the picture, wondering what it was, though of course I knew. Oddie had kept dinner waiting for me, and we sat down to eat together. I was waiting for her to say something—I could see, behind her eyes, a bright, hopeful smile, though she need not have worried; in my heart I had already agreed. But it was Oddie's way to wait, patiently letting an idea sink in before it was announced.

Finally, I spoke. "So," I said, "I see you've been house-hunting." I picked up the photo. "Pretty fancy, Miss McFadden." I put the photo down, and decided to have a little fun. "I can't say that I think we need it. We have plenty of room here."

Oddie smiled. "Not with the new baby," she said.

We moved three months later, and in the summer of '52, our daughter Helen was born. The house, in a leafy neighborhood of mostly older homes northwest of Philadelphia, felt as big as a palace, though in many ways it was quite ordinary. The neighborhood around our house in Drexel Park had not escaped the rapid development of the postwar housing boom, and the open land behind us had become crowded with new houses during the time we lived there. I was relieved to be out in the country again. I could stand in the backyard at night and see not a single light; holding my breath, I could hear nothing but the creak of crickets and cicadas in the trees and, at a distance, the gentle whoosh of traffic on Spring Avenue, and beyond it, on Bethlehem Pike—the road where my father had died. Behind me in the dark house, my family slept. Then the baby would cry—startled awake, as babies are, by nothing, by hunger, or by the unpleasantness of a soggy diaper—lights would flick on, there would be footsteps within, and life would resume again.

We were bursting at the seams at work, too; the time had come to expand the plant. I had avoided this, too, thinking it an extravagance and worrying in a cautious way about taking on the extra debt. (Tangentially, I was also concerned about the inevitable interruption in production while we moved our facilities; we never kept more than a few weeks of product on hand, and to keep up with demand, we had to keep cooking. It presented a logistical problem I could not quite solve.) Then the property next door at 177 East Street came up for sale, and I had no more excuses; we could expand without moving, taking our time to renovate the facilities and join the two together. The building, like so much else in Manayunk, was over a hundred years old, and had worn a number of hats, though most of its history had been long forgotten. It had stood vacant for a while; in its last incarnation it had been a stable, and on a warm day, the walls and floors exuded the telltale tang of its former occupants, the horses, now long dead, that had carted the milk from the local dairy. We gutted the building, then broke through the wall between the two properties to join the two first floors, making one large production and storage area, including a pair of large walk-in freezers. (By this time we were renting freezer space at several facilities in the city, but we still needed to freeze the bulk of our product on-site.) No more standing in the front window or sitting out on the curb to conduct business: we renovated the second floor to make my first real office, a spare room with a desk, chair, and telephone.

One morning, just after we had moved into the expanded plant, one of those things happened that usually only happens in novels. I came into work about seven-thirty, parked my car down the block on East Street, and as I approached the building, I saw a figure, strangely familiar, waiting on the front curb. A light rain was falling, and she huddled under an umbrella, clutching a purse to her chest. Then I saw, peeking from beneath the kerchief that covered her head, a bright flame of red hair, and instantly I knew who I was looking at. It was Sally Williams, the same woman who had coached me and protected me all those years ago in the Control Cage at General Electric.

"Sally, my God." I was thrilled to see her, and we embraced. Her body felt thin, almost birdlike. As I pulled away, I saw that her eyes were still bright, her smile as luminous as it had been all those years ago. But her face was gaunt and drained. She looked like she hadn't slept in weeks.

"Edward, I. . . . " Her voice trailed off, and she gave a wan smile. "It's really you, isn't it? Oh, it's so good to see you."

I could still feel the lightness of her bones where they had pressed against me. "For goodness sakes, let's get you out of the rain," I said.

I brought her into the building. The early morning shift was already in full swing, and she looked around the room with a wide, happy smile. "I always knew it would happen for you."

"Oh, we were just lucky. All this is pretty new, actually. We just expanded."

She took my elbow and squeezed it. "No, it was more than luck, Edward." I thought she was about to say something more, but she paused, and a look of pain fell over her face, like a shadow crossing a field. She began to cough, lightly at first, then more deeply. Soon her body was wracked with it. I had never heard such a cough and was seized with horror. Her face bloomed a violent red. Around us, the early shift workers stopped what they were doing and watched. The moment felt frozen. I held her by the arm, uncertain what to do. At last it passed, and Sally removed a handkerchief from the pocket of her raincoat and dabbed at her moist mouth. The color left her face like water going down a drain.

"Sally—"

"I'm sick, Edward."

I didn't know what to say. "Well, of course, standing out in the rain like that."

"I wish that were all it was," she said. "Please. Is there somewhere we can talk?"

I led her upstairs to the office. The stairs were steep, and she took them one at a time, pausing on each like an old woman and clutching the banister tightly. I got her into a chair and barked down the stairs for someone to bring us up a glass of water.

"Drink," I said.

She took the glass and sipped at it. For a while we just sat there.

"Edward, do you remember, years ago, back at GE, you told me . . ."

I never let her finish her sentence. "That someday I'd be running a business, and you'd come work for me?" I smiled at her. "Of course I remember."

"Edward, I have tuberculosis. I have it bad."

In fact, I had already guessed this. But to hear it said—it stopped me flat. "Oh, Sally."

"I haven't worked for four years. I get these needles in my back and they wear me out. My doctor thinks I should just lie down." She paused, and I thought she might cough again. But she didn't. A tear welled in her eye, and she brushed it away. "Edward, if I do, I think I'll die. I shouldn't be asking you this, because I'm not in good shape. But if I do as they say, I think I'll die. I can't just stay home and wait to die."

I understood what she was asking. I wasn't a doctor and didn't know a thing about tuberculosis. For all I knew, I could have been hastening her death. But if Sally wanted to work—if that was what she thought would keep her alive—then she would work for me.

"Sally, when can you start?"

Finally, she began to weep. "I thought I was going to have a good day. . . . I waited for weeks to have a good day to ask you . . ."

"Sally, it's all right. You're hired. When can you start?"

She fixed her damp eyes on me. "Ed, are you listening? I have T.B."

"Of course I'm listening. For the last time, Sally, *when can you start?*"

She smiled at me through her tears. "Now?" she asked.

What occurred then was, in my opinion, the one and only miracle I have ever witnessed. I had seen amazing things in my life. But what happened to Sally Williams was nothing less than the hand of God at work.

She became well.

Not right away, and perhaps there were medical reasons for it. (Of course, there had to be; but that doesn't mean it wasn't a miracle.) Some years later, when the fight against tuberculosis became an important cause in my life, I would read about a European treatment, new in the early 1950s, that went against the prevailing medical opinion of the day and said that the patient should remain active, not stay bedridden, as Sally's doctors wanted her to do. Whatever the explanation, almost from the first day Sally came to work as my secretary, her health improved. The roseate color came back into her face; her appetite returned; the coughing spells abated, then vanished altogether. Within a month, she was flying up and down the stairs to my office like a teenager, the same old Sally again, the Sally who had captivated and charmed so many young men back at GE.

Three months later she went to visit her doctor. She told me the story the next day. The doctor was dumbfounded by her improvement; he listened to her heart and lungs again and again, checked his charts, made her stand on the scale twice. He scratched his head like a man taking a test he had not studied for.

"OK," he finally said. "What did you do to yourself?"

"I went back to work. Exactly what you told me *not* to do."

"That must be some job." He shook his head, checked his chart again. "Weight, respiration, heart rate. It's the damnedest thing I ever saw. Sally, you don't even seem sick."

"I don't think I am," she said.

"You should have seen him," she told me that afternoon, laughing with pleasure. "It was as if I'd disappointed him somehow. What do the experts know?"

"You did the best thing for you," I said. "You made yourself well."

And she had. A month later, the doctor made it official. He put her chart in his files and pronounced her cured.

That year, the sixth since I had traded in my Dodge for three hundred fifty dollars, Mrs. Paul's Kitchens reached one million dollars in sales. Again, no champagne corks flew, no toasts were raised, no wild party of celebration burned into the night; I think now of that number as a border, and we crossed it silently, without remark, like passengers in a car moving from one state to another in the middle of the night.

That same year, 1952, we introduced a novelty item, something new: fish sticks. People in the industry told me I was crazy. We tripled our sales to three million.

Then doubled them again to six million.

And so the car became a rocket, hurtling skyward; ten million in 1955, twenty million in 1960. Fifty, seventy-five, a hundred million dollars.

I swear, that is exactly how it happened.

Chapter Ten
Stranger in the Rain

By the early sixties, Mrs. Paul's was a major national company. Frozen food, a novelty when I had first started, had grown to become a billion-dollar industry, and Mrs. Paul's was one of the most recognized brand names in the business. Our product line had expanded to some four dozen items. We owned our own processing plant on the Eastern Shore of Maryland, bought fish by the ton from foreign governments (Iceland was our major supplier for the cod we used to make fish sticks, a mainstay in kitchens and school cafeterias across the country and by far our most profitable product). Our East Street plant, outgrown in just five years, had been replaced by a new office building up the hill on Henry Avenue and by a large factory down below in Manayunk, a former Philadelphia Electric Company power plant perched atop a slender island between the Schuylkill River and the weed-choked Manayunk Canal. With our national sales force headed by my old boyhood friend Jack Kelly, we completely dominated the high end of the prepared frozen food market; television ads had replaced radio, and at night, folks who tuned in would hear our warm and fuzzy sales pitch: "Good things come from Mrs. Paul's . . . where flavor begins!" (Shades of Pepsodent, all those years ago.) Most significant, against all opposition, we had managed to maintain our one-price policy, thus avoiding the "discounts" that were like an anchor around my competition's neck. (Old Joe Gaudio never did forgive me.) Our rate of growth was off the charts: 20 to 25 percent each year. Our margins were devastating; the profits, simply dazzling.

Around town, I had become known as "The Fishcake King," a name given me by Philadelphia newspaper columnist—and later close friend—Tom Fox. At times, the inaccuracy annoyed me. ("They're crab *cakes*, fish *sticks*," I groused.) But the truth was, I hardly minded.

Yet, Mrs. Paul's remained, at least in spirit, the company it had been since we started. Though our Henry Avenue office was definitely a step up, it was still appropriately modest—an innocuous brick building on the edge of a residential enclave of typical Philadelphia working-class row homes, with a front door that looked across the street to a sandwich and pizza shop and a park where kids from the neighborhood played football on autumn weekends. The management staff was small for an operation our size. In addition to myself, Jack Kelly, Sally, and Hal Montgomery (though, technically, he did not work for me, it was easy to forget that; we were by far his largest account), there were just a few others. My friend John Ritchie, who had worked with me at GE, joined us in '58 to head production. A neighbor from Drexel Hill days, Joe Lash, became our accountant and later assistant treasurer. My sister, Cecilia, ran our test kitchen (a job that she would pass along to my daughter Helen in 1974); Bill Wehmeyer, who took over kitchen operations from John Paul, still moved the production line along. Jimmy Flately, who had worked as a mailboy in a local ad agency, came aboard as a jack-of-all-trades and became our purchasing agent. There was barely a college degree in the bunch. Our "executive staff meetings" were held at my house on Saturday mornings over coffee and doughnuts; a "power lunch" was takeout cheese steaks and bottles of soda pop from the shop across the street. We were, in sum, a family business in every sense of the word.

By then, Oddie and I had also moved again, into the home I live in still. Spring Avenue proved to be just a pit stop for us. We had lived there just four years when, in the spring of '56, Oddie heard that Emlen House was for sale.

I knew it well. I could practically see it from my front yard—a wide, parklike swath of green, lying at the base of the next hill just beyond Route 309, with a large stone house at the end of a long, tree-lined driveway that curved past a running stream. There were fields and outbuildings—stables and garages, I guessed—and what looked like a barn. We had no idea who lived there; from the looks of things, it was pure Philadelphia blue blood, more like the horse tack and tennis clubbing Main Line set than the rest of Montgomery County, which back then was a mix of working-class people, farmers, and small-town shopkeepers, with a few new middle-class developments sprinkled in the mix. A historical marker by the road identified the estate as George Washington's headquarters during the Battle of Germantown, just before he had moved his troops to Valley Forge. I had stopped once to read it and had a little laugh, remembering the groundskeeper who had chased Oddie and me away twenty-five years before, when we were just a couple of teenagers from grubby little Nicetown looking for a place to smooch. Whenever we drove past it, Oddie and I would joke about that day. "C'mon, let's just turn in," Oddie would say, reaching for the wheel. "See what they think of us now, a couple of old married folks like us."

The price, I learned, was sixty-five thousand dollars—a lot of money, even then, but cheap for the size of the place. When Oddie told me, I gasped. Thirty rooms! What would we do with thirty rooms? It seemed too much for one lifetime, to travel from an apartment over a grocery store to a thirty-room mansion with a plaque by the road.

For a while I put it out of my mind, until one Saturday when I was driving to the office, and I found myself coasting slowly past the entrance to the estate. It was a warm spring day, and I pulled the car over by the side of the road, out of the way of oncoming traffic. For a while I stood there, my back against the driver's door, looking. The house was set far back from the road and hidden by a thick nape of green trees. To the right of the driveway gurgled the old millrace and past it the stream that fed it just as they had when Washington had headquartered there. I gazed at the water and was seized by a memory or, rather, a feeling—a deep, inexpressible calm. My life was hectic, crazy, consumed by the world. When had I last been out to Quakertown? I looked out at the vast, green lawns of the estate, so like the farm fields of my youth; I heard in the water the sound of my own heart and knew at once that I had found the place where I would live the rest of my life.

Oddie made the arrangements for us to look the place over; I didn't tell her that I had already made up my mind, but I am sure she knew. The realtor escorted us through the house, room after endless room. When I asked her if the house had always been so large, she explained that only the front four rooms were part of the original structure. The rest had been added later, including the large dining room added by the estate's current owners, a family named Cheston.

"Reading Railroad money," she explained, lowering her voice reverentially. "Very, *very* old." I wondered what she was driving at, though I could guess. Emlen House was not the sort of place she thought just anyone should buy.

At the foot of the stairs, she turned to me. "I meant to ask. What is it that you do, Mr. Piszek?"

I was about to speak, when Oddie cut me off. "We sell fish," she said.

"Ah." The realtor searched for something else to say, but could not find it. For a moment we all just stood there. I wanted to laugh. Who cared what the realtor thought of us? "Well, I hear that's a fine business," she said finally.

"You could say we sell a lot of it," I confided.

At the foyer, she left us alone to wander the grounds. Before she left us, though, she gave us some bad news: somebody had already made an offer on the place. She was not certain of all the details, but the offer came from a woman who wanted to turn it into a restaurant—"a wonderful country inn," the realtor said, her voice telling me how much she thought of the idea, and how little she thought of us. The deal was on hold until the bidder could secure a liquor license, which would probably happen in due course. If we wanted to make an offer, we would have to make up our minds right away. The window of opportunity was just forty-eight hours long.

It was a relief to get outside. When we were out of range, Oddie laughed and squeezed my arm. "Can you believe that woman? I guess she doesn't think we're good enough."

"Apparently not." I stopped and took her arm. "Does it matter, hon?"

Oddie smiled at me. "No. Of course not. Why should it matter?"

"Well, a place like this. Our lives will change. People will think of us differently." I tipped my head toward the house, where the realtor was standing by her car, scribbling into a notebook. I noticed for the first time that the driveway was circular. Strange, but it was this detail that made me suddenly aware of how incredible all of this was. I couldn't imagine I was about to make an offer on a house with a circular drive.

"So what if they do? Let them think what they want."

"I don't mean just her. And I guess I don't mean the blue bloods, either. I seriously doubt they'd ever take to us." I rubbed my head, gathering my thoughts together. Around us, the lawns and gardens of Emlen House, all thirty-four acres of them, sprawled like a parkway.

"You think some of our friends won't like us anymore? Because we have a house like this?"

"Money changes things, hon. It's one thing when it's in your bank account. But this is out in the open. Can you really see people from the old neighborhood just dropping by? Asking to play a few hands of gin rummy on the porch?"

Oddie thought for a moment, frowning. "It shouldn't matter. Not if they're our real friends." She sighed heavily. "God, Ed, I don't know what to think. All of this has happened so fast. And we have to make up our minds so quickly."

"Well, do you want it?"

She laughed then. "Of course I want it. It's beautiful. It's like heaven." She raised her index finger. "No, it's better than heaven. Heaven should be this nice. But you know the rules, Ed. Do *you* want it?"

"Yes. I want it, too."

It was entirely possible, of course, that all of our hand-wringing was for nothing; we could offer them the moon, but the owners had to agree to sell the place to us. One thing I was certain of: there would be no dickering on the price. On the streets of Nicetown (or, for that matter, the hotel rooms and crap tables of a frozen food convention) a price was something fluid, as words and ideas are fluid. But not here, on the lawn of blue-blooded, colonial-era Emlen House. "Old money," as the realtor had called it, didn't get that way by negotiating.

As we talked, Oddie and I worked our way around the house to the rear, where a large stone patio filled in the corner-shaped space formed by the house's old and new wings. It was a lovely spot, and we didn't notice the man sitting at the iron table until we were practically upon him.

"Excuse us," I said. "We didn't mean to disturb you."

He rose and, even before he spoke, I knew who he was. The high, wide forehead, the thick eyebrows over piercing black eyes, the slightly pointed chin; in his sixties, Radcliffe Cheston was the spitting image of his grandfather, whose portrait I had seen hanging on the wall by the stairs.

He introduced himself and shook my hand, his palm still moist from the sweating glass of iced tea that sat on the table. He wore a plain white shirt and loose khaki trousers, their knees smeared with the same dark dirt that blackened the crevices under his fingernails. A trowel and claw lay on the patio by a bed of irises, and I guessed that he had been gardening. I had seen him from the windows inside and had assumed he was another groundskeeper.

"I hope the realtor has answered any questions you may have, Mrs. Piszek," he said to Oddie.

"Yes, thank you," she said. "It's a beautiful home. It must break your heart to sell it."

In the moment before he answered, Cheston's eyes seem to glisten with tears, though perhaps it was the bright sunlight bouncing off the stones of the patio.

"Yes, well. It's time, I'm sad to say." He cleared his throat and slid his hands into his trouser pockets. "There's just me now, you see, and it's really much too big. None of my children wants to take it on, and I can't blame them. Tell me. Did you have a chance to see the gardens, Mrs. Piszek?"

In fact, we hadn't gotten the chance. "I'm sure they're very lovely," Oddie said.

"It's the gardens I'll miss the most." His voice was far away, and I felt suddenly guilty to be hovering over his house. "I hope whoever buys it will take good care of them." He looked at his feet and frowned. "Somebody wants to turn all this into a restaurant, you know."

"The realtor told us," I said.

Cheston shook his head. "Do you have a family, Mr. and Mrs. Piszek?"

"Oh, yes." Oddie laughed. "Two boys and two girls. Ann is eighteen, Ed is fourteen, and George is twelve. Our youngest is four years old. That's Helen."

"Four children." His face curled into a faint smile, and I knew he was smiling at the memory of his own children, now grown and gone. What image flashed before him? I imagined two children, a boy and a girl, floating down the long driveway on their bicycles or chasing butterflies across the fields that sloped away from the house. "How wonderful. A home like this needs young people in it, I think. To keep it alive."

Around the corner of the house, I saw the realtor appear, waving to us. I knew she wanted to get us away from Cheston as quickly as possible.

Cheston looked at her, then at me. "That's what you want it for, isn't it, Mr. Piszek? To raise your family?"

I nodded. "Yes sir. It reminds me of a place I loved when I was a boy, a farm in Quakertown."

Twenty feet away, the realtor stopped, clutching her pad.

Cheston leaned toward Oddie and lowered his voice. "I don't want to see it turned into a restaurant," Cheston said. He took Oddie's hand; his voice was almost a whisper. "It needs to be somebody's home. It needs life and love and warmth again. Not strangers." He cleared his throat and looked at me. "Mrs. Paul's Kitchens, am I right?"

For a moment I was stunned; but of course he would know. "That's right, Mr. Cheston."

"I've read about it. You've done very well." He winked at me. "For the asking price, the house is yours."

Nineteen sixty-four, a rainy Friday evening in early spring: I was working late at the office on Henry Avenue, as I often did in those days. Nearly everyone else had gone for the day; I had just told Sally to take off, too. In the morning, I had plans to go down to Bellhaven, North Carolina, to see Captain Clyde Potter, whose fleet of boats supplied most of our crab. Clyde and I had become the closest of friends—we lived strikingly different lives, but our origins were not so far apart—and I took any chance I could to visit with him, especially in the fall, when he would demand that I drop everything on the spot and take the boys down for a weekend of duck hunting. He was a good deal older than I was, a wise man who understood the sea and much else besides, and I welcomed his influence in my life and in my boys'.

That weekend he would be christening a new boat, the *Edward J. Piszek*. It was a stirring tribute. But as excited as I was, my mind, that Friday evening, was not on the trip but on the mountain of paperwork on the desk before me. Around me the office was empty and silent save for the sound of traffic pushing through puddles outside on Henry Avenue, half-flooded after a daylong rain. Spring comes slowly in Philadelphia, and April of 1964 was no exception.

I was startled, then, when Sally buzzed me. "Mr. P?"

"I thought I told you to go home, Sally."

"There's someone here to see you. A Mr. Sykes?"

I looked at my watch; it was already 6:00 P.M. Under low clouds, the light outside my window was as dark as night, though the sun had not set. I remembered the name—Sykes—but couldn't place it.

"Does he have an appointment?"

For a moment Sally didn't answer.

"Yes. I'm sorry. I forgot to remind you." I heard a second voice, then Sally came back on. "He says he's with CARE?"

At once I remembered. He had called a week before; we hadn't spoken, but Sally had given the message to me. He was looking for money, of course. Usually, I passed such things along to a company vice president who took care of charitable giving. But Sykes had been adamant about speaking to me personally.

"All right." I heard the weary tone in my voice. "Send him in."

A moment in my life that changed absolutely everything: into my office walked Bill Sykes, soaked to the bone. He was a tall man, African American, with close-cropped hair and thick-framed glasses fogged with moisture. The image was both handsome and comic. I found him impressive, though I was still planning to make short shrift of our meeting. In fact, our association would last more than a decade.

We shook hands, and I offered him a chair. The subject of our meeting, as I recalled, would be some philanthropic activities in Poland. Bill had learned through the grapevine that I was Polish American—a Polish kid who had done well. He thought that I might be interested in chipping in for some kind of ambulance in the Polish countryside.

And he was right; I was or at least would be. But the truth was that, at least at first, my Polishness had nothing to do with it. In fact, in those days—the heydays of the Polish joke—my own ethnic roots were nothing I advertised. I knew little about my own heritage and remembered only bits and snatches of the language. Being Polish was, in some ways, a dirty secret. The majority of my Polish friends felt and acted the same way; we were as quick to tell a Polish joke as anyone and were much more interested in how the Phillies were doing than in who was in charge in far-off Warsaw.

Shedding our heritage, as for many different groups in American life, was part of the price we had paid for full membership in the economic and social mainstream.

But something happened as Bill was talking to me—something like a door opening, a door to the past and a door to who I was.

Bill explained the project, giving me some background on CARE in general and the organization's work in Poland. His voice was calm, almost magnetic. Did I know about the devastation that Poland suffered during the Second World War? Was I acquainted with the way that Poland had been handed over to the Soviets, despite the Polish partisans' brave resistance to the Nazis? He handed me some literature, full of maps and charts and dates, detailing the Allies' failure at the end of World War II to guarantee the free elections in Poland that had been agreed upon by Joseph Stalin, Harry Truman, and Winston Churchill at the Potsdam Conference.

"What happened to Poland, it was a crime," Bill Sykes said. He shook his head mournfully and put the tips of his fingers together. "Perhaps it was inevitable. It isn't really for me to judge. But Poland was the ransom the Allies paid to Stalin after the Second World War. We could have stood up to them. And twenty years later, Poland is a communist prison. In 1776, we could have done something about slavery in America, but we didn't—it seemed like a price that had to be paid at the time. But it was paid by real people, Mr. Piszek. My great-grandparents were slaves. Their story isn't really so very different."

"I see your point," I said. And I did. I would have written the check for the ambulance right then, but Bill Sykes went on.

"Do you have family there, Mr. Piszek? In Poland?"

I thought about my uncles and aunts, the brothers and sisters my parents had left behind. Growing up, we had rarely talked about them and, eventually, not at all. They were like pictures in a photograph that had faded over time, their images swallowed by the ghostly white of the photographic paper.

And I remembered then that there really was such a photograph. My mother kept it on her bedroom dresser, a formal family photo taken in the early 1900s. The people in the photograph would be old men and women now if they were even still alive. I realized that after the war my mother had never spoken of them again.

"Some. I don't really know who, though. My father visited in the thirties. I know he found some."

"You should ask him. Perhaps you could find them again."

"I wish that was possible. He died when I was a teenager. He was killed in a car wreck when I was fifteen."

As I said it, I was struck by the number. Fifteen! My father had been gone for almost three decades. He, too, was a ghost from the past, though the image of him was still etched sharply in my mind. For a moment, sitting there with Bill Sykes, I was a boy again, running down the driveway of the Quakertown farm, my tongue bitter with the dust that boiled up from under the wheels of my father's car.

"I'm sorry," I said to Sykes. A long moment had passed, and I smiled, embarrassed. "Just for a moment there, you caught me thinking about him."

He waved a hand. "No apologies necessary. My father passed away a few years ago. It's strange, how they seem to come back to us like that, isn't it? It's like they're not really gone at all." He began to gather his things together. "But it's late. I've taken too much of your time as it is. I'm sure there are people at home waiting on you."

"It was no trouble, Mr. Sykes." I rose to shake his hand, realizing I hadn't really asked him any details about the ambulance, though of course by then, I was happy to pay for it. It seemed the least I could do. "How much do you need for the ambulance?"

"Well, about five thousand in all. We were hoping you could pay half. It would be a great benefit, Mr. Piszek, to the people of Tarnow. That's the town where the ambulance would be based, in southern Poland."

I was thunderstruck. The coincidence was just too great.

"Where did you say?"

Sykes raised an eyebrow, studying me. "Southern Poland."

"No, no, the town. Its name. Say that again."

"Tarnow."

I sat back down in my chair. It couldn't be. From my desk drawer, I removed my checkbook—a personal account, not one tied to the business. I wrote the check out to CARE in the amount of five thousand. But it felt like far more than money.

"Mr. Sykes, Tarnow is where my family is from. It's where I'd be right now, if my parents hadn't emigrated. If I'd survived the war and the Communists—which, to hear you say it, I doubt I would have."

Sykes took the check and looked at it. "This is very generous, Mr. Piszek. I have to say I'm as amazed as you are. I had no idea." His eyes rose and met mine. "Perhaps it's a message."

"Maybe so," I said.

A message: but what could it all mean? I slowly drove home that night, through the rain-washed streets, in something very close to a trance, still under the spell of the past and Sykes's calm voice telling me a story about myself I hadn't realized was still true. I started to head out of the city toward Ft. Washington but found I could not. A few miles up Henry Avenue I slowed, then stopped the car, and wondered for a moment what I was doing, then doubled back toward Manayunk, gliding through the narrow streets of shoulder-to-shoulder row homes that rose from the Schuylkill River: the old Polish neighborhood where I had sold soup, then fish, and made my fortune—made my life, and my children's lives, as far away from the rocky farm fields of southern Poland as the moon was from the earth. For a hundred years men had descended the hill in the morning and trudged back up at dusk. At a stop sign, I paused to let a figure pass— a young man, his raincoat buttoned to the throat, hunched down against the rain on his way home from work or else leaving for a night shift some- where, his long hours of work still before him. The wipers slapped across my windshield, turning my vision of him into something like an old movie, the sequence of frames just slightly out of synch. In the beam of my head- lights, his raincoat seemed to glow, its luminescence captured then frac- tured in the drops of moisture on the glass through which I watched him. He stepped onto the opposite corner, and as he did so, he uncurled a hand from his jacket pocket to give me a little wave and thank me for letting him pass, though of course, there was no reason to—the right-of-way had been his.

It was an unsettling, almost hypnotic, vision. The man might have been me, after all. Only chance and time separated us. I had always be- lieved that my life was something I had earned—a methodical assault on the future, each move built on the last and aimed at the next. But sud- denly, it didn't seem that way anymore. The term "self-made man," that most deeply American idea, appeared to me as a kind of fraud. Just like the man across the street (I watched him hurry on his way, the glowing rain- coat fading like the taillights of a car pulling away), I was living inside of history, was *made* by history. And I had no idea what that history really was.

When I got home that night, Oddie looked in my face and knew right away that something momentous had happened. We sat down to the din- ner she'd kept waiting for me and, afterward, took our coffee into the living room, our customary ritual after a long day.

"Ed, what is it?"

I shook my head. "I don't really know."

"Is it good or bad?"

I thought for a moment. "Good, I think. I'll let you know as soon as I do." I sipped at my coffee and returned the cup to its saucer. "Listen. What would you say if I said I wanted to go to Poland?"

"I'd say go. If that's what you want. Is it business?"

"No. Well, in a way. I don't know yet."

"An opportunity then."

"Something like that. I might be gone a while. A few weeks, anyway. Here's a question. Why did I build the factory in Manayunk, do you think? And keep the offices there? We could have gone anywhere—downtown, out in the suburbs maybe. Probably it would have been easier to build from scratch, out here somewhere."

She laughed. "You're asking me? It was a business decision. That's what you said. What's on your mind, Ed?"

"Maybe I wanted it to be there for some other reason."

Oddie reached out and touched my arm. "What does all this have to do with going back to Poland?"

"I think I need. . . ." I stopped. "I think I need to go home."

Her eyes found my face. "This is your home, Ed. *Our* home. What's going on with you?"

"I'm not saying this right." I shook my head. "Oddie, does this all ever seem to you . . . I don't know. Like it's all just luck, and we had nothing to do with it?"

Oddie laughed again. "All the time, Ed. Didn't you know that? You've worked hard, you're the hardest-working man alive. Your success is yours. But sure. It's luck, too. Who knows how these things happen?"

"I gave five thousand dollars to a man today. Just for making me sad."

"Well." Oddie paused. "He must have made you *very* sad. Five thousand is a lot of money. Was this someone I know, so I can thank him?"

Pure Oddie. I laughed with her then and finally said, "I'm sorry. I'm not really making much sense tonight."

"You've made sense all your life, Ed, even when other people thought you weren't. Maybe what you need is a vacation from making sense."

"I was thinking about my father today."

Oddie nodded, and looked into my face. Her hand lay once again on my elbow. "I thought maybe you were. I can tell when that happens, you know."

"Did I ever tell you he went back to Poland?"

"I think so. Tell me again."

I thought for a moment. "When was this? Just before we sold the farm. It was . . . well, he was just about the age I am now, come to think of it."

"So, there." Oddie smiled. "You have your answer," she said.

"I do?"

"Maybe you need to visit *him*."

I packed a bag that night before bed, and well before dawn, as Oddie slept, I crept from the house to drive down to Belhaven, North Carolina. Usually, I took one or two of my sons with me, but not this time; that day

I was alone. For weeks, I had been looking forward to my visit with Captain Clyde, but the journey this time seemed to have a special urgency, as if this trip—like Bill Sykes's visit, like the man I had watched crossing a rainy Manayunk street in the glare of my headlights—was one more part of a developing new direction in my life, some cosmic plan unfolding. In just twenty-four hours I had been transformed from the most logical, methodical of men to someone bordering on mysticism.

The rain had blown through overnight, the low, heavy clouds of April yielding to sunshine and a high blue sky like a dome over my head. I drove the seven hours in a cheerful, almost thoughtless haze, stopping only for gas, and arrived at Clyde's place a little after noon. A small crowd had gathered by the dock, black and white faces mixed in equal numbers. Clyde saw me pull in, waved, and moved spryly to my car. Clyde was a big, barrel-chested bear of a man, and his crushing hugs always left me a little dizzy.

"Well, sir. Edward J. Piszek, in the flesh. And not a minute late." A tall black man with a haze of beard emerged from the crowd and joined us at my car. Clyde motioned toward him. "Eddie, you know my captain, Henry Dubois?"

"Sure thing." We shook hands. "Good to see you, Henry."

"Likewise, Mr. Piszek."

"Henry's bought himself a boat," Clyde explained. He slapped Henry's chest lightly with the back of his hand. "All those years I'm wondering what he does with the money I pay him, so when I retired the *Jenny G.*, who pulls out a wad of cash but Henry here."

I knew the *Jenny G.* She was one of Clyde's older boats. But she was a good boat, too, with many years left in her. "That's great news, Henry," I said. "I guess you're in business for yourself now."

"Yessir. I reckon that's right," Henry said.

"Trust me, there's nothing like it. You and me should talk." I looked back to Clyde. "That okay with you, Cap'n? A little friendly competition?"

Clyde let loose a big throaty laugh. "Aw, hell, Ed. That's the *idea.*"

I was pleased for Henry and just as happy for Clyde, who seemed as proud as any father could be of Henry's accomplishment. The black-and-white politics of North Carolina were nothing I knew about, far removed from the neighborhoods of Manayunk or Nicetown where I had grown up. On those rough streets, the biggest distinction people made was whether someone was Polish or Irish, and color was never an issue for one simple reason: white people and black people had almost nothing to do with one another. But in North Carolina, race was a fact of life and not always a happy fact. Yet, Clyde was different. He was coarse, and sometimes I had heard him say things that made me blush, but he was no bigot. He respected his men, and they respected him. And now that Henry had bought a boat of his own, Clyde was only too happy to cut him a piece of my business. Thinking about the conversation that had just transpired, I realized he had made sure of it.

Three of us went down to the dock, where the *Jenny G.* was tied up next to Clyde's new boat, its bow facing the shore. She was a good-sized vessel, thirty feet or so, with a cabin wheelhousing and twin booms suspended over the stern for nets. Freshly painted, her white metal surface gleamed in the sunlight, ricocheting off the water of the inlet. On the port bow, written in block letters, was her name: *Edward J. Piszek.*

"Folks around here have been wondering how in thunder anybody's supposed to pronounce it," Clyde said. "You should hear what they come up with. So to make it easy, we're just calling it the Eddie."

"It's quite an honor," I managed. And it was. When Clyde had first told me about it, I had been pleased, of course, and terribly flattered. But to see her shining and new and large as life—it took my breath away. "I really don't know what to say."

"Don't say anything." Clyde laughed, and loomed up on his heels. "Hell, you paid for it."

From somewhere Clyde produced and then handed me a quart bottle of soda water. I gauged its solid weight in my hands, imagining the crash and splash it would make on the side of the Eddie.

"You know," I said, "I've never done this, but aren't you supposed to use champagne?"

"Not for a working boat," Clyde said. "Why waste it? If I had champagne, you and I would be drinking it right now, not making a mess of it. Besides, you're getting ahead of yourself. A man can pay for a boat, but he can't christen it."

Clyde took the bottle from me, and a woman standing next to Henry stepped forward. Clyde introduced her to me as Henry's wife, Elizabeth. She was a startlingly pretty woman, with wavy black hair and skin the color of butterscotch.

"It seemed right that the day Henry takes over the *Jenny*, Lizzie here should christen her replacement," Clyde said.

I nodded. "Sounds good to me."

Elizabeth moved to the bow, and with Henry holding her waist, stretched her slender form over the flat water. "I christen you . . . the *Eddie*," she said, and smashed the bottle on the bow. She looked around with a smile, a bit of bubbly soda clinging in her hair. From the crowd came a sprinkling of applause.

Clyde nudged me in the side. "C'mon," he said to me. "Let's give her a run."

The four of us—myself, Clyde, Henry, and Lizzie—spent the day out on the *Eddie*, taking her out to Bluff Point and back, then returned for dinner at Clyde's house: not crab or seafood of any kind ("I fish it, I don't have to eat it," Clyde always said. "It'd be like eating my *job*) but thick steaks cooked out on the grill. Henry and Lizzie left early—Henry was taking the *Jenny* out in the morning, his first time out as owner-captain, and wanted to get to bed—so Clyde and I put on jackets and went down to the dock to drink a beer and enjoy the rest of the evening, sitting on the transom of the *Edward J. Piszek*. I was languorous after a day on the water and a big meal and happy to be out of Philadelphia for the day. I hadn't even phoned home.

We talked business for a while, then when the moment seemed right, I raised the subject of Bill Sykes. I was curious what Clyde had to say about it.

"Sounds to me like Oddie has it right."

I shrugged. "She usually does."

"You know, Ed, I've always thought one thing about you. You want to hear it?"

I laughed. "Sure."

"I've always said to myself, 'There's a man who's chasing something. Don't know what it is, but he's doing it. Won't be happy till he gets it.'"

I thought for a moment. "I don't know. I think I've been happy. I think I've got most of what I wanted. Hell, Clyde, I've gotten way more."

"What you mean is, you've got a lot of money."

I felt embarrassed. Money was never anything we really talked about. "Well, sure. I guess. Money's part of it."

"Guess nothing. You do. And money ain't a bad thing to want, not by a stretch. You've taken good care of Oddie and the kids. Hell, you've taken good care of *me*. For most folks, it'd be enough. Most folks'd sit on a mountain like the one you've got and look at the world and say, by God, this is it. *Look at me, I'm the Fish Cake King!*" Clyde paused and sipped his beer, content for the moment with his performance. "What I'm saying is," he went on, "you're not most folks. Money can't make you happy, and all the money in the world isn't going to change that, much as you'd like it to."

For a while we sat in silence. Beneath us, the boat rocked gently on the tides that washed in and out of the inlet.

Finally I said, "That was a nice thing you did today, with Henry."

"You mean the boat?" Clyde waved his beer bottle dismissively. "Hell, he gave me a good price for it."

"You know what I mean. I get the feeling some people around here don't really care for the way you do things."

Clyde thought a moment, his lips curling into a frown. "Maybe not. Old ways die hard." He gestured again with his empty beer out over the inlet. "You know, my daddy and Henry's daddy grew up together on these waters."

"I guess I'm not surprised. Roots go pretty deep down here."

He gave a curt nod. "Now, that's a fact."

Clyde rose, disappeared into the wheelhouse, and returned with two more beers, cold and sweating. He passed one to me and remained standing, rocking back on his heels.

"You see, Ed, to some folks that'd mean things should stay the same. Just because my daddy called his daddy a nigger, I shouldn't let him captain my boat, or help him get his own start. Now, what I'm thinking is my daddy just didn't know any better. He was just born to it, the way he understood things. So, to me, it means the opposite. Time to set things right. Learn from the past and get on with it."

"That's just what I'm saying. You have. Learned from the past, I mean. Almost no one ever does."

Though it was dark, I could tell I had embarrassed him. "Aw, don't go giving me any medals." He turned his gaze away from me and gestured up and down the shoreline. "Down here, folks might think I'm another L.B.J. But a couple of hundred miles north? It'd be a different story, that's a fact. So the way I see it, I'm just a waterman trying to do all right by the folks in his backyard."

"It's more than I've done." I felt strangely hollow. "I don't even know where my backyard *is*."

"Oh, don't worry now. You'll get your chance. Sounds to me like you're about to go looking for it." Clyde sat down beside me again. "So, this Sykes fellow. He wants you to go to Poland? See this ambulance thing for yourself?"

"You know, the funny thing is, we didn't actually talk about it. I just gave him the check and away he went. But somehow I almost feel as if we did, like he's expecting me to go." I shook my head. "I can't explain it. Two days ago I thought I knew exactly what I was doing with my life."

"Man gets a message, he should listen to it."

"You sound pretty sure."

He gave me an amused look. "Ed, things are different down here. We read the signs, you know? It ain't all logic. You're a smart businessman. From what I can tell, you're a pretty smart man, too. You know what's bothering you as well as anyone, and it's the same as the rest of us."

"It is?"

"Sure. You want to know what it all *means*. What it meant before you were born, and what it'll mean after you're six feet in the ground." He stamped his foot on the deck. "And you're scared to death it don't mean anything at all."

And that, of course, was exactly right. That was exactly what I was afraid of.

"Seems to me, Ed, it's the only question worth asking. We're *supposed* to ask it." He blew out a little puff of air. "If we don't, God help us. So good for you."

"My father went back to Poland," I said. "He was about the same age I am now."

Clyde nodded with satisfaction. "What'd he find?"

"I don't really know, not the details. A few relatives, I think. He died before I could ask him about it."

Clyde smiled at me in a way that told me he had known this; he just wanted to hear me say it. He extended his bottle to mine and clinked them together, sealing a bargain I hadn't realized I was making until the moment it was done.

"So maybe that's part of the plan, too," he said. "Now you'll have to go and find out for yourself."

Chapter Eleven
Tarnow

I awoke to a vision of green, acres and acres of it, as lush and succulent as any landscape I had ever seen, forests and fields of green undulating to a far horizon in the early light of dawn. Below me I heard the whine of the landing gear descending then locking into place, and felt a jolt in my stomach as the plane dipped; over the loudspeaker a voice announced first in English, then in French, and finally in Polish, that we had been cleared for our final descent into Warsaw.

The trip had taken two months to assemble. From the day I returned from North Carolina, I had pointed all my energies to this moment, setting my business affairs in order and making arrangements with CARE. Sykes had surprised me yet again; though I had expected it would take months to cut through all the bureaucratic red tape to get the ambulance up and running, in fact, it was all ready to go the day he walked into my office. At the last minute, it had been cut from CARE's budget. "Not the ambulance itself," he explained. "But the money to make it happen. Cooperation was the issue." I understood immediately: CARE needed five thousand dollars to bribe officials at the Polish health ministry. No matter, I thought. It was my first lesson in dealing with the communist government of Poland, but at the time, I was only happy that I would not have to wait to go.

I was traveling alone. I had asked Oddie if she wanted to go, but she had said no: "This is your pilgrimage," she said.

I had prepared for the trip by reading everything I could about Poland—in effect, giving myself a crash course in Polish history, life, and culture. My expectations had been low. Though Polish, I, too, had been brainwashed by prevailing ideas about Poles and Poland—namely, that Poles were plodding, simpleminded peasants for whom domination by foreign powers was inevitable. All was a lie, except the last. From the four-teenth to the seventeenth centuries, Poland had been one of Europe's greatest powers, a society of culture and refinement producing some of the world's finest music, art, and architecture, as well as some of the most significant scientific advancements of the day. But Poland's strategic location at the crossroads between Europe and western Asia made it a valuable military prize; by the end of the eighteenth century, Poland, as a nation, had disap-peared, its lands apportioned among Prussia, Austria, and czarist Russia. Not until the Treaty of Versailles, at the end of World War I, had the modern nation of Poland emerged—only to be overrun, once again, in 1939, by Hitler's army. In the five years that followed, six million Poles, half of them Jews, had been murdered—with scarcely a tear shed by anyone in the world. Virtually no Jews at all remained in Poland after 1945.

The end of the war should have restored a democratic, independent Poland to world maps, but that was not what had happened. In the scuffle to reorganize Europe, Poland had fallen under communist domination; though the West recognized a London-based Polish government in exile, official "elections" in 1947 were completely dominated by the Commu-nists, puppets of Stalin's regime in Moscow. Formal protests by the Allies were just that—empty formalities. The following year, the Soviets block-aded West Berlin. Though the Berlin Airlift would ultimately force the Soviets to release that captive city, and cement the U.S. role in safeguard-ing Western Europe against the Soviet threat, it also made it clear to every-one that no interference by the West in Polish affairs was forthcoming. The stakes—global war—were simply too high. And so, behind the Iron Curtain, the forgotten nation languished.

But not entirely. Centuries of domination by foreign invaders had taught the Poles how to resist. For a decade, the Stalinists did their best to transform Poland into a model communist nation, collectivizing its agri-culture, nationalizing its industries, secularizing its schools, and jailing its clerics. But by 1956, the communist experiment already seemed to be failing; farm production had fallen apart, and workers had begun to riot against oppressive conditions on farms and in factories. A new politburo was installed, one that distanced the Polish Communist Party from the Soviets, with Wladyslaw Gomulka as first party secretary. Immediately, Gomulka ended collectivization of agriculture and restored basic religious liberties to the nation—provided the church made no moves to involve itself in the nation's one-party politics.

Gomulka's reforms, in effect, made Poland distinct among all the na-tions of the Warsaw Pact. With the end of collectivization, 85 percent of Poland's lands returned to private control. As he had before the days of

Stalin, a Polish peasant in the mid-1960s owned the land he worked. It might have been just a few acres, but it was *his*—affording him an independence that no central authority could organize or corrupt. The restoration of religious liberty also had the effect of subverting central authority. Ninety-five percent of the nation was—and remains—Roman Catholic. Though officially apolitical, the Catholic Church in 1964 functioned at the local level as a kind of second government. The Communists would not admit it, but a great deal of the power in the country actually resided with the church.

What else had I learned? That Poland, since the nineteenth century, provided free, compulsory education that had produced one of the most literate populations in all of Europe; that Slavic tribes in the area were converted to Christianity in the tenth century; that Frédéric Chopin, the great composer, was Polish, as was the astronomer Nicolaus Copernicus, whose theory that the Earth revolved around the sun forever changed the course of human understanding; that a Pole, Thaddeus Kosciuszko, had served as a brigadier general of the Continental Army in the American War of Independence but was unsuccessful two decades later in his attempt to repel occupying Russian forces from his own country (the Kosciuszko Insurrection of 1794), spent five years in a Russian prison, and died in exile in Switzerland, still planning the war that would restore his nation to freedom; that Joseph Conrad was Polish, and Madame Marie Curie, and the pianist Artur Rubinstein; that the country was mostly flat, situated on the northern tier of the European Plain, but that the Carpathian Mountains in the south rose to more than eight thousand feet; that it had been overrun by armies of the Austro-Hungarian Empire during World War I, but that in 1920, Poland had been strong enough to turn back a Soviet push intended to conquer all of Europe; that during the Nazi occupation, Warsaw's underground resistance movement held concerts, lectures, poetry readings, and plays, graduated 9,000 students from high school, published 270 different newspapers, launched 800 armed actions against their occupiers, and held courts that tried and executed traitors to the Polish cause; that during the Warsaw Uprising of July 1944, fifty thousand Polish insurgents rose up against the Nazis, though only one of ten possessed a firearm; that in retaliation, Adolf Hitler had ordered the total destruction of the city, "not one stone left atop another stone"; that at the end of the war, the Poles had rebuilt Warsaw's Old Town, reconstructing it exactly as it had been before Hitler's first bomb fell in 1939; that Auschwitz, in the country's southwest corner, was called *Oswiecim* in Polish and had once been the deadliest place on Earth; that the country was officially "classless"; that five classes—communist officials, Catholic clergy, members of the intelligentsia (writers, artists, teachers), factory workers, and peasants—

actually made it a rigidly stratified society; that, in sum, I knew next to nothing about the country I was going to.

Bill Sykes had arranged for me to spend a day in Warsaw before traveling to Tarnow, about two hundred miles to the south. Weary from my night of travel, I stepped from the plane in a haze of excitement and exhaustion. We deplaned straight onto the runway, where armed soldiers stood watch, languidly smoking cigarettes and laughing to one another in a quick, clipped Polish I could not understand. I followed the other passengers as we trailed into customs; the guard who examined my bag was a young man, his face pale and soft, and he barely peeked into it before waving me through with a mocking laugh.

Once in the terminal proper, I was met by a representative from CARE, a friend of Bill Sykes's. His name is lost to me now; though I would travel to Poland continually for another thirty years, I saw him only once. Like the guard who inspected my luggage, he was a young man, almost boyishly youthful, and he spoke English with the choppy imperfections I remembered from childhood days when my Polish relatives would gather at the Quakertown farm for Sunday afternoon picnics. The sound of his voice made me instantly nostalgic, three thousand miles from home.

"Mr. Piszek. Welcome to Varsaw." We shook hands. "I am hoping your trip was very vell."

I made a mental note never to pronounce it Warsaw again. *Varsaw.* "It was fine, thank you."

He scooped up my luggage. "Bill Sykes is asking me to your hotel I take you, please. You are tired? From the flight? My car is just outside."

We drove into town in his tiny automobile, a sputtering contraption that had my knees pinned up against the dashboard. It was a gray morning, damp and drizzly. Traffic was light; all the other cars on the road looked the same as ours, as cramped as hamster cages. We passed through the outlying sections of town, then into the city proper, where nondescript apartment complexes, hulking government ministries, and bland office buildings dominated the skyline. Everything was new, but depressingly stale-looking, as if all the buildings had been conceived as monuments to state-run efficiency.

"We are taking you to the hotel in the Old Town," my guide advised me. "*Very* nice. I live most nearby there."

Suddenly, the city seemed to change; we crossed a bridge over a wide river and entered a maze of narrow, twisting streets like something from a children's tale. Elegant old buildings with red-tiled roofs pressed close together, punctuated by open squares and chaotic roundabouts. It looked like London or even Rome. We turned and emerged onto a wide thoroughfare with a park of green grass and flowering trees dividing the lanes. My guide brought the car to a skidding stop in front of my hotel.

"You are the American with the ambulance, yes?"

For a moment, I was so dazed I didn't answer him. "That's right."

Then he did something that surprised me completely. Sitting in the cramped car, he threw his arms around me. Before I could say anything, he had kissed my cheek. "You have many friends here," he said.

He left me standing on the curb, and I never saw him again.

At the front desk, two messages waited for me: one from Bill Sykes welcoming me and another from an Ernst Raszewski, whom I knew to be the health ministry doctor who would be taking me down to Tarnow. I called his number from the lobby, worried that whoever answered would only speak Polish. My fears were unfounded; the woman who answered spoke English with a crisp, British accent and seemed to know exactly who I was. Dr. Raszewski was out for the day, she told me, but he was planning to meet me at the hotel the next morning.

I settled down in my room and tried to sleep but discovered that I was too keyed up. Here I was, in Poland at last—and I had nothing whatsoever to do. I was exhausted from the trip and the time change, but every time I managed to relax enough to approach sleep, my mind would suddenly spin out in a new direction. Finally, I rose, took a shower—*hot water!* I marveled, still half imagining that I had left the civilized world behind—and set out on foot.

I did not return until dinnertime. Warsaw had left me stunned, exhilarated; in the eyes of its people, in its buildings and parks, everywhere I had seen the same thing: Poland was alive. Gray-faced communism had failed to kill its spirit. All around me, the city buzzed and hummed: schools, houses, offices, restaurants, shops. For two hours in the afternoon I had sat at a cafe on the banks of the Vistula, and what had I seen? Lovers holding hands across a table; schoolchildren teasing one another, carrying their books home from school; women chatting over lunch, shopping bags clustered at their feet; men in suits, holding forth to one another; old people playing chess in the sunshine. Ordinary things, and yet, nothing I had expected.

But the day had not been without its reminders of unhappier truths. Late in the afternoon, as I had been returning to my hotel, I turned a corner and saw the largest building I had ever laid eyes on; rows upon rows of windows dominating a city block, eyes that seemed to stare outward with a stern and monumental countenance. The sight of it froze me in my tracks. I wanted to ask someone what it was, but I didn't even know how to ask the question, so I circled the building, feeling its eyes beading down at me, until I came to the front entrance. The words on the sign meant nothing to me, of course, so I took out my guidebook and tried to figure out what it said, though I had already guessed. I quickly found what I was looking for. There, on the corner of Nowy Swiat Street and Jerozolimskie Avenue was the headquarters of the Polish United Workers' Party Central Committee: the seat of Polish communism. Was it just my imagination, or did the other people on the street turn their faces away from its gaze, as I had?

In the hotel, I soaked my aching feet in hot water, dressed for dinner, and went down to the restaurant in the hotel lobby. I had barely eaten a thing all day. I struggled to make sense of the menu, finally guessed, and received an overcooked slab of beef, pickled cabbage, and boiled potatoes. I ate it all ravenously, and when I was done, I realized I was finally ready to sleep. Raszewski would be coming to the hotel at 7:00 to pick me up. I paid my check (guessing again; Polish money still felt like play money) and went upstairs to call Oddie before bed.

It took nearly a half hour to get the call through. Finally, just as I was about to give up, the phone rang, a Polish operator said something I couldn't make out, and there was Oddie.

"Hon! I'm here!"

"Ed? Ed? I can barely hear you."

"I'm in Warsaw, hon," I said. We were both practically yelling.

"What time is it there?"

"It's late. It's bedtime here. Oh, you should see it, hon. I spent the whole day just walking around."

"Ed? I'm having trouble hearing you. There's some kind of echo. Wait a minute. Helen and Bill are here." I heard murmurs on the other end. "Bill wants to talk to you. We looked at Poland on a map this morning."

Bill was our youngest, just four years old. "Put him on," I said.

His small voice burst onto the line. "Dad, are you there? I saw Poland today!" He pronounced it with two syllables: Po-land.

"That's great, son."

"Dad? Dad, are you there?" His voice, whining, pulled away. "Mom, I can't hear *anything!*"

"Give the phone back to your mother, Bill."

But it was too late; the line was dead. I looked at the phone in my hand, feeling helpless. It would take another hour at least to get the call back through. I returned the receiver to its cradle, missing them all, and promised myself to call the next day.

I awoke feeling strangely, deeply refreshed; my jet lag was over. I ate breakfast in the dining room, checked out of my room, and sat myself in the lobby to wait for Dr. Raszewski. Though he was a friend of Sykes's, I also understood he was a government official—in other words, a Communist. Mentally, I had prepared myself for . . . what? What did a Communist look like? Like most Americans, I was thoroughly versed in the evils of communism as an institution but had no idea what a Communist actually looked like, what face it wore. The only image I could summon was—who else?—Nikita Khrushchev, banging his shoe like a gavel at the UN.

I could not have been more wrong. At precisely 7:00 A.M. the front door swung open, and into the dim lobby strode a small, even dainty, man, perhaps forty-five years of age, wearing a stylishly cut tweed suit. He approached me directly, wearing a warm, slightly surprised smile. The thick lenses of his glasses made his eyes seem unusually large.

"Ah. Mr. Piszek." His accent, like his secretary's—who I later learned was his wife—was British, though he pronounced my name as other Poles had, running the *s* and *z* together into a kind of *sh* sound and turning the *e* into an *i*: Pisz-ik.

"Dr. Raszewski."

"It's Ernst, please." With a graceful and alert gesture, he lifted my bag and gestured toward the door. "My car is just outside."

We stepped into the early morning sun. Though it was technically rush hour, the streets were quiet. By the curb was parked yet another tiny car. I stifled a groan.

"I know what you are thinking," Raszewski said, lifting my suitcase into the cramped trunk. He looked at me and frowned. "And you are quite correct. Polish cars are simply horrible. But the trains are worse, be assured."

I folded myself into the passenger seat and off we went, sputtering down the boulevard. I liked Raszewski immediately; he seemed, somehow, like a kindred spirit. Dangling one arm out the window, he lighted a fat, sour-smelling cigarette, and puffed away as we sped across the Vistula and out of the Old City.

"I'm sorry I was unable to meet you yesterday," he said. "There was a bit of a mix-up."

I told him that I hadn't minded; a day on my own had given me the chance to look around Warsaw. "It's a remarkable city," I said.

A grin unfolded around the cigarette clamped in his teeth. "Not what you imagined?"

"Not at all." I shook my head. "Why doesn't the world know about this place?"

He tipped one shoulder, spinning the wheel to guide us through the dense traffic that had suddenly appeared from nowhere. "Half of it does, you know. But you mean in the West, of course. And there are many misconceptions, to be sure."

"I had no idea it was . . . well, so *old.*"

He laughed, puffing out acrid smoke. "Forgive me. I remember thinking the same thing when I moved to London."

"You lived in London?"

"Yes. Well, I was a student there. For college, then for medicine. My wife is English." When I didn't answer right away, he turned to me and wagged his eyebrows. "You are surprised? That an Englishwoman would marry a Pole and live in Poland? Everyone is, you know."

I didn't know how to respond. "Yes, a little," I admitted.

"That is wise." He gave a little sigh. "I miss London. I was just a poor student, but I owned a little Aston Martin. You know this car?"

I wasn't sure that I did. "I think so," I said. "Isn't that what James Bond drives?"

He nodded, then sighed again, grieving for his lost Aston Martin. He tapped the steering wheel with the butt of his fist. "Polish cars are shit," he said.

We sped on toward the edge of the city. The landscape began to open, the crowded blocks of the city's core yielding to faceless industrial parks, huge monolithic factories, and tracts of barren land strung with massive utility poles and batteries of humming high-tension wires. Traffic thinned until we were practically alone on the road; here and there, clopping along the edge of the highway, was the improbable sight of a horse-drawn wagon. Smokestacks chuffed on the horizon.

"Is Tarnow much like Warsaw?" I asked finally.

He considered my question a second or two, then gave a curt nod. "Not at all," he said.

The trip took us nearly half a day. Outside of Warsaw, the highway disappeared, ceasing abruptly at a barricade of orange cans. Flashing arrows pointed to the left, taking us onto a second-class road that wove through forests and fields. I waited for the highway to reappear, but it never did. For another six hours, my long legs tucked painfully under the metal dashboard, we bounced our way toward Tarnow.

Raszewski explained a little more about our destination. Tarnow, he said with a wry grin, was "a bastion of the Polish peasantry."

"My parents were from there," I offered. "I was hoping to track down some relatives, actually, while I'm there."

He chuckled mysteriously. "Oh, I think that should be no problem."

We arrived just around lunchtime. Raszewski was right: Tarnow was nothing like Warsaw. It was a small industrial city, old and worn, situated in the green foothills of the Tatra Mountains. The sides of the buildings were caked with soot, and I felt none of the hum and bustle that had so enchanted me in the capital. There were few cars on the roads, and everywhere I saw piles of dung from the horse-drawn carts that clopped through the streets. It was like traveling back in time.

We checked into the hotel, then headed over to the hospital. On the drive down, Raszewski had explained that he was one of a half-dozen doctors on staff—the fact that he actually lived in Warsaw struck me as odd, but I let the question wait—and that the ambulance, which was really more of a mobile health care unit, was his to oversee.

"My luck," he said mournfully. "But without it, there would really be no way to take care of many of the people in the hills. They don't like doctors, and they have no way to get into town."

I was taken aback. "Why don't they like doctors?"

"Well, they are peasants," Raszewski said. "They don't like very much." He waved the remark away. "No, really, it is a general distrust of politics. Doctors are political figures, you see. We all have to work for the government. In Warsaw, everyone understands that this means nothing, that party membership just comes with the job. But in Tarnow?" He shook his head. "No. In Tarnow, a Communist is a Communist."

The hospital was within walking distance from our hotel, so we left the car and set out on foot. The air had a bitter, faintly sulfuric smell: the remnant, I realized, of centuries of burning coal. Black soot seemed to glaze every surface of the city like a skin of grease. Soon we came upon a small, one-story building, about the size of a suburban public library back home.

"This is the hospital?" I asked. I was incredulous. How could it be the one and only hospital for the whole city of Tarnow?

"You should have seen it before," Raszewski said.

Inside we were greeted by stale air, a tart combination of ether, perspiration, cleaning fluid, and the sour smoke of Polish cigarettes. At the desk, a nurse looked up as we entered; the two of them spoke briefly in Polish, then Raszewski left me in the lobby, reappearing a moment later in a white coat. It was strange, but I had almost forgotten he was a physician.

"I'm afraid I have to see some patients before we can go see the ambulance. It should be just a few minutes."

I took a seat in the waiting area. No one else came in. From time to time, the nurse at the desk would look up at me, smile vaguely, then return to her work. There were no magazines to read, I realized, but what good would they have done me in Polish?

An hour passed before Raszewski returned, looking harried. He scribbled on some paperwork at the desk, then approached me.

"I'm sorry for the delay. One of the other doctors didn't show up today. It looks as if he won't be back. The ministry is always doing this to us."

"The health ministry, you mean?"

Raszewski rolled his eyes. "Yes. Well, that is what they like to call themselves. If they were a health ministry, they would leave us a few doctors, don't you think?" He shook his head. "Never mind. I'm being petulant. It is really nothing unusual. Come see your ambulance."

Raszewski led me outside, around the rear of the hospital. The truck, a step van, was parked by a back entrance. The insignia of the Polish health ministry was emblazoned on the side; beneath it was some writing in Polish and then my name, *Edward J. Piszek*. It reminded me of Clyde's fishing boat.

"What's this?" I asked.

Raszewski frowned, obviously flustered. "Ah. Well, I see you noticed the writing." He laughed nervously. "It means 'gift of.' "

"But it's an ambulance! I don't want my *name* on it. I gave the money to be helpful, not to parade my name around Tarnow."

Raszewski shuffled his feet in the dirt. "I said that perhaps you would feel this way. But they thought that, because you were American, you would like it. The ministry, I mean. They think all Americans are like your John Wayne."

I fumed. "Well, maybe some Americans would. But I don't. Can't we get it changed?"

"I'm afraid that is perhaps more easier said than done."

"Tell them anything. Tell them I wanted to be anonymous. Or put it in small letters, somewhere less noticeable. Anything but this."

Raszewski paused and lit a cigarette. I could see my anger had embarrassed him, and I was instantly sorry. The situation certainly was not his fault.

"I'm sorry," I said. "It just seems . . . well, in bad taste, is all."

"You're quite right," he said. "By the end of the week, it will be gone, as you wish. Just a little name on the back door, perhaps?"

"As long as it's little," I said.

"You will need a microscope," Raszewski assured me.

Just then, two orderlies appeared through the hospital's rear entrance. Pausing to light cigarettes, they stopped by the truck, tipped their heads toward the words on the side, and had a hearty laugh before walking off.

"What was that all about?" I asked.

Raszewski smiled. "Are you sure you want to know? It is like . . . what do you call it? A Polish joke. One said to the other, 'I wonder who gave us that ambulance.' " Raszewski laughed. "So you see, you are already famous!"

That afternoon Raszewski drove me up into the hills outside town in the panel truck to visit patients. At first I had declined, thinking I would only get in the way, but finally, my curiosity had gotten the better of me. Somewhere in those hills, I believed, were members of my father's family.

Before leaving for Poland, I had asked my mother about my Polish relatives. She professed to know little; it had been years since she had heard from anyone. But eventually she had told me that one of my father's brothers still probably lived somewhere around Tarnow. He would have been an old man by then, she said, assuming he was even still alive.

It was a warm, sunny afternoon; Raszewski, still in his white coat, drove the truck with obvious pleasure, spinning the wheel this way and that to negotiate the ruts and potholes that gouged the roadway. We ascended the hills south of town, gently folded mounds of earth covered with hay and grass, like a landscape painting. Every so often we passed a stone cottage or saw one tucked into the folds between the hills. Horse-drawn plows dotted the fields, a sight I had not seen since I was a boy in Quakertown.

We stopped in a half-dozen homes during the afternoon. At first, I offered to stay in the truck, but Raszewski would have none of it: "Come and be useful," he urged. At each house where we stopped, Raszewski would introduce me, then add (as he later explained) that I was an observer from America come to learn about the Polish health system. ("Anything to get them to trust me," he explained.) Mostly, he seemed to be delivering routine care: vaccinating children—thousands of them, it seemed, crammed into the tiniest cottages!—examining old people, delivering medicine, looking in on a man who had broken his ankle in a fall from a horse. After he had done his work, it was always the same: an offer of coffee or pastries (which we had to accept, even though we had other patients to see), gentle excuses to get us back on the road, final exhortations to keep off the leg or use less salt or keep the children's vaccinations updated. And we were on our way again.

By four o'clock I was thoroughly exhausted, though I had drunk so much coffee and eaten so many sugary cakes I wondered if I would ever sleep again. "Is that all?" I asked hopefully.

"One more house," Raszewski said.

Our final stop was a cottage buried deep in a thick pocket of woods. Raszewski knocked, then entered without waiting to hear an answer.

The interior was dark and damp; stepping in, I waited a moment for my eyes to adjust. In the stone fireplace, a kettle chuffed out steam, exuding a vaguely sweet and pepperminty smell. No children greeted us in the tiny room; for a few seconds, I thought perhaps that no one was home. A wooden bedstead had been pushed next to the fireplace, where an old man, pale and thin, struggled for breath. One hand lay on the sheet, and in it he clutched a rag, stained with dark blood. At Raszewski's approach, his eyes flickered; the old man nodded, though he did not speak.

"What's wrong with him?" I whispered.

"Tuberculosis."

Raszewski tended to the old man, asking him quiet questions, listening to his lungs and heart, helping him to drink a cup of tea. But that was all. The old man seemed not to notice me where I sat at the rough wood table. Ten minutes later, we were back outside.

"Isn't there anything else you can do for him?"

"I'm afraid not." Raszewski opened the door of the van and put his bag of instruments on the driver's seat. "I don't imagine he'll live much longer. His sister and her family live down the hill and see to most of his needs. Food and whatnot. But his lungs are very, very bad. Did you know that he is only fifty-five?"

I thought of Sally Williams, going about her business back in Philadelphia, as if nothing had ever been wrong with her. "But I thought T.B. was curable."

"It is. Or, it's treatable, I should say. But in Poland, things are different. Here it's an epidemic. No one knows how many have it, because we don't test everyone, but some people think that the infection rate may be close to 5 percent. Most of those who are infected will die, especially out here. We can't catch it in time. We simply don't have the equipment."

"What would you need?"

Raszewski laughed ironically. He opened his bag then and removed a small flask. He drank and passed it to me: vodka. I felt my chest burn with it.

"What don't we need, you mean. Well, X-ray machines would be helpful. There's only one in all of Tarnow."

We got back in the truck and headed down the hill. Five percent, I thought. One person in twenty. It was appalling.

"Can't the ministry do anything?" I asked.

"Of course it can," he said bitterly.

I spent my week in Tarnow bouncing around the hills with Raszewski, combing the countryside for anyone who knew of anyone named Piszek.

The problem, it turned out, was a surprising one. Piszek was hardly "Smith" or "Jones" back home, but in Tarnow, it was a common name. Using local parish registries, I found close to thirty different families with the name. Dutifully I tracked each one down, only to find the same thing. Around town, the word was out that a rich American named Piszek was looking for his relatives.

"Cousin!" they cried as I introduced myself on their doorsteps. "It is our long-lost American cousin, come home at last!" But when pressed, none could provide a shred of evidence that we were related. Bloated on coffee and sweets, I would go on my way again, untangling children from my legs, declining invitations of marriage or business partnerships, buying my freedom off with a few American pennies and vague promises to return someday soon.

"You can't blame them for trying," Raszewski said one night at dinner, after I'd regaled him with one more tale of a narrow escape.

"This is awful," I moaned. "I feel like I should check my wallet when I leave."

"That wouldn't be a bad idea," Raszewski said.

It was terribly frustrating—to come so close, and not find one relative. As the days went by, and my departure loomed, I began to lose hope. But something else was happening to me, too. While the wheels of Mrs. Paul's were turning, three thousand miles away, I began to feel deeply at ease. The Polish part of me, long buried, was beginning to rise to the surface. Pausing to eat an apple perched on a hilltop overlooking the rolling countryside, memories of my youth in Quakertown came bubbling up—or rather, the texture of feeling they invoked. And with these feelings, to my surprise and wonder, came a smattering of the Polish language itself, a tongue I had not used at all since I was a very young boy. As I hunted for my relatives, in cottage after cottage I would search for the right words—and find them. *"Czy to jest dom Piszka?"* I would ask. *"Czy jest Wladek Piszek? Jestem jego bratankiem, przyjechalem z Ameryki."* ("Is this the Piszek home? Is there a Wladek Piszek here? I am his nephew, come from America.") The answer was always *"Nie, nie ma go tutaj"* ("No, not here"), but to hear myself say the words—it was like listening to a different man entirely or hearing my real voice for the first time.

On my last day in Tarnow, I spent the morning and early afternoon meeting with local health ministry officials, then left with Raszewski for a final ride into the hills. While he was going to visit patients, I was on my way to investigate one last Piszek family I had heard about. Their names weren't in any registry; I had learned of their existence indirectly from a nurse at the Tarnow hospital. They were said to live at the end of an unmarked dirt track off the main road to the south. With patients to see, Raszewski deposited me at the crossroads, agreeing to meet me back there in three hours.

It was five o'clock by the time I set out on foot. The pathway wound between fields of tall hay and pressed on to a cluster of low hills in the distance. Smaller pathways forked off the main branch, leading to a series of cottages. I stopped at each, always getting the same reply: "No, but Piszek . . . up further." I trudged on as twilight descended, bringing with it a cool breeze that pushed the grain of the fields into smoothly undulating shapes like waves on water. The path grew muddy, its rough form dotted with pools collected during a fierce rain the night before; still, it did not end. At last I crested a small hill and saw the final cottage, nestled in a copse. Glinting firelight flickered from its windows. It seemed like my last hope. I would try this one final house, then return to the main road to meet Raszewski.

I knocked on the wide plank door and waited. Inside, I heard murmurs, then the scrape of a chair on a hard dirt floor. The door inched opened, revealing a woman, wearing a plain dress and apron, her hair twisted up in a rag. She looked at me fearfully, not comprehending—what visitor would knock on her door at this hour, in such a place?—and for a moment I forgot the words. Behind her in the dim interior, I glimpsed the shape of a child moving across the room.

At last I opened my mouth to speak. "I am . . ." But then the door pulled open wider, revealing a man beside her.

My heart stopped.

Standing in the doorway was my father.

His name was Antoni Piszek, my cousin. His father, Wladek, had been my uncle—my father's brother. Antoni had lived in Tarnow all his life and married a local girl, his wife Genevieve, the woman whom I had so badly frightened by knocking on the door. They had four children; the two boys were Wladek and Josef, the two girls Krystyna and Sofia. All were luminously beautiful. They asked me for nothing. We sat by the fire, drinking sweet tea, the children clustered around us. I do not remember what we said to one another that night. It seems possible we said nothing at all. But somehow we made ourselves understood. And in the warm light of the cottage, I saw Antoni smiling at me, wearing my father's face.

At the end of my visit, they all escorted me down the path to the road, lighting our way through the darkened fields with oil lamps. Stars smeared across the blue-ink sky above. I worried that I had taken too long, that Raszewski would already be gone. But as we approached the crossroads, I saw the headlights of the panel truck, then, stepping into the beams, the shape of my friend, waiting to take me home.

Chapter Twelve
Wojna on Tuberculosis

T wo years later, a bright, damp morning in May: I awoke just as the sun was rising, drank a cup of coffee in the quiet kitchen, then set out on my bicycle down the long drive of the Emlen House grounds. Around me the wide fields of the estate gleamed with the scattered jewels of the night's dewfall, beneath a gauze of rising mist. The bicycle was a gift from Oddie the previous fall, and since then I had come to love my morning rides, to depend on them; with each pump of the pedals, my mind would achieve a deeper, more crystalline clarity, and I had found that, under the spell of the bike's familiar childhood rhythms, I felt a closeness to the world around me that was like a kind of prayer. All the distractions, all the clutter, all the thousand decisions that made up my life were washed away by the bright morning air that breezed past me.

But that morning I set out with more on my mind than usual. My life was approaching a crossroads. In just a few months, I would be turning fifty—for any man a moment of deep reflection, but I felt its poignancy with an extra sharpness. My father, after all, had been fifty years old when he died. I was not one to dwell morbidly on my own mortality, but I also found myself thinking that my years beyond fifty were a lucky break, a gift I should not squander.

What to do with the rest of my life? On one level, the answer was obvious. Later that morning, I had an appointment with an investment banker, a man who had been courting Mrs. Paul's for some time. The subject of the meeting was expansion. In a way, the conversation was long overdue. The law of the market was simple: grow, or die. And a company like Mrs. Paul's—arguably one of the most successful companies of its kind—had only one place left to go. I had received offers for the company nearly every quarter since the early sixties and always scoffed; selling Mrs. Paul's—or merging it into another company—would be like selling one of my own children, I said. There was no price I could put on it. But the gentleman I was meeting that day had something else in mind: through a strategic series of acquisitions, transforming our family-run business into an international food company to rival the giants of the industry, the Heinzes and General Foods and Krafts of the world—those very companies I had dared compare myself to, and dream of, all those years ago, selling crab cakes over a Kensington bar. The leap the gentleman had described was nothing shy of the leap from millions to billions. And in my heart, I knew it was possible.

But I also wondered: *What would it get me?* Captain Clyde knew me well; money was not enough. A billion dollars. It was a dizzying, intoxicating sum, like the weight of a planet. But I had no idea what I would do with it. And Mrs. Paul's—the company *was* like a child to me. It is a marvelous thing to see the child you have raised go off into the world and exceed your wildest expectations. But what if that child is no longer really yours?

I pumped the pedals and mulled. Although it was still early, the sun warmed my neck and face, and when my thirty-minute ride was over I parked my bike in the foyer and entered the kitchen, where Oddie was drinking coffee at the table.

I poured myself a cup and sat down across from her. "Hon, what would you say if I said I was going to give away a billion dollars?"

Holding her cup to her lips, she paused, then sipped—as if I had asked a completely ordinary question. "Well," she said finally, "I didn't realize we had a billion dollars."

"We don't."

"Then it wouldn't cost you anything to give it away, now would it?"

It was my answer. I rose across the table, took her face in my hands, and kissed her. She smiled and narrowed her eyes at me. "This is about that meeting, isn't it? I could tell you hardly slept."

"Well, it is," I said. "Or it was. I think I just canceled it."

Upstairs, I telephoned Sally, and did exactly that. ("What should I tell him?" she asked. And I said, "Tell him anything.") Then I asked her to get Bill Sykes on the phone.

In the two years since I had been to Tarnow I had received regular reports from Bill and returned to Poland twice to ride with Ernst Raszewski up into the hills in the ambulance. I had even begun to make arrangements to bring Wladek and his family to the United States. In a way, Poland had become a kind of secret second life for me, at least as far as most of my friends and associates in the United States were concerned. It was, after all, still a communist country. Though I knew better—communism was just a fraction of Poland's story—my visits there were not necessarily something to discuss. I simply didn't want to explain, and how could I?

But that morning in May, I decided that it was time to bring my Polish life out of the shadows. Before I hung up the phone, I asked Sally a question.

"Tell me, Sally," I said. "How are you feeling?"

"Me?" She laughed. "I've never felt better, Mr. P. You know that. My doctor still feels a little cheated, I think."

"When did you last have an X ray?"

"I used to have them all the time. But not for years now." She paused. "What's this all about, Mr. P.?"

"I'll let you know."

I did not forget my first ride into the hills with Ernst Raszewski two years earlier, and the dark cottage where a man—just fifty-five years old, but looking like he was eighty—gasped for breath on a stained cot by the fire. On subsequent visits, I had seen the same scene dozens of times in different cottages. In the rest of the industrialized world, the disease was just a memory, a remnant of the nineteenth century that cropped up from time to time and was quickly controlled. But in Poland, T.B. had raged virtually unabated since the end of World War II. Tens, maybe hundreds, of thousands of people were afflicted—dying of a communist bureaucracy that could muster neither the resources nor the will to combat it.

I had also learned a little more about Polish history, and in particular, the composer Frédéric Chopin, whose music—lilting, beautiful, like something from a dream—I loved. A great patriot, the exiled Chopin was dying of T.B. in Paris when a group of his fellow countrymen sought him out to help them raise money for an insurrection against the czarists. Though his health was poor, Chopin did his duty, traveling from European capital to European capital, giving concerts for the Polish cause. During his last years, his health failing him, he had played with a blood-splattered handkerchief in his cloak, pausing to cough into it between songs. Death had taken him at just age thirty-nine.

On my second trip to Poland, I had visited the great composer's home outside of Warsaw. Pausing at his piano, I had run my hands over its smooth white keys, drinking in through my fingertips the memory of this towering genius, as great as Mozart, struck down in midlife while playing on behalf of the imprisoned country he loved. I was moved practically to tears. And now, over a century later, red tape and ideological arrogance had restored T.B. to its lethal ascendancy over the countryside.

At my office, I phoned Bill Sykes and told him succinctly what was on my mind.

"Bill, I want to cure tuberculosis in Poland. I'll provide a mobile hospital, X rays, whatever we need. I'll need CARE to pave the way, though."

"The whole *country*, Ed?"

"That's right. All of it."

For a moment, Bill was speechless. Finally, his voice came back on the line. "Do you have any idea how much money you're talking about? Because I don't."

"Well, I'm not sure." I had thought a bit about this. "I'm not sure I much care. Half a million? A million dollars? What, you don't want it?"

Bill laughed. "Oh, we want it. I'm just not sure the Poles do."

"Then we'll talk them into it."

"Ed," he said, his voice lowering, "these are *Communists*. You know how they operate. They're not just going to let some American capitalist waltz into their country and fix the health system. One ambulance in a provincial city no one cares about is one thing. We're talking about every man, woman, and child in a country of thirty million people."

"Right." I'd already done the math. "About the size of Pennsylvania and New York."

"Ed, I'll say it again. This isn't Pennsylvania and it sure isn't New York. Now, I grant you, the infrastructure is probably there. If we were talking about Africa, I'd tell you to just forget it and go back to bed. But you can't buy a loaf of bread in Warsaw without permission from some deputy minister. You know that as well as I do."

"So we'll get his permission, whoever he is." I thought of old Joe Gaudio, his warehouse full to bursting with frozen cherries. "We'll . . . negotiate."

Bill laughed again. "You know, if someone told me I was going to get a million-dollar phone call this morning, I would have told them they were nuts. And here I am, telling you just that. Okay, Ed. I'll get the ball rolling at this end. This should be quite a ride."

I spent the next few weeks doing some digging of my own. For all of my sudden passion, I didn't have a clue, really, what I was asking to do; only someone who understood the disease, and the public health issues involved, could answer that. I phoned the Montgomery County Health Department, and after a few messages back and forth, found myself on the phone with a doctor at the University of Pennsylvania, a professor of public health and a specialist in respiratory disease. I told him what I wanted to do and asked if it was possible.

"From a medical standpoint, it should be," he explained. "But it wouldn't be cheap, and you'd have to move pretty quickly. You'd have to x-ray the entire population in less than a two-year time period, treat everyone with the disease, then go back and x-ray everyone again within another two years. In theory, by then, it could be gone. But you'd have to get to *everyone*, Mr. Piszek. Not just people in the big cities."

I asked again: "But it *could* be done?"

"Yes," he told me. "Technically, I'd have to say it could."

It was all I needed to hear. It *could* be done. But how could you x-ray everyone in an entire country in just two years? And Bill was right; Poland wasn't Pennsylvania. I had seen that well enough. Government officials that I had met all struck me, to a one, as remarkably ineffective; the general assumption seemed to be that very little could be accomplished, so why bother? And the government would not be the only hurdle. Especially in the countryside, suspicion of doctors—of any state-run enterprise—was general. Getting fifteen or twenty million Polish peasants in front of an X-ray machine, even one with CARE written all over it, would be no small trick.

An answer came quickly from Bill Sykes, and I was in luck; CARE had a mobile X-ray unit that was, in fact, sitting unused in storage. The unit had been slated for a country in West Africa, but problems had arisen— "just another goddamned civil war," Sykes said grimly—leaving the unit with nowhere to go and CARE stuck with the bill. It had cost CARE forty-two thousand dollars; for twenty-five thousand, Bill said, I could buy it outright from them. Bill had also talked to Ernst Raszewski, who said that the ministry would accept the unit on two conditions: only Polish doctors and nurses could operate the unit (which I had planned for anyway—it was the most cost-effective strategy, and from what I had seen, Poland's doctors were first-rate) and the ministry would retain the power to send the unit wherever they saw fit.

The last troubled me. I had hoped to start in Tarnow. We were also talking about only one unit; spread too thin across the country, sent here and there at the inscrutable whim of the party, it had no chance of doing any good. But my reasons for wanting to base the unit in Tarnow were, I had to admit, mostly personal. I was thinking of Wladek and his family, his friends, the people he knew. If I was truly serious about eradicating the disease from the entire country, I would have to put such sentimental considerations aside. And in any event, the one unit was just a fraction of what I had in mind. Making such a concession to the health ministry would cost me little, for now, and be a sign of goodwill that I could use to my advantage later.

"Sold," I said to Bill. "Tell them yes." I added, "You might want to add that there might be a few more units on the way, too."

"How many?"

"For now, let them wonder. But I'm thinking about a dozen."

The number was actually eleven. By my best estimates, confirmed with the help of the doctor at Penn, eleven units working seven days a week, twenty-four hours a day (assuming 25 percent downtime), could examine the entire population in about a year. Doubling that figure—a 100 percent margin for error, probably necessary, given the thousand myriad details (supply shortages, bad weather, negotiations over salaries, bullheaded communist intransigence) that I couldn't predict—still brought the project in under the two-year deadline. Adding in the costs of shipping, supplies, and buying and maintaining support vehicles, I estimated I was about to spend three-quarters of a million dollars.

It was time to call the family together. We gathered at Emlen House on a Sunday morning: Oddie (who knew most of what was going on), my oldest daughter Ann (twenty-eight years old, married, and well into her adult life), Ed Jr. (twenty-three, and vice president of manufacturing at Mrs. Paul's), George (just two years behind his older brother, and a VP of marketing), Helen (a spunky thirteen-year-old at Germantown Academy), and Bill (only in the first grade, but in his own way, a force to be reckoned with). At Mrs. Paul's I never had to answer to a board of directors, but with the family the situation was different, and I found myself uneasy. I had never done anything like this before. Or rather, *we* had not; whatever I was going to spend was money out of their pockets, too. And the argument against my cause was compelling: Why try to help *Communists?* The Polish communist state was, after all, a wing of Soviet communism—the same government that had pledged, on the floor of the United Nations, to bury us. They had money for guns and bullets and bombs—why not X-ray machines? Wasn't I, by taking on the costs myself, inadvertently supporting the communist cause?

The truth, of course, was far more complex, as I had learned. Polish communism and Soviet communism were not the same things at all. In two years of dealing with the government, I had yet to meet a single state official who seemed to believe what he was saying. The official communist party line was like an ill-fitting suit of clothes the country was forced to wear, like a costume in a play. It was all fakery and pantomime, performed with tight-lipped dutifulness under the ominous shadow of Soviet tank turrets. (Prague Spring and the Soviet invasion of Czechoslovakia, just two years away, would prove this point, at least to me, in short, brutal order.)

In any event, I didn't believe it was the government I was helping, but the Polish people, captives to one invading army after another since well before the Cossacks.

My family gathered around me; I told them what I hoped to do, and what, as best as I could guess, it was going to cost. ("Is that a lot of money, Dad?" Bill asked, and I had to say, "Yes, son, it's more than a lot.") My older children listened carefully, asking the sorts of questions they had every right to ask: *Would it work?* ("Maybe.") *Would it affect the business?* ("Some.") *Would people think I was a Communist? CIA?* ("No one with any brains.") Their encouragement was important, and to a one, that Sunday morning in July 1966, they gave it.

Later that night, as we were about to go to sleep, Oddie turned to me. She had barely spoken a word that morning—because (or so I assumed) she had already made it clear to me that she supported the plan and wanted to let the children make up their own minds.

"You know," she said, her voice rising in the darkness, "what you're doing, it's important work. More important than anything you've done before." She sighed sleepily. "I just wanted you to hear it."

"I hope so," I said. "I hope it works."

"It will," she said. "In a way it already has, you know."

I realized what she was talking about. Whatever happened in Poland was far away, a gamble that might or might not pay off. But under our roof, I had already won. We had become, that day, a different kind of family, one with a mission in the world that was far larger than ourselves. I remembered then something Bill had said to me when our family meeting had adjourned. Just seven years old, he was always full of questions, and like all children, had a way of cutting straight to the heart of the matter.

"Daddy," he said, "if we don't do this, will people die?"

Struck by the unflinching frankness of his question, I had not answered right away. What did he know about death? It seemed to me that it had not yet touched him, though he had asked several times about my own father, whose framed picture stood atop my bureau. It was the photo taken of him on the deck of the ship that had carried him back to Poland a year before his death. Daddy's daddy had gone far away, I explained to Bill, to a better place, but he could not come back from it; that was death.

"Yes, son," I said at last. "I think they may."

He frowned, looking away and biting his lip in deepest concentration, then affixed me again with his gaze. A child's vision of things is often the clearest, and in his eyes I saw that he had decided something. With a curt, businesslike nod, he concluded his ruminations.

"Then we have to," he said.

The key official in the communist hierarchy, at least for me, was the deputy minister of health, Comrade Jan Sieklucki. Twenty-five years later he would rise to become the director of the Health Ministry's Department of Foreign Relations. But back then, he was an up-and-coming hotshot, brash and eager to make a name for himself, and interested in the ways I might help to make that happen for him. Though I wouldn't say we ever became friends—the gaps between us were just too great—I think it is also true that we grew to respect one another. And one thing we shared, without question, was a fervent hatred of T.B.

Sieklucki surprised me often; despite his youthful appearance—a shock of blond hair fell over his forehead, making him look like a schoolboy—he was, like many communist officials, a sly negotiator, quite accomplished at getting what he wanted. The irony was profound; in this regard, nearly all the communist officials I dealt with over the years reminded me far more of American businessmen than state officials of any kind. And perhaps that was why, in the end, I fared better than my counterparts in government. Two decades in the trenches of free-market American capitalism were excellent training for my new, public life cutting deals behind the Iron Curtain.

The negotiations began in August 1967, when I returned to Poland for a series of meetings with Sieklucki at his office in Warsaw. When I entered his office for the first time, I was immediately hopeful that the negotiations would proceed quickly. On the wall behind his desk, a large sign read *"Wojna Z Gruzlica"* ("War on Tuberculosis"). Shaking his hand, I thought, *At last, someone on my wavelength. This is going to be a snap.* I was right, and wrong. Sieklucki was on my wavelength, at least as far as T.B. was concerned. But in other important ways, we would differ sharply.

I did find, though, that I had two things on my side. Communism, as an institution, is surprisingly materialistic. With the average communist official, moral arguments will get you nowhere; he simply has too much to protect in terms of personal reputation and the appearance of obedience to the rigid pecking order that organizes communist society. But use the language of business—"leverage" and "bang for the buck" and all the rest—and he will snap to attention. If you can make him look good on the bottom line, you have won an ally.

I was also a new creature in Sieklucki's experience. I had no pecking order, no "upstairs," no board of any kind to answer to. I look back now on those initial negotiations and think how odd it must have been, how confusing for him to face an independent entrepreneur who was completely free to make a decision on the spot. And, though I had never worked so closely with a communist official, I understood Sieklucki's position rather well; it was not altogether unlike dealing with a local union chief, caught between his national office and the union rank and file. In other words, Sieklucki had little room to move, whereas I had all the room in the world. Though of course, it wasn't what I wanted, but in the end I could simply take my money and go home if it came to that.

Our negotiations proceeded, then, as a kind of mutual education, a crash course in the differences between East and West. At first, we found ourselves in agreement. The subject of our first day's conversation was the number of vehicles I would provide, and Sieklucki's number matched my own: eleven mobile X-ray units. Poland did not have such units and would be glad to welcome ours. Then the discussion turned to the number of support vehicles. I gave him my figures and calculations, which called for forty-two cars of various sizes to transport materials and doctors and to travel ahead of the mobile units to arrange for T.B. screening in each town.

Sieklucki looked the paperwork over, nodding and making some notes to himself. Then he spoke in rapid Polish to the interpreter, a woman provided by the ministry for the duration of my visit.

"Forty-two vehicles is acceptable."

"Fine. Tell him it's a deal."

She did so. Sieklucki leaned back in his chair and again delivered a battery of rapid Polish. In those days, I could make out some of the words, but not all.

"We will now break for three days," Sieklucki said through the interpreter, "so that I can make my report. Then you will receive new instructions."

I was dumbfounded. "What is he talking about? A deal's a deal." I turned to the interpreter. "Tell him I said I'm not waiting for three days."

Sieklucki gave the interpreter a blank look as she spoke, then gave the same look to me. "Things are not done that way," he replied calmly, as if he were remarking on a simple fact of nature.

"Oh, yes, they are." *Three days!* I thought. For what? I pointed at his desk. "Get whoever it is you need to talk to on the phone. I'm not sitting in my hotel until Friday."

For a moment, nobody said anything. Sieklucki made no gesture toward his phone, but leaned back in his chair, placing the tips of his fingers together. I realized he was giving me the chance to recant—to save face, in other words, because there was no way he was going to do what I was asking him—no, *telling* him—to do. In the eyes of his superiors, picking up the phone would be tantamount to giving away the store. *Slow down, boy*, I thought.

"Never mind," I said to the interpreter. "Tell him three days is fine, as long as we can continue to meet. There are other details to work out, right? So we can work on those. Let's at least assume we're going ahead."

She repeated my words, and Sieklucki nodded, smiling with satisfaction: he had won. I had read him correctly, without his having to tell me how to behave. So both our dignities had been preserved. The first test had been passed.

"I know that you are used to things happening quickly," Sieklucki said. "I wish that could happen here. But it is simply different. The epidemic isn't going anywhere, is it? It has been going on for forty years. So three days isn't so much."

"I guess not."

"We are making excellent progress," he said, and yawned. His gaze drifted past me to the window. "Come back tomorrow."

I did. And the next day, and the next. On the third day, as he had promised, the report came back from the foreign office: eleven X-ray units and forty-two support vehicles, paid for by the Polish American entrepreneur Edward J. Piszek, would be gratefully employed by the Polish Health Ministry to combat tuberculosis.

"You see?" Sieklucki said, showing me the letter. "It all works out in the end."

We had, by then, ironed out every detail but one: the make of the support vehicles. I had already arranged to order forty-two station wagons through a Ford distributorship back home for about two thousand dollars apiece. They were roomy and reliable, and having spent countless hours on Polish backcountry roads, I believed they were up to the job. The last thing I wanted was to have the whole operation bog down in the muck of rural Poland.

"I do not think we can take Fords," Sieklucki announced. "I do not think that will be acceptable."

I sighed wearily. A week of his vague pronouncements—this was acceptable, that was not, all in the passive voice—had worn me down. But I had no intention of rolling the dice on an Eastern European car of any kind. It was, after all, my money.

"What's the problem?" I said finally.

"Mr. Piszek, you are a businessman, yes?"

I looked at him, surprised to find him smiling. Usually, his face was as blank as the face of a master poker player. Why, after a week of this, he was still having fun, I couldn't guess.

"Right," I said.

"And that means you're not afraid to save a little money?"

I saw where he was going, or at least thought I did. I remembered my long, bumpy ride to Tarnow two years ago, my legs folded like a chicken's wings under the dashboard of Raszewski's go-cart of a car. They were the only vehicles that ordinary citizens seemed to own, though almost no one outside the inner circle of the party had a car, anyway. There were long waiting lists, often a dozen years long, for ordinary Poles to buy one. If you put your name on the list at age twenty, you were considered lucky if your car was delivered by your thirty-fifth birthday. Even then, a cramped box like Raszewski's would cost the average Pole the equivalent of his life savings.

"If you're thinking of those little tin cans you call a car, you can forget it."

"Tell me, Mr. Piszek, are you familiar with our Warshava?"

I conceded as much. I had been in a Warshava several times, when the health ministry had sent someone to pick me up at my hotel. They were a good deal larger than Raszewski's car—actually they were a dead rip-off of a 1939 Ford. Primitive by modern standards, lacking any amenities, but tough. The engines were the size of a tractor's.

Sieklucki went on. "And is it not built like a truck? A tank? Hard-lasting for our roads?"

Again, I was forced to concede that this was true. "But I thought only communist officials got those," I said.

Sieklucki shrugged. "Generally, yes. But I have just this day received word that perhaps forty-two can be made available. You can purchase them for twelve thousand dollars apiece. And because these are Polish cars, you will not have to ship them here."

Who would be getting a cut from this I did not know—maybe even Sieklucki himself. But the cars would do the job.

"I won't take them unless they're station wagons."

Sieklucki's face brightened. "As a matter of fact, they are."

"And they have to have a rack on top. With a tarpaulin, so when it rains all the clothing and luggage can be kept dry."

Sieklucki nodded. "It is already in the letter."

As long as I was bribing him, I thought I would at least take care of the details. "And strong hooks bolted to the front and back. With a long rope two inches thick, no less than sixty feet long, so they can be pulled from the mud."

"I see you know our roads well. Of course, I would never think of providing you with anything less."

We shook hands, and out came the vodka. Could it be that we were beginning to like each other?

I flew back to Poland a month later, when the vehicles were delivered to the Health Ministry. It was an exciting time; things were coming together quickly, communist foot-dragging or no. The doctors and nurses them-selves proved supremely competent—not only Raszewski, who rode with us the first few weeks, but all the other medical staff besides. They checked out the X-ray vans—"Gift of the American People" written boldly on their sides—and the Warshavas, proclaimed everything ready to go, and soon we were on our way.

Each unit was staffed by two doctors, a T.B. radiologist, and three nurses. The doctors came in two categories: generalists, like Raszewski, and heart and respiratory specialists, who would examine the plates for evidence of other diseases as well. Strangely, this was officially kept secret from me (though Raszewski explained everything), as if I would object to my money being spent combating illness other than T.B. Of course I was delighted. We began in the south, near Tarnow after all, then fanned out across the countryside.

Ours was a complex enterprise. An advance team would go on ahead to a small town or city, often leading the way by as much as a week, then the medical team itself would arrive and set up shop in a school or town hall for one to three days. We slept in tents, private homes, hotels—whatever was available. Our arrival always had a kind of carnival atmosphere; Poles, especially rural Poles, were completely unaccustomed to the sight of four or five brand-new vehicles, including a large van, roaring down main street like a mud-spattered parade. Many of the most isolated communities hadn't seen more than one car at a time for years, nor more than a single doctor on duty. We might have come from Mars. But suspicion inevitably gave way to curiosity, curiosity to warmth and welcoming; and before long, our arrival in each town was eagerly anticipated, like the rumors of a circus traveling the countryside. People lined the street as we pulled into town; sometimes, they even cheered. Each team operated sixteen hours a day—not the twenty-four I had originally planned, but enough. At the end of each day we collapsed on our cots in utter exhaustion.

Because I was not a doctor or nurse, and spoke only rudimentary Polish, my duties varied. In each town, I would meet with local officials, receiving with embarrassment their thanks, then try to make myself generally useful. With civil authorities or with the parish priest, I would examine records to verify that the team doctors examined everyone. It was hardly glamorous work, but it was necessary, and as the weeks went by, it introduced me to a notion that would later become very useful to me: state atheism, at least in rural Poland, was a myth. The Catholic Church actually functioned as a kind of local government. As a visiting medical observer, you shook hands with the mayor, had dinner at his house, took his boastful tour of the run-down city hall, library, school, or hospital; but if you wanted to know anything serious about the town and its people, clerics were the people to ask. And I was personally meeting with all of them.

What problems we encountered were surprisingly ordinary. Weather bedeviled us; the rains came, and the ropes and hooks came out every day to haul one vehicle or the other out of the ditch. Tarpaulins leaked, soaking everything, and stranding us for days at a time while everything dried out. The van I traveled with—the first one, which CARE had originally slated for West Africa—had no heater, and we froze until a heating unit caught up with us and we found a mechanic to install it. Most humorous—and time consuming—was the very human problem of the Polish Peeping Tom. Somehow word had spread that in order to receive chest X rays, the women would have to remove their shirts. Crowds of young men and boys would gather by the van, trying to sneak a peek through the side doors and bringing the operation to a halt. We hung extra curtains, blocked the door with a table, but in the end, they still came, giggling and laughing until we chased them off, threatening to make them strip head to foot for their own X rays and sell tickets to all the women in town.

I had planned to stay only a month, but all my calls home assured me that Mrs. Paul's was doing fine without me, so I decided to extend my stay. By this time the team had worked its way north and east toward Warsaw, into the flat farming country between the country's capital and the Soviet border. It was the same patch of ground across which, twenty-three years earlier, the Soviet army had pushed back the Nazis, then marched on to Berlin. Poor little Poland, always caught in between; though the nearest Soviet tanks were several hundred miles to the east, it was as if they had never left.

On a Monday morning in October I awoke at my hotel in the town of Siedice, ate a quick breakfast, then hurried to the small health clinic in the center of town, where we had parked our van the night before. It was a raw morning, damp and blustery, and as I walked the dozen or so blocks to the clinic I began to wonder how soon winter would set in. Certainly in the worst of January and February, we would have to slow down, if not stop altogether; but so far, we were proceeding on or even ahead of schedule, and I had included in my calculations sixty days of downtime to account for impassable weather.

I arrived at the clinic expecting to see a crowd, but to my surprise, no one was around. On the side of the van parked by the clinic door, a sign had been posted: "No X rays Today." Inside, I found the team leader, a doctor named Marcin Stanislaw, drinking coffee at a table in the lobby. Like Raszewski, he had done some of his training in the West, and spoke English passably well.

"What's the problem?" I asked him.

He shrugged and pushed his coffee mug toward the center of the table. "New orders from the ministry. We're supposed to stop for the day. All the teams, not just ours." He sipped his coffee and frowned. "It's probably nothing. Some mix-up with the paperwork."

"Orders? Whose orders?"

He reached into the pocket of his coat and removed a piece of paper. "Well. It doesn't say." He handed it to me. "It's from Sieklucki's office. But the orders aren't his."

"How do you know?"

He gave a mysterious little laugh. "I know Sieklucki."

I wasn't sure if this was praise or damnation—whether he meant that Sieklucki wouldn't give such an order or he was a coward who wouldn't take credit for his own actions. In Poland it was often hard to tell the difference.

"Where's the phone?"

He tipped his coffee cup toward the front desk. "You can try. I already did. The orders are confirmed. It's best for now to wait." He rose and drained his coffee. "Do what the rest of us are going to do. Sleep. We all need it. Tomorrow we'll hear something."

But the next day it was the same: "Suspend all activities until further notice." By midweek, when nothing had changed, I called the ministry and was told that Sieklucki was not available. Was there a number where he could phone me back?

"Never mind," I told the secretary. I hung up the phone, and went back to the hotel, where Stanislaw was playing solitaire in the lobby.

"Can you spare me for the day?"

He laughed. "Why not? My guess is they're expecting you." He rose, slapping his knees. "Come on. I'll take you."

We drove into Warsaw and went straight to Sieklucki's office. It was nearly five by the time we arrived, and we caught him just as he was packing up for the day. Stanislaw was right; Sieklucki did not seem at all surprised to see me. But when he saw the look in my eyes, his face went white with alarm. This time, the vodka stayed in the cabinet.

"Why did you pull us off the road?" I demanded.

"The work . . . it is going well? Ahead of schedule?"

He smiled weakly and gestured toward a chair. "Please, sit down, gentlemen."

"You know it is. And thank you, comrade, I'll stand. I've been in a car for five hours."

Sieklucki sighed and eased himself back down into a chair behind his desk. "I'm sorry. The teams will have to cut back to four hours per day." He shrugged, not really looking at me. "It isn't really my idea. But it's the vehicles, you see. Some people are concerned. They are causing quite a stir."

"Four hours a day is nonsense," I barked. My Polish language skills suddenly failed me completely. I looked at Stanislaw. "Tell him that's what I said: nonsense. Make it even stronger if you can think of something."

Stanislaw raised an uncertain eyebrow at me. "Really?"

"Just tell him."

Stanislaw delivered the message. I heard him use a word that, roughly translated, meant "rotten horse sausage." Sieklucki nodded, listening.

"Well," he said finally, "I admit it is not ideal. But you must understand. There are many factors here. Eleven vans and forty-two Warshavas, all with 'Gift of the American People' written on the side. It is disturbing to people."

"Not to anyone I've met," I said. "They're pretty happy to see us."

But of course he knew this as much as I; it wasn't the well-being of the people in the towns we visited that he was really thinking of. People were wondering: How could the Americans get Polish cars, when we have to wait our whole lives for one? It was a fair question, but not one the government wanted to answer. We were just fifty-three vehicles, but in Poland in the 1960s, it was enough to foment discontent.

"It won't do," Sieklucki said. "The writing will have to go. We need to be . . ." He searched for the word, found it, and smiled. "More *inconspicuous,* yes? And besides, it isn't true, what it says on the vehicles. The gift is yours alone. Now, if we could repaint the vehicles, so that only your name . . ."

I was weary of this discussion, the silliness about my name. Fifty vehicles driving around Poland with my name written prominently on the side was hardly what I wanted. One ambulance in Tarnow was more than enough.

I cut him off. "Comrade, do you know anything about American tax law?"

Sieklucki stopped, his eyes widening. "I don't see why that is relevant."

"Well, in the United States, a gift like mine doesn't really come from one person, you understand. Seventy-five percent of what I earn goes to the government in corporate income taxes. It was Mrs. Paul's, my company, that made this gift, a tax-deductible donation. That means that 75 percent of the value of this equipment was actually paid for by the American government. So when you say the American people didn't give it to you, comrade, you're wrong."

I said all of this rapidly, hoping that Stanislaw would fudge it a little; it was, I'll admit, a slightly slanted interpretation of the situation. But it wasn't altogether wrong, and my goal was to put Sieklucki off balance. One thing I had learned about Sieklucki; like many communist officials, he was reluctant to admit that he did not understand the West. In effect, he would have to pretend that he had actually known this all along—that the complexities of American tax law were an open book to him, and he had simply forgotten.

For a long moment, Sieklucki didn't say anything, a good sign. Then at last, he spoke: "We'll put it in English," he announced.

"In *Poland?*" I was outraged. "What's the percentage who read English?"

"Mr. Piszek. Please. I am looking for a solution. Let us be fair."

"You call this fair?" Somewhere along the line I had taken a chair; I took this moment to rise again, using my height to hover over Sieklucki's desk. I reminded myself of the juicy kickback that Sieklucki had no doubt pocketed when the Warshavas rolled off the line. "You'll put it in English. Operate four hours a day. You call this fair?" I was waving my finger a foot or two from his nose. "When I make a deal my handshake is my word. It's worth a trunk full of signed contracts. You're talking about fairness, comrade?"

Sieklucki's eyes narrowed. I seriously doubted he was used to this kind of talk. Such directness was anathema to Polish bureaucracy, its euphemisms and vagaries.

"Mr. Piszek. I will ask you to sit down, please. And lower your voice."

"I will not sit down, comrade. As a matter of fact, I think I've about had it with what I'm getting from you people. Hah!" I snorted. "Four hours a day. You think I'm not serious? I'll take it all back to the United States."

Sieklucki shoved back his chair and shot to his feet. He looked at me sharply. The shock of blond hair over his forehead seemed to sway with his anger.

"Then take it," he said, his voice seething. "Fine. Take it all back!"

For a long moment we stared at one another in silence, a silence so palpable I could almost hear it throb in the air of the room. From the corner of my eye I glimpsed Stanislaw beside me, his face gone white as the lab coat he wore to examine his patients. He must have thought I had gone mad.

And I wondered: *Had I? What the hell did I do now?* Sieklucki had called my bluff. But I could also tell that he was frightened. We had both forgotten ourselves, forgotten what the stakes were, and gone at each other like a pair of street-fighting Poles.

Thirty years ago I would have said that it was Sieklucki who blinked first—that American grit triumphed over communist petulance. But now I think that what happened next was another example of Sieklucki's cleverness.

"Of course," he said, "the return of your equipment would have to be done according to all the legal laws of the great Republic of Poland."

He sat, not taking his eyes off me, and so did I. "Of course," I agreed. What was he up to?

"Which will, presumably, take some time. There will be many lawyers involved, which we will be glad to supply."

"Commie Polish lawyers," I said, nearly laughing. "I wouldn't trust them."

"Very fine men," he assured me. "But slow, I must concede. Not like your American lawyers, who are, I expect, a model of efficiency." He waved his hand in the air. "A great deal of trouble for everyone, in the end."

I chuckled, and so did he, each of us imagining a dozen or two dozen Polish lawyers trying to sort out the return of the equipment. Beside me, I heard Stanislaw exhale a breath that he might have been holding a full minute. The moment had passed. I knew now that nothing would happen, that our threats would go nowhere and the project would go on. I looked at Stanislaw, whose complexion had returned to its usual rosy color.

Then it hit me that we were both sitting on the answer; or rather, looking right at it. It was staring us in the face, there on the wall above Sieklucki's desk: the sign that read, in bold red letters, *Wojna z Gruzlica.*

"Comrade," I said, after a moment, "isn't it true that the Poles know more about war than any people on earth?"

He gave me a quizzical look. "Well, yes, I think that's true."

"Comrade, turn around." Sieklucki's eyes followed my own to the sign over his desk. "Now, I don't read much Polish, but I know what that says. *War on Tuberculosis.* Like the Cossacks. Like the Nazis. Every bit as deadly."

Sieklucki nodded. "Agreed."

"Your own government *calls* it a war. And what do you do when you're in a war, comrade? You throw out the rules. You throw them out for the duration, so you can *win.* It's always true."

For a moment Sieklucki said nothing, then I saw a smile nudge across his lips. I was speaking his language at last—giving him something he could tell *his* boss, and his boss's boss, and so on, right up the line.

"So are we going to win this war or not?" I asked. "Win it, or sit here talking about numbers of hours or what gets written on the side of a Warshava?"

The smile broke into a grin. "Mr. Piszek, you have made an excellent point." He placed a slender finger to his chin. "This is something to consider."

"How quickly can you consider it?"

He nodded. "Come back tomorrow."

Outside on the street, Stanislaw released another long sigh of relief. It was the end of the workday; the sidewalk was jammed with people.

"Did you really mean it? About taking everything back?"

I stopped and thought a moment. "Maybe right then, right at the moment I did." I looked at the doctor. "No, not really. It was just . . . poker."

"Poker?"

"A card game." I laughed. "I don't know the Polish word for it."

He shook his head. "I really thought you two were going to hit each other," he said. "The craziest thing I've ever seen."

The next morning, a message was waiting for me at the hotel: by order of the Polish Health Ministry, all the X-ray vans would immediately resume operation, to run twelve hours per day. It wasn't sixteen or the twenty-four I had originally envisioned, but it was enough. The matter of the writing on the vans was yet to be settled, and in the end, we compromised. Instead of "Gift of the American People," the wording would read "Gift of the Polish American People to the Polish People." Quite a mouthful, and not exactly true—there was only one Polish American involved, me—but I figured that as long as the word "American" was included, the point had been made. And the wording was in Polish.

I returned to the United States a week later. There was no grand send-off, no ceremony to mark my departure; one day, Stanislaw simply dropped me off at the airport in Warsaw, scurrying away to rejoin the X-ray van, and I boarded a plane for London and the United States. I returned to Poland again in the spring, later the following summer with Oddie, once again in fall. But by then, everything was running so smoothly there was really nothing for me to do. Sooner or later, there comes a time for the benefactor to step aside and let the experts do their jobs. It was a testament to the success of the project that my presence had become irrelevant, just as the sight of eleven X-ray vans and forty-two mud-streaked Warshavas combing the green countryside had become an unremarkable part of the Polish landscape. But it made me a little sad, too. When I left that last time, I knew that when I next returned to Poland, it would be for a different reason.

Twenty-five years later, I found myself with a small group touring a new health facility in the city of Krakow. Our group paused by a door on which was written, in faded red paint, "T.B. Ward." An Englishman next to me asked the young resident who was conducting our tour if T.B. was a problem in Poland.

"No," he answered in Polish. "That's an old sign. But before my time, it used to be." The doctor shook his head. "A terrible scourge after the war. Whole towns perished. My own grandfather died of it."

"What happened?" the Englishman asked.

"Well, the story is, an American came over and cured it."

"An American doctor?"

"I don't know. It was an American, that I do know. But it was a long time ago." He gestured dismissively toward the door and its ghostly red lettering. "Now T.B. is something we hardly think of anymore."

I had spent close to a million dollars. As we left the hospital and walked across the courtyard into the tart, autumn sunshine, I thought to myself: *What is it worth to overhear something like that? One million? A hundred million? How do you put a price on something that is priceless?*

Chapter Thirteen

The Novelist, the Churchman, and the Patriot

Who knows when it happened? My memory says it was 1968, perhaps on that last trip back from Poland, leaving the doctors and nurses to finish their work without me. Perhaps it was earlier, perhaps later. No matter; it was one of those moments that ought to mean nothing but later turns out to mean everything; it assumes a place in memory outside the flow of time.

What I do remember is this:

I was flying home, exhausted but pleased. I had changed planes at Heathrow, with a long layover, and by the time we were airborne again the day had already gone on too long. I slept most of the way; when dawn came, I rose and moved around the quiet cabin to stretch my legs. Eventually, I fell into a conversation with an American from California, headed home from Europe, where he had been traveling on business. Insurance, aviation, pork bellies—I don't recall what he did, only that we fell into the sort of easy conversation that business travelers do. He told me about his work, his family in Los Angeles (San Francisco? San Diego?), then asked me about my life. I told him I was in the frozen food business, and that I was returning home from Poland.

"Poland?" He frowned sourly. "What could you be doing there?"

But before I could tell him, he did something that I had come to expect from Americans, even Polish Americans (though he was not one; his name was Irish, Italian, something else).

He told a Polish joke.

"Say, did you hear the one about the Polish pilot who landed his plane at JFK?"

I admitted that I had not.

"Well, it's one of the first Polish planes ever to land in the States. So there's a big fanfare for it, and lots of news people, and after everyone gets off, a reporter asks the pilot, 'What do you think of our airport?' 'Oh,' the pilot replies, 'it's a marvelous airport. What a wonderful runway. However, I thought it was very short.'

" 'Short?' the reporter asks. 'At JFK?' 'Yes indeed,' the Polish pilot says. 'But is it ever wide!' "

He burst into laughter. To be polite, and because I was too tired to give a speech, I bit my tongue and mustered a chuckle or two of my own.

"Isn't that a good one?" he said, lowering his voice again so as not to awaken our sleeping fellow travelers. " 'Is it ever wide!' Wait, here's another. Stop me if you've heard it. So, there's these two Poles walking down the street, and one of them has a pig on a leash—"

"That's OK," I said, rising. (Was it me, or was it my blood pressure?) "That one was plenty."

I returned to my seat and stewed the rest of the way home. What could that fellow have been thinking? Hadn't I just told him I was returning from Poland? Hadn't I given him my name, obviously Polish? But of course these obvious facts, and the discourtesy they implied, did not matter. At that time Polishness was synonymous with stupidity.

And the more I thought about it, the more I thought that the jokes *themselves* were the enemy, even more than the prejudice they revealed or supported. Nothing travels faster than a joke. It was—and is—axiomatic to the business world that any successful sale includes at least one. How better to warm up a room full of buyers, to take the edge off a tricky negotiation, to tame a sour relative at a family reunion, than with a joke? Comedy is the great icebreaker, the currency of familiarity between strangers. The man on the plane had meant no harm. Just the opposite; he had told me a joke to narrow the distance between us. If I were to complete the transaction, I would carry his joke back with me to Philadelphia, tell it to two or three people before I forgot it, and if they laughed (and even if they were Polish, they probably would; I had, too) they would do the same. By phone, by plane, by rail, across the bar or the boardroom or the washroom, the joke would travel, greasing the gears of commerce and spreading the news that Poles were Polacks, and Polacks were stupid.

Hear the one about the Pole with the pet pig? That was what people remembered.

Jokes were . . . advertising.

And who knew more about the power of advertising than I did?

It might have been that very day, flying home from London, that the next idea was born. I would change the way that Americans, and everybody else, perceived Poles and Poland. The most beautiful diamond needs the right setting; no matter how glorious the stone, unless it is placed in the proper way, it will reflect only a fraction of its beauty. It is the same stone, but it is *perceived* differently. In the same way, all that was noble and beautiful about Polish history and culture was hidden from the world; unless someone told the world otherwise, Poland would continue to languish.

Restoring the public image of Poland, selling the *idea* of it, became the core of my life at that instant, and I gave the idea a name: Project Pole. It began with a weekend meeting at Emlen House in 1971; though I hardly expected it at the time, it would end nineteen years later, when a Polish shipyard electrician named Lech Walesa became president of his newly freed nation.

At Emlen House, I gathered together a critical mass of influential Polish Americans, including the leaders of several major Polish cultural organizations. We agreed easily on one thing: debunking the Polish joke itself would be our "hook." The Polish joke was, after all, ubiquitous; even *All in the Family*, one of the most popular television shows of the day, featured a rednecked working-class American making ceaseless jokes about his "meathead" son-in-law, a "dumb Polack." (No matter that Archie Bunker was, retroactively, the butt of all the jokes; what the show's writers intended and what the audience understood often were two totally different things.) So, whenever and wherever possible, Project Pole would take the Polish joke head on, refuting it with the facts. ("Poles are dumb? How about Madame Curie or Nicolaus Copernicus?")

We also agreed that the most effective campaign would attack on several fronts at once. To get attention, Project Pole would need to blitz the media. We wrote a press release announcing the formation of the initiative and sent it to every major paper and news organ in the country. Attached to it was a pamphlet that we called, simply, "Poland," filled with facts about the history of the country and its contributions to culture, politics, and science. We created posters, brochures, and four large newspaper ads that I was prepared to put in any paper in any market that wouldn't cover our story. (In essence, if a major paper declined to cover the story as news, I was prepared to buy space to run our own ads.) At the close of the meeting, I agreed to underwrite the project myself, as a corporate cultural project of Mrs. Paul's, for five hundred thousand dollars. Though some people warned me that the company itself would suffer from its connection to Polish boosterism, I didn't think it would. Though such corporate cultural projects were rare at the time, my hunch was that, if anything, Project Pole would increase our visibility and associate the company with a good cause.

And I was right, in several ways. Sales never suffered; in fact, for the period of time when Project Pole was most active, in the early seventies,

Mrs. Paul's grew faster than ever. And our paid ads barely made it out of the drawer. Except for a few major papers, Project Pole was covered nearly everywhere as news. We formally kicked off the project in Orchard Lake, Michigan, at the Center for Polish Studies and Culture of St. Mary's College, in September 1971. All through the next year, the story was picked up across the country. I even found myself on the *Today* show, chatting with host Frank McGee about Polish history and culture. Afterward, I thought, with amazement: *Ed Piszek, you have become one of America's most famous Poles.*

Concurrently, circumstances would place me in contact with several men who would change my life—and the life of the Polish nation—forever.

The first was Jim Michener. Even back then, before he had written several of his biggest books, Jim Michener was easily one of the most important and prolific writers in America—a "serious" writer who was a best-selling author, too. *Tales of the South Pacific, The Fires of Spring, Iberia, The Source,* and of course *Hawaii;* with each novel Jim had established himself as that rarest of writers, one with a global vision to match his epic storytelling skills.

For a decade, I had admired his work from afar. Though I was no writer, our ambitions and interests seemed not so very different. What was Project Pole if not a kind of story being told about a long-forgotten place? What were Jim's novels, if not a form of mass communication, brilliantly disguised? And I knew, too, that Jim and I came from similar backgrounds. Orphaned in infancy, Jim had been raised in Doylestown—a few miles from Quakertown—in a state-run home.

Our meeting was propitious. At the time of our first visit, in the late sixties, America was going through a period of terrible social turbulence. Student demonstrations against the war in Vietnam challenged the nation to reassess its most deeply held values. It seems long ago now, but in those days, it was impossible to feel anything like certainty about where the nation was headed. I, too, grappled with these changes. As part of the generation that had weathered the Depression and the Second World War, I found myself deeply torn. On the one hand, my immigrant heritage made me fiercely patriotic in the most old-fashioned ways. If my parents had not emigrated, I would have been tilling a field in Tarnow—or else moldering in a Russian prison. As it was, America had given me the opportunity to achieve, to grow, to prosper. Corny, perhaps, but true. The American dream was not an empty promise; it was my life, and my patriotism was an expression of appreciation for that fact.

But like most Americans I also understood that the nation found itself at a terrible crossroads. Vietnam was a horrible, contorted affair, and the students who were marching on the nation's campuses—though I sometimes disagreed with their methods—spoke with an idealistic passion I could not easily dismiss. In raising their voices, they were exercising their most cherished right, a right so fundamental to a democratic way of life that is in essence a kind of duty. I could quarrel with their clothing and hair and music but not with their purpose. They were speaking up for what they believed. I had spent too much time in a communist country to wish them to be silent.

For myself personally and for the nation, there seemed to be no answer. Between 1968 and 1970, the country seemed bent on a kind of madness. The assassinations of Martin Luther King Jr. and, a few short months later, Robert Kennedy; the contentious Democratic National Convention in Chicago; riots in Newark, Detroit, and Los Angeles; the gunning down of innocent students at Kent State by National Guardsmen young enough to be college students themselves: each story in the news was more horrifying and disturbing than the last. In the thicket of so much national pain, it was impossible to see what the solution might be. I had begun, quite seriously, to wonder if there was any purpose at all in what I was doing in Poland, when the country I loved most of all was coming apart at the seams.

It was then that I came across a slim volume written by Jim Michener, entitled *The Quality of Life*. Though Michener himself was well known, the book was obscure. It had been privately written and published for Girard Bank in Philadelphia for their employees and stockholders. I read it and was entranced. Somehow, in just a few slender pages, the author had managed to put into perspective all the upheavals of the day. It spoke with a clear, ringing voice I hadn't heard in all the fray of the nation's violent self-examination. I wondered at the kind of man who would write it—it was, after all, completely noncommercial—and I got it in my head to find some way to put it in the hands of a wider audience: business and political leaders, educators, journalists, opinion makers.

Ironically, it turned out that the book itself was actually the brainchild of Hal Montgomery—the man who first put Mrs. Paul's on the radio and who had handled our advertising for nearly twenty years. I called Hal on the phone and asked him to communicate my admiration for the book to its author. Would it be possible, I asked, for the two of us to get together?

Thus began one of the most important and valued friendships of my life. I met Jim for lunch in Doylestown, and it quickly became apparent that we had more in common than either of us knew. Beyond our mutually humble origins, Jim also had an abiding interest in Poland, the Balkans, and the rest of Central Europe. To write *The Bridge at Andau*, he had become deeply involved in the 1956 Hungarian uprising, even helping to smuggle refugees into Austria. As both a historian and a geographer, Jim was well versed in the particularly painful plight that Poland faced, and its geopolitical origins—especially, the high price it had paid for its lack of any defensible borders eastward with Germany or westward with the Soviet Union. In the thirties, on the eve of Hitler's invasion of the Polish heartland, an older geographer had neatly framed for him Poland's precipitous circumstances with one dire sentence, which he repeated for me that day over lunch: "Either Germany or Russia could invade Poland by merely sending a postcard saying 'We'll be coming on Friday,' and there would be nothing Poland could do to prevent it."

We talked for hours into the long afternoon, well past the time when both of us had other engagements to meet. As for *The Quality of Life*, it turned out that, although he had written the book for Girard, he had reserved the copyright to himself. (A brilliant writer and erudite thinker, Jim was no less a shrewd businessman.) I was delighted to hear it. We agreed over lunch that I would find a publisher (which I did) and send it to anyone I could think of.

"I'm very complimented," he said. "You think people would really be interested?"

"Well, if they're not, they ought to be. They will be, when they read it."

We shook hands, and the deal was done. The waiter came to refill our coffee cups, then I said, "Listen, Jim. Did you ever think of writing anything about Poland?"

He sipped his coffee and returned the cup to its saucer. "A novel, you mean?"

"Sure. Though it wouldn't have to be. But a book, anyway. You're just the kind of writer to do it." I shook my head. "Listen to me. We just met, and I'm telling you what books to write. I should just drink my coffee and keep quiet."

"No, no." He thought a moment, rubbing his chin. I could practically hear the gears turning. "Poland, you say. There may be something to that. It's a possibility."

"There's a lot of good to be done there, Jim. And the country itself—well, it *feels* like a novel."

Jim smiled with amusement. "Now, right there, you sounded like a writer, Ed."

I had to laugh. What had I said? What did a writer sound like?

"You know, maybe I'm not the only scribe at this table," Jim went on. "You might be the one to do it."

I shook my head, embarrassed. "Words are your business, not mine."

He held up his hand. "Trust me. You're too modest. It's not so hard, what I do. Even so, you may be on to something. Poland, huh?"

I nodded. "Poland."

In the years to come, as our association deepened and we found our-selves traveling around the world together, Jim and I often joked what an unlikely pair we made. Jim was wrong; I was no writer. A night business school graduate, I was hardly a literary man, and the circles in which Jim traveled were ones I did not know at all. The kind of work he did was utterly beyond me; I could no more have sat at a typewriter for days at a time than Jim could have run Mrs. Paul's. But I think we saw in one another a more profound commonality, far more important and lasting than the surface of our daily lives. It was something Jim knew, and that his slender book for Girard had put into words for me, ringing bells of recog-nition: ideas had power to change things, and ignorance froze the world the way it was.

I was not a literary man. Nor was I a religious man. So it happened that, during the same period, to my list of most valued friends and advisors was added a second, a third, then a fourth man, all unlikely, all from a world as foreign to me as Michener's.

In those years in Poland—the darkest period, before Lech Walesa and Solidarity and the sweeping changes they would bring—it was impossible to understand the country without appreciating the key role in day-to-day domestic affairs played by the Polish Catholic Church, and in particular by Stefan Cardinal Wyszynski, the Polish Primate. Traveling the countryside with the X-ray vans, I had learned this much. Of all the countries under the Soviet sphere of influence, Poland alone had an active church, and Wysznyski, its spiritual and nominal leader, was decidedly anticommunist. Wyszynski's authority and the authority of the Polish Catholic Church were histori-cally synonymous. As a unifying force against communism, Wyszynski had been so threatening to the government that, in the mid-1950s, he had been imprisoned for three years, shuttling back and forth among four dif-ferent prisons between September 1953 and October 1956. (Like all such regimes, the Polish government of Boleslaw Beirut, a Stalinist puppet, prac-ticed the philosophy that the simple incarceration of political prisoners was not enough; a man like Wyszynski had to be kept in motion, lest he become an international jailhouse cause célèbre. The wonder of it is that they didn't simply kill him.) But the death of Stalin in '53 and a deep economic crisis in '56 initiated a thaw; Beirut left power, replaced by the considerably more liberal Wladyslaw Gomulka, who ended the crackdown on the church and returned Wyszynski to his role as active Primate. For his freedom, Wyszynski had "only" to guarantee that a revived Polish Catholic Church would keep out of the nation's political affairs.

In all likelihood, Gomulka let Wyszynski go more as a concession to political reality than as a humanitarian gesture. Indefinitely imprisoned—

or dead—he would have achieved martyr status in a country where communist rule was already tenuous. Serious civil disorder would have invited a Soviet invasion, as it had in Hungary. As it was, a free Wyszynski at least was where the Communists could keep an eye on him. (Interestingly, an almost identical scenario would be played out some twenty-five years later, when workers' strikes led communist First Secretary General Wojciech Jaruzelski to crack down on the upstart Solidarity Union and declare martial law. Like Wyszynski, Solidarity leader Lech Walesa would spend a year detained, a hostage against the threat of a Soviet invasion; like Wyszynski, Walesa would also be freed when that threat had passed.)

But as a religious leader in a country that was 95 percent Catholic, Wyszynski's influence was nearly as great as any political figure's. His concession to keep out of national politics was, on its face, laughable. As a model of faith and personal resolve, he had no peer. But the real genius of Wyszynski was that he understood how to read any situation precisely. He knew not to challenge directly the power of the state but, rather, to subvert it quietly. The injunction not to enmesh himself or the church in politics was, ironically, the very source of his power. Officially apolitical, he operated outside (though *just* outside) the structures of state bureaucracy—wheedling here, cajoling there, applying the unspoken moral influence of his personal stature to loosen the ties of state communism. Though he would not live to see his country freed, no man was more responsible for the sweeping changes that occurred in Poland and across Eastern Europe in the late 1980s than Wyszynski. To this day I think of him as the father of democratic Poland.

My relationship with Wyszynski was both personal and professional; beginning in '67, I counted him as both an important colleague and something akin to a moral advisor. Time and again, when I encountered some difficulty with the government, I would later find that Wyszynski, working quietly behind the scenes, had simply solved it. His reputation for a steely countenance was well deserved—he was not a man to cross—but he also brought to all our encounters a personal warmth that made me always feel that my work in Poland was important.

"It will add up," he always told me. "And not just in the life to come."

At that time, in the early seventies, the focus of my energies had diffused to several areas, all bringing me back to Poland on a regular basis. It was the era of détente, and doors of cultural and humanitarian exchange were beginning to open. In February 1971, I financed a trip to the United States for a Polish heart surgeon and his patient, a man who needed an artificial artery; later that year, I arranged for and sponsored a concert tour of the U.S. by the Polish Boy's Choir of Poznan, culminating with a performance at the White House. All these activities began to outstep the formal boundaries of Project Pole, and I decided in 1972 that it was time to form a private, nonprofit foundation to house my charitable and educational projects. I chose the name "Copernicus Society," honoring Nicolaus Copernicus, one of Poland's greatest minds. Our first major undertaking was fitting; in November '72, the society, after lengthy negotiations with the Polish government and the Jagiellonian University Museum in Krakow, sponsored an exhibition of the original Copernicus instruments at the Smithsonian to celebrate the great astronomer's five-hundredth birthday.

Concurrently, I was deeply involved in a Polish cultural project in my own backyard. Early in '69, it had come to my attention that the American home of General Thaddeus Kosciuszko, located in Center City Philadelphia, was about to be razed. A central figure in Revolutionary War history, Kosciuszko, a Pole, was largely unknown by most Americans; except for one aging bridge in upstate New York, there wasn't a single public memorial to celebrate him. Yet, Kosciuszko's contributions to the American cause had been astounding. An engineer as well as a military man, he had designed the fortifications at West Point, a key American stronghold throughout the war, and later at Saratoga, site of the first major American victory of the war. Following the British surrender, Kosciuszko—by then a decorated brigadier general of the Continental Army—returned to his native Poland to lead his own people in a similar struggle against their Russian occupiers. But a second victory was not to be. Though his army of seven thousand volunteers won a stunning, early triumph at the battle of Raclawice, Kosciuszko and his men were eventually overwhelmed by the substantially larger and better armed forces of the combined Russian and Prussian armies. In 1794, gravely wounded, Kosciuszko was captured by the Russians.

Kosciuszko spent the next two years imprisoned in Moscow under Catherine the Great; freed by her successor, Czar Paul I, in 1796, Kosciuszko returned to the United States, his adopted homeland. He could not return to Poland, then or ever. Under the terms of his release, the great patriot was barred forever from setting foot on his native soil—though, formally speaking, Poland no longer existed. During Kosciuszko's first year in captivity, Russia, Prussia, and Austria had divvied up what was left of the country, erasing it from the map of Europe.

Kosciuszko spent the next two years at his modest Philadelphia home at 301 Pine Street in the heart of a neighborhood now known as Society Hill. His second American sojourn was brief, but during that time his friendship with fellow patriot Thomas Jefferson became the center of his life. The two were said to meet almost daily. What their conversations must have been like! When Kosciuszko finally embarked again for Europe, he named Jefferson the executor of his will and directed that, at the time of his death, all of his American assets be used to purchase the freedom of slaves. Ironically, Kosciuszko never could secure for his own homeland the freedom he had helped America to win. Still plotting a Polish insurrection, he died in Switzerland in 1817. Only in death could Kosciuszko be repatriated; his body was returned to Poland to be interred at the Royal Crypt in Krakow's Wawel Cathedral. Of his friend, Jefferson said, "He was as pure a son of liberty as I have ever known."

A noted Polish American historian, Edward Pinkowski, had tried in the mid-sixties to establish a private Kosciuszko museum at the house. But the Philadelphia Zoning Board had rejected the plan. Meanwhile, the house had fallen into disrepair. Its doom seemed certain.

What else could I do? I bought the home outright.

My plan was to turn it over to the National Park Service for it to administer as a historic and educational site. I assumed, incorrectly, that simply donating the house would be enough—it was, after all, the home of a major American patriot. But dozens of petitions, bills in both the Senate and the House, and hundreds of pages of congressional testimony lay ahead. The obstruction was actually quite technical. Because nothing historic had actually happened *at* the house per se, the Park Service could not designate it a historic site but had to use the designation "national memorial" instead—a title reserved to a comparatively small number of structures, typically those honoring the most major of American figures. (The Lincoln, Washington, and Jefferson Memorials in Washington, D.C., fall under this category.) Before long, I found myself enmeshed in bureaucratic red tape that rivaled anything I had encountered in communist Poland. Not only did I have to secure the resources, both public and private, to support the site's ongoing operation, I had to convince half of official Washington that Kosciuszko, a relative unknown, was worthy of such an honor. (I also had to buy the house next door to solve a traffic flow problem. But by this point, I would have bought all of Society Hill from Third to Front Street if that was what it took to get the job done.) All told, it took four years—far more time than I had ever expected. But the effort was surely worth it. In February 1976, I turned over the keys to the Park Service, and the Thaddeus Kosciuszko Memorial Site became a reality—a monument, in the fullest sense, to one of history's most undercelebrated patriots, a hero of two revolutions who just happened to be Polish.

In all of these projects, I had come to rely on my connections to the Polish Catholic Church, at least as much as the government itself. I traveled to Poland constantly and was always careful to pay my respects to local church leaders, whom I had come to regard as the real power in the country. What I did not fully comprehend at the time was the way in which, simply by making these connections, I was participating in the process of historic change in that country.

What I did know was that Poland was ripe for something new. Communism felt like a failure, exhausted and spent. No one I met in the country actually seemed to believe the empty promises and vapid propaganda that issued in "official" statements from the government, like a stream of tepid water from a hose. Authority was generally obeyed but rarely, if ever, respected. The general population seemed to view the affairs of government with the wry, dispirited amusement of an audience at a boring, vaguely comic play. There remained always the "Russian question"—the threat, largely unspoken, of invasion—but I found that on this subject most Poles were deeply fatalistic. Foreign powers had overrun Poland so many times in history that the image of Soviet tanks pouring over the border elicited little more than a shrug.

Poland *felt* different from its neighbors, too. Unlike East Germany or the Soviet Union, life in Poland was not governed by suspicion. There was no KGB; there were no microphones in the coffeepot, no video cameras behind the bathroom mirrors. (At least I never noticed any.) Poles didn't prey on other Poles; though I am sure it happened, never did I hear directly of Poles turning one another in for "counterrevolutionary thinking" (or some such trumped-up nonsense). Poland was a communist country, but it was not, in the strictest sense, a police state; people were more or less free to think what they wanted, and for the most part, they thought communism was nonsense. Even party officials and high-level ministers would confess their misgivings when I gave them the chance.

At the same time, though, the nation was suffering. For all intents and purposes, Poland was bankrupt. The nation's standard of living, although significantly higher than other nations in the Soviet sphere, lagged far behind its neighbors to the west. And on this subject, the party was running out of excuses. I thought of it as the "invisible tractor" problem; you can only tell the people so many times about the glorious increase in the production of tractors before you have to show some tractors to prove it. Thirty years of state communism, and the Poles had very few tractors to back up the rhetoric.

Clearly there was a change brewing; the only question was when. Still, if someone had told me in 1974 that Polish communism had less than fifteen years left—indeed, that communism itself would vanish from all of Europe within my lifetime—I would have told them they were dreaming.

Chapter Fourteen
The Cardinal from Krakow

Some say that history is a line of dominoes—that, viewed in hindsight, the events and personalities that comprise the sweep of human affairs reveal themselves as a tidy chain of cause and effect. It is a comforting notion, but like most comforting notions, it says more about the seer than the thing seen. The truth is that history is more like a thousand marbles falling from a broken paper bag to bounce across the pavement. It is anything *but* tidy, and the forces that collide and ricochet to make history happen are too many for any person to claim to know them all.

Yet, there are moments that are simply greater than others, moments of connection, of synergy, when history is made in a rush. Every child knows the rhyme that begins with the nail: "For want of the nail, the shoe was lost; for want of the shoe, the horse was made lame; for want of the horse, the message was too delayed; for want of the message, the battle was lost; for want of the victory, the empire fell." Communism was such an empire, hollow and rotten to the core, and I trace its spectacular collapse, in part, to a morning meeting in Warsaw in the spring of 1972, when for some unknown reason—indigestion? exhaustion? a bad mood?—I dropped my guard, threw diplomacy out the window, and simply blew my stack.

I was meeting that day with a certain Professor Scarczinski, the Polish government's top man for negotiating with the church. In any other country, a man with such a role would have had very little importance. But not in Poland. In effect, he acted as liaison to a kind of internally exiled government-in-waiting. The subject of our meeting was mass communication—the success I was having at home with Project Pole and the ways that success could be exported and enlarged. More and more I had come to believe that the source of Poland's woes was its failure to make itself known to the world. All the humanitarian and relief efforts would amount to very little if Poland failed to help itself—to *sell* itself, in effect, to a world that had forgotten it existed.

For nearly an hour I regaled the professor with my theories. He sat and listened, saying next to nothing, occasionally pausing to refill his glass of water from the pitcher on his desk. It was clear that he was under orders to treat me with respect, but it was evident that he also thought very little of what I was saying. Finally worn down by his silence, I stopped.

"What you are telling me, Mr. Piszek, makes a good deal of sense. And yes, if it were possible, I would agree that this is a matter to warrant our attention. But you see, we have no money. So it is all moot, I'm afraid."

"Of course you have money. You have a budget. This is an *investment*."

His face curled into a frown. "You are talking about millions of dollars. For what? We have no budget for this sort of thing. None whatsoever."

I felt my temples pulse. "Comrade, I don't think you're listening. Think of Germany, think of Japan. Enemies of the U.S., destroyed by the war. Now they're two of the richest countries in the world. Why? Because they *sold* themselves. They convinced the world that they were worth the trouble. No one would ever think twice about investing in either country now."

Scarczinski leaned back in his chair and sighed impatiently. "As I said, we have no money. Mr. Piszek, you are a smart American capitalist. A rich man, too. If you're so smart, you should be telling me how we could be getting this for free. Yes, for *nothing!*"

Perhaps it was the smug smile on his face; perhaps I had simply lost all patience with the Communists' backward way of doing things. Perhaps it was just that I hated the idea of something for nothing. *Everything* cost something. Anything worth having required a sacrifice, a risk. I had been negotiating with communist officials for nearly a decade, but it wasn't until that morning in Scarczinski's office that I realized the full depth of cowardice that lay at the heart of the communist system.

"Comrade Scarczinski . . ." I began. But then I stopped.

Maybe there *was* a way.

"Mr. Piszek, forgive me, but I have other people that I must see this morning." Scarczinski shuffled some papers around on his desk. "I thank you for taking the time to share your ideas with me, but now, if you'll excuse me—"

"Comrade, how would you like to buy one hundred fifty million . . . no, make that two hundred million dollars' worth of positive communication to the world?"

He sighed resignedly. "Yes, well, all very interesting. However, as I believe I made clear to you—"

"I mean for nothing, comrade. Not one zloty!"

His hands paused over his papers. He leaned back in his chair again and placed a pen to his lips. "Go on."

"It's simple. Invite Pope Paul VI to visit Poland."

For a moment, Scarczinski said nothing. Not a muscle seemed to move. He was utterly impassive.

"You're joking."

"Not at all. Think of it, comrade. Hundreds of journalists would cover it. *Hundreds*. Not just from Europe and the United States, but from all over the world. And while they're here, you could show them your cities, your transportation, your airports, your museums. You'll be able to show them all of these things, and they'll fill the papers, the television news, the radio, with stories about the country. Poland will be the center of the world's attention. And all of it will cost you *nothing*."

I stopped and found that I was standing. I was practically out of breath. All of it had come out in a sudden rush, the idea forming even as I put it into words. To me, it felt like the answer.

Scarczinski eyed me from his chair. What was he thinking? The moment seemed to turn on whether or not I would sit down again. I stayed where I was.

"This is . . ." he said finally, "a possibility."

"Comrade, it's better than that."

For a moment, I thought I almost saw him smile. "You are friends with Wyszynski, no?"

"Yes. We're friends. He's been very helpful to me."

"This will be useful. Come back tomorrow, Mr. Piszek," Scarczinski said.

The next morning I returned to Scarczinski's office with one thing on my mind. All night, unable to sleep, I had replayed our conversation in my head; by dawn, I was convinced that I had hit upon a once-in-a-lifetime idea, something even the Communists could not back away from.

In any event, I also knew that the moment I entered Scarczinski's office I would have my answer. In eight years of such visits, I had learned to read the signs. An unimportant visitor warranted only tea or coffee; someone of moderate station, perhaps a plate of cookies besides, or even, if the politest refusal was forthcoming, bottled water. But a man to be dealt with, a man with ideas that mattered—no matter the time of day, the brandy would be waiting.

In Scarczinski's office, at 9:00 A.M., I found coffee, water, cookies—and a bottle of the best Cognac—perched atop a tray on his desk beside two snifters.

"Mr. Piszek, good morning." Scarczinski rose with a smile on his face and directed me to the small sofa. "Please, make yourself at home. May I offer you a drink?"

It was a little early, and my stomach was unsettled from a restless night. But I could hardly refuse. If the brandy meant what I thought it meant, I had good enough reason to celebrate. Scarczinski blew the dust from the snifters and poured, then handed one to me. He took a chair across the small coffee table from the sofa.

"Mr. Piszek, I want you to know that your idea has been discussed at the highest levels since we met yesterday. The *very* highest."

"I'm glad to hear it." *It's a lock*, I thought. What did you wear to meet the pope?

"And I'm glad you're glad. But all the news is not so good, I'm afraid. All things considered, it's been decided there are simply too many problems to be overcome. You must understand—"

I never let him finish. "God damn it!" I banged my snifter on the table. "A few problems, and you cave in like a house of cards. Just like a Communist, you want everything done for you. Of course there will be problems, with something as large as this! Twenty-four hours and you're ready to throw in the towel!"

"Please, Mr. Piszek." He held up a conciliatory hand. "There is no need to shout."

"Oh, you bet there is."

He shook his head. His demeanor was strangely unruffled, I thought. If someone had yelled in my office like that, I would have kicked him out already.

"I understand you're disappointed," he gently said. "It is sometimes very difficult to get things done here, I admit. And believe me, I liked your idea. But perhaps there is another way—something I have devised."

I saw then that the brandy wasn't for nothing; Scarczinski had a plan of his own in mind and needed me to help him.

"All right," I agreed. "I'm listening."

"Tell me," he went on. "A papal visit—you said yesterday that it would be worth . . . two hundred million, yes? And I agree with the figure. So. A papal visit is not possible, but the idea is still there. The principle, you understand. Free advertising, in your own words. I have given the matter some thought, Mr. Piszek. What I am driving at is that perhaps there is someone else we could invite."

I sipped my brandy and thought. "Who did you have in mind?"

Scarczinski smiled and held up one finger. "You see, here is the genius of it. Not the pope, but almost as good. A cardinal. An American cardinal. A *Polish* American cardinal, in fact. I am thinking, of course, of your own John Krol of Philadelphia."

I had to admit, the idea was brilliant. Cardinal Krol wouldn't bring as much coverage as a papal visit, not by a long shot, but it had several advantages. Krol was in every way a major figure; he would be the first religious leader from the West to break the Iron Curtain, and he was an American. That in itself was news. But because he was Polish, too, his visit would represent a kind of homecoming, an East-West reunion much in the spirit of détente. The human-interest possibilities were tremendous.

"How much, Mr. Piszek, do you imagine such a visit would be worth in free public relations?"

I had to grin. "Millions, probably. With all the coverage, it would be like taking out an advertisement in every major paper in the world."

"As I thought." He clapped his hands. "Then, we do it!"

But watching Scarczinski raise his brandy snifter in a toast that April morning, there was already in the back of my mind a seed of doubt, a hitch in the plan I did not dare to mention. Scarczinski was assuming that because I was from Philadelphia and knew so many Polish clerics that I also knew Cardinal Krol. From the tone of his voice, it seemed he thought we were great friends, and that all I would have to do was pick up the phone. But I had never met the man.

The reason was simple. I had never had a reason to. My involvement with the Catholic Church in Poland was purely practical; to get anything done there, I needed the guidance and influence of men like Wysznyski. I was not a religious man in the slightest, and my life in Philadelphia made virtually no reference to organized religion, either personally or publicly. Though my parents were—or had been—nominally Catholic, religious faith was part of the life they had left behind in Poland, and they had rarely taken me to mass. My mother, in particular, viewed the Catholic Church with the gravest suspicion. As a girl in Tarnow, she had earned her passage to the United States in part by working as a clerk for the local parish priest, a hard-hearted and smugly superior man, and the experience had turned her off organized religion entirely. I was baptized in infancy, but I had received no other sacraments, and by the time we moved from Quakertown to Philadelphia, I was a completely secular boy. On Sunday mornings in Nicetown, I would sit on the stoop and watch as our neighbors, Catholic to a one, emerged from their houses in their Sunday finest, tugging their reluctant, overdressed children down the street to mass at St. Ladislaus Church. I had felt no envy; my Sunday mornings were my own.

But it was not true to say that, as a grown man, I experienced no spiritual feelings at all. To the contrary; the older I became, the more I had begun to feel the tug of forces unseen and to yearn for a spiritual context in which to understand my life. Clyde Potter was right; I wanted—no, I *needed*—to know what it all added up to. And as every man eventually must, in this matter, I often turned to prayer; not the rote prayers of childhood (because I had none to use), but a silent contemplation, in the late hours before sleep, of what I felt to be true: that everything was connected, and that all meaning flowed from that connection. It was a prayer that was, in effect, a kind of yearning: the most fervent wish that my life could be of use.

So, although I considered myself a spiritual man, I was not a religious man, and I did not know John Cardinal Krol. In his Moscow office, Professor Scarczinski spun his plans. For once, I was the listener; Scarczinski had thought everything through, like a safecracker planning the heist of his life. I would be the linchpin, the connective tissue between Wyszynski and Krol.

"First, you must get many people from the United States and from Poland to write to Wyszynski, asking him to invite Krol. The mail must pour in! Then, in a month's time or so, you will approach Krol himself. By then, he will have already heard of the plan but not directly. You will say, 'My friend, wouldn't it be nice if you took a trip to Poland?' Already the road will be open, and when someone says to Wyszynski, 'Why would you want to bring Krol to Poland,' he can say, 'Look at all these letters! It is the will of the people to receive such a man.'"

I didn't have the heart to tell him, and how could I? He had called my bluff.

I returned to Philadelphia and got to work. Both from Poland and the United States, the mail, as Scarczinski said, poured in. In June, Wyszynski called me in Philadelphia: did I know something about all these letters? I explained the plan. We agreed that he should wait to hear from Cardinal Krol himself before he contacted him. Then I called Krol's people and set up the meeting.

It would be, like my lunch meeting with Jim Michener, one of the most propitious visits of my life. My worries proved irrelevant. Though I did not know Cardinal Krol, he certainly knew me. Some of this I expected; I was, after all, a Polish American operating a large and very successful corporation in his own hometown. Certainly he would have heard of me, at least. What I failed to realize was the extent to which he had taken an interest in my work abroad.

He received me at his office adjacent to the Cathedral of Saint Peter and Paul in Philadelphia—a hale, energetic man in his late fifties. He seemed glad, and not very surprised, to see me. Without much ado, I launched right into the subject of his traveling to Poland, following Scarczinski's script. There was reason to believe, I told him, that he would be welcome.

"I know of your work with T.B. in Poland," he said. "It is very laudable. That is why I'm concerned that perhaps you are working with someone in Poland whose standards of integrity are not up to your own."

I was dumbfounded. Did he mean Scarczinski? He rose from his chair and went to a file cabinet, returning with a thick manila folder. He placed it on his desk to show me. It was marked "Piszek, Edward J./Mrs. Paul's." All along, I had wondered if he would receive me, and here he had an entire folder!

He raised an eyebrow. "You're surprised?" he asked. "You shouldn't be. Take it as a compliment."

"I guess I am, a little." I nodded toward the folder. "Is that all about me?"

The cardinal shrugged. "We've taken an interest. You've become an important man, Mr. Piszek." At this, he chuckled. "We're not the CIA, but we do pay attention."

He opened the folder and leafed through it, finally finding the document he was looking for. "The man I'm speaking of . . . Leopold Dende? He has done some work for you?"

I breathed a sigh of relief; it wasn't Scarczinski after all that he was speaking of. If it had been, the whole plan would have been derailed, right then. As it was, I had little to worry about. Dende was someone I had used on a few occasions; he was fairly well connected in the Polish government and had helped cut through some red tape on a number of projects. I didn't know very much about him; he did come across as something of an operator, but on the other hand, he had been helpful to me. In any event, he was no one very important.

"I know Leopold. What about him?"

Cardinal Krol closed the folder. "The details aren't important. He's a well-connected man, to be sure. But his past is less than exemplary. I simply wanted to advise you of that fact, in case you were unaware." He gave a broad smile. "If I'm going to Poland, after all, such things must be thought of in advance."

The trip was on. After a frantic summer of arrangements, we embarked for Poland in October. Michener came with us—still thinking, he told me, about a Polish novel—as did Oddie and my oldest children. As I had predicted, Cardinal Krol's trip was big news. The passenger complement swelled to sixty, filling half of a good-sized jet, including reporters from a number of major papers. At Philadelphia International, television crews jammed the waiting area. The air crackled with excitement. In the papers, headlines read: "Prince of the Church Breaks Iron Curtain," and "Philadelphia Cardinal Makes Historic Journey Home." From Poland, our group was scheduled to travel on to Rome. The word that everyone seemed to be using was "pilgrimage."

The historic nature of the trip was deepened by Cardinal Krol's own history with the Polish Communists. When I had visited his office in the summer, I did not know that a number of years earlier, he had tried to engineer his own trip back to Poland. Twenty-four hours before he was scheduled to fly to Warsaw, his visa had been revoked. It had been a terrible embarrassment, and I was honored that he had put so much trust in me. (Even so, it was not until we had finally arrived in Warsaw, and disembarked onto Polish soil, that I allowed myself to relax.)

I need not have worried. For a week, we traveled in a caravan across the country, and everywhere he went, Cardinal Krol was met by joyous throngs. Even the Communists warmed to him; several days into the journey, we were informed that a brand-new jet, named the Thaddeus Kosciuszko, had been reserved for our use. And Cardinal Krol was magnificent. Whether offering mass or stepping from his car to shake hands with the people or meeting in conferences with church and government officials, his message was always the same. He had come to Poland to preach the idea of universal brotherhood—to offer comfort without confrontation. I had never met a man so personally magnetic or politically astute.

The highlight of the visit was a mass to be held at the Birkenau Concentration Camp, outside the city of Krakow. By then we were all exhausted, but not Cardinal Krol; with each passing day, his energy seemed to increase, feeding on the adoration of the people who turned out to see him. As our car approached the camp, we heard a roar, and looking out the window, I saw something that astounded me: a sea of people, filling the fields around the camp, as far as the eye could see. In all, nearly half a million Poles had come to hear him speak.

We disembarked and moved to the dais, where an altar had been set up for the mass. Behind us, the weathered buildings of the camp stood in mute memorial to the pain of Poland's past. I looked out over the crowds, now silent, then at Cardinal Krol.

"It's quite a crowd," I said.

He placed a hand on my shoulder. "And in such a place, my friend," he said.

The mass began. Is it implausible to say that there are moments when the world stops, when history pauses, when the truth of what we are is consecrated?

But the greatest moment of the day was yet to come.

When Krol finished, Wyszynski mounted the dais and delivered his thanks. Then a third man rose, took the microphone, and began to speak; beside us, our translator began to hurriedly put it all into English. It took me a moment before I understood what I was hearing. This was no minor figure; he spoke with a clarity and force to match Krol's own, and his words were even more daring. There, in communist Poland, before an audience of four hundred thousand Poles, this man was speaking about freedom.

Oddie shook my elbow. "Who is he?" she gasped. "He's electrifying."

I knew who he was. I had met him many times. His name was Karol Cardinal Wojtyla, of Krakow.

The world would soon know him by a different name: Pope John Paul II.

When I had first met Karol Wojtyla six years before, when he was Archbishop of Krakow, my reaction was peculiar. I thought him poorly dressed.

Not tastelessly dressed: literally, *poorly*. The edges of his shirt cuffs were badly worn and his collar frayed to wispy threads. Even in the most impoverished countries, all the high church officials I had met dressed impeccably—as, indeed, befit their stations as high-ranking officers of a major global institution.

I met with him off and on throughout the T.B. project. His message to me was always the same; he wanted my commitment that Krakow and the countryside around it would get its fair share of attention. I always assured him it would but was also struck by the force of his claim. By Polish standards he was astonishingly direct.

Each time I visited, I would leave an envelope with a monetary contribution to his diocese. This was the custom, though I was also glad to do it. But the dismal state of his wardrobe nagged at me. It seemed a slight upon his office, and it troubled me that such an important man would lack the resources even for a new shirt. Finally, on one visit, as I handed him the envelope, I offered the suggestion that perhaps he could use some of the money for himself.

He shook his head, motioning to the two sisters in his office. They were there to tutor him in English, which we always used in our meetings. It was one of six languages he spoke.

"I believe they need it more than I," he said.

"But wasn't it St. Francis who said something on the order of look to yourself first?"

Archbishop Wojtyla smiled. "As I say, the sisters are much in need of aid. Their thanks to you."

I never asked again.

At critical junctures in world history, certain individuals can emerge who embody both the spirit and the best natures of their times. Even in the early days of our friendship, I sensed that Karol Wojtyla was such a man. In his person were joined two overwhelming traits: a devout and deeply felt religious faith and an uncanny sense of social and political realities. Added to that were a tremendous physical constitution, a thespian's sense of self-presentation (he had been an actor as a youth, performing with an underground theatrical group during the Nazi occupation), a philosopher's range of mind (he received his Ph.D. in 1948), and a poet's gift for language. As the number two churchman in Poland, he operated to a certain extent in the shadow of his mentor, Stefan Wyszynski. But even by the late sixties, it was clear to all who knew him, Wyszynski included, that Karol Wojtyla had the potential to emerge as a figure of global importance. That afternoon at Birkenau, no one could have disagreed. In Wojtyla, the Polish people had found a new and stirring voice to challenge the communist orthodoxy and speak openly about freedom of conscience and worship.

I did not see him again until December 1974, when Jagiellonian University in Krakow awarded me an honorary doctorate. Like my visit with Cardinal Krol two years earlier, the ceremony was sufficiently newsworthy to warrant American television coverage—an opportunity that Wojtyla immediately seized. Meeting with me after the ceremony, he used the presence of American film crews to deliver an impromptu, twenty-minute address on political and human circumstances in Poland and the resolve of the Catholic Church to better conditions for the Polish people. I found myself standing to the side, watching and listening; I was struck by the powerful look in his eye, by the whole quality of his bearing. He was absolutely magnetic; I had never met a man who understood so well the power of mass communication.

When I returned to Philadelphia, I immediately had copies made of the tape and mailed it to church leaders and journalists across the country. Watching it myself, I said to Oddie, "Doesn't this man talk like a pope? Listen to what he's saying. He's talking like a pope." I was surprised to hear myself say it, but already I was convinced. When Cardinal Krol asked me the next year to help with the planning of a Eucharistic Congress to be held in Philadelphia, I jumped at the chance; wouldn't it be a fine idea, I suggested, to invite this little-known cardinal from Krakow? Wouldn't he make a fine keynote speaker? It wasn't an event that drew much attention in the general media, but for the church leadership itself, Wojtyla's address was tantamount to a coming-out party. Even Cardinal Krol, always a skeptic, admitted that Wojtyla was increasingly looking like a force to be reckoned with.

At home, Mrs. Paul's continued to roar ahead; the economy, as a whole, was on shaky ground, but each year we had managed to push forward, opening new markets. I was glad but barely thought about it; in my new life, I had found something far more valuable than money. I had found a purpose.

The project that most occupied me then was a joint venture with Jim Michener, whose PBS television series, *James Michener's World*, I had helped to sponsor. In '77, when Reader's Digest, the principal sponsor, dropped their funding, I agreed to take it on myself. It was a natural role for me. I suggested to Jim—and he agreed—that our first joint venture should be a one-hour film called *Poland: The Will to Be.*

No project I had yet attempted seemed to have as much potential to do good; all the news coverage in the world could not hope to match the worldwide audience that we could reach with a successful documentary carrying Michener's name. For a year, I shuttled back and forth to Poland, making arrangements and meeting with the show's writers and production staff. By then, my influence in Poland was such that few doors were closed to me, and the filming went off without a hitch.

The film debuted on American public television in early autumn of 1978. Included in the film were lengthy interviews and profiles of both Wyszynski and Wojtyla. All the reviews were positive, and the audience was large.

Following the American screening, Jim and I were invited to take the film to Poland (ironically, no one there had seen it) to host a special screening for high-ranking communist officials and members of the country's cultural establishment. The screening was held at a government building in Warsaw, and afterward, we adjourned upstairs to a reception. It was the evening of October 16, 1978. Pope John Paul I, after only thirty-four days in office, had died two weeks before. Jim and I had actually stopped in Rome en route, hoping to be there when the new pope was named; after ten days, with no puffs of smoke forthcoming, we had abandoned Rome for Warsaw. There was some talk that Wyszynski might be named his successor, but I ignored these idle rumors. Wyszynski was too controversial, too political, too openly anticommunist. And, he wasn't Italian. For five hundred years, an Italian had occupied the Vatican. Most of the big money (and yes, there was betting) was on Dionigi Cardinal Tettamanzi, Archbishop of Genova.

The party had moved upstairs when a messenger pulled me aside to say that I had an urgent call. He directed me to an office downstairs, where I found the phone waiting; it was my friend and colleague Dick Baker, an administrative VP at Mrs. Paul's, who had told me he would call as soon as there was news from Rome. I heard the excitement in his voice.

"Ed! The news just came out. The new pope is John Paul II."

"That's his *new* name," I said. "Who is it?"

"Ed, you won't believe it! It's Karol Wojtyla! Karol Wojtyla, Cardinal of Krakow, is Pope John Paul II!"

I sat down, stunned and disbelieving. "Dick, you better not be kidding me. I'm going to have to go upstairs and tell the top people in the country—the top Communists—that a Polish cardinal has been elected pope. They'll hand me my head if it isn't true."

"I'm telling you, it's no joke. Wojtyla has been elected! Call the TV stations, call the radio! I'm telling you the facts!"

I sat awhile in the office, considering what it all meant. Here was the first pope in half a millennium who was not Italian—and it was my friend, Karol Wojtyla. No pope had ever set foot in a communist country, let alone come from one. I made some more calls. It was no joke. Maybe, I thought, it was a miracle.

What would happen when I took the news upstairs? Fearful, I entered the room, and looked for Jim. I found him chatting with a deputy minister of culture and managed to catch his eye. He came over to where I was standing.

"What's up?" Jim's eyes searched my face. "You look like you just saw a ghost."

"You'll never believe it," I said. "Hang around. This should be really something."

I cleared my throat and called for silence. All eyes in the room rose toward me.

"Ladies and gentlemen . . ." I began. And I told them.

For a moment there was silence. Then another moment. Silence stretched to a minute, maybe longer. Beside me, Jim held his breath. I heard him mutter, "Good God."

Then something remarkable happened. Everyone began to applaud.

For the rest of that night, the talk was of Wojtyla. People dashed for the phone, dashed back, reporting: yes, it was all true, the Cardinal of Krakow was the pope.

But Jim was strangely quiet. Usually ebullient and sociable, he had spent the rest of the evening speaking to almost no one, despite the infectious excitement of the room. In the cab on the way back to our hotel, he finally broke his silence.

"In Hungary, you know, I saw the same thing happen. Well, not quite the same. But Hungary was ready to break free. It seemed unstoppable." He paused, and let his gaze drift out the window of our cab. His voice was distant, ominous, and strange. "You know what this means, don't you?"

"I think so."

"They'll kill him," he said. "Or they'll have to let it go."

I swallowed hard. It was not what I had been thinking at all. By "they," he meant of course the Russians, the KGB. They could never allow this to go unchallenged, I realized.

"Or let what go?" I asked.

At last he looked back at me. "Poland," he said. "The whole country. They'll have to let it go."

Chapter Fifteen
The Four Disasters

To watch Poland in the late 1970s and early 1980s, in the new era of Solidarity and John Paul II, was to watch a sleeping nation rise and take its first steps into the modern age. The only comparable event in world history that I can think of is our own War of Independence—though, in the end, Poland would win its struggle without a shot being fired. And perhaps that is the most stunning fact of all. Revolutionary ideas are the first link in a chain that inevitably leads to war; the clearest lesson that the past teaches is that freedom's bill comes due in blood. But in Poland, liberty was taken without a single broken window.

That is not to say that it couldn't have happened that way. The threat of civil disorder, and Soviet invasion, was palpable. And I have often wondered why the KGB didn't do the logical thing: kill Lech Walesa, the force and inspiration behind Solidarity. Many times, he told me, he wondered the same thing—always augmenting his point by touching the place on his chest where the bullets would have struck if they had ever come.

"That I am still here is a miracle as much as Poland is a miracle," he told me.

It was an exciting—and dangerous—time, and the election of Karol Wojtyla was its inauguration. Never in modern history had the world had such an activist pope or one so keenly aware of the political and social circumstances of his age. Pundits have long since dubbed him "the pilgrim pope," referring to his restless itinerary of international visits. But to my mind, he was—and remains—the "media pope." By the end of his first year as pontiff, he had visited Mexico, Poland, and the United States, where he met with President Carter and addressed the General Assembly of the United Nations; by the end of 1990, he had set foot in forty-four different countries.

Most provocative of all was his trip to Poland in June of '79, less than eight months after his coronation. For Karol Wojtyla, as for John Cardinal Krol, a Polish visit was as much a homecoming as a demonstration of political clout. But to the communist leadership, guardians of official state atheism, the message was clear: from that point forward, the Polish Catholic Church had the full weight of the entire organization behind it.

On that visit, he also took the time to meet and speak with Lech Walesa, an electrician at the Lenin Shipyards in Gdansk. No action could have been more politically astute. The Lenin Shipyards were the flashpoint for growing labor unrest. Walesa and the fledgling Solidarity Union had begun to challenge the prevailing communist order. Around Walesa, Poland's historic struggle was beginning to coalesce, and Karol Wojtyla's visit gave that struggle an additional global visibility, linking its fate to the church itself.

I met Walesa at about the same time, on a visit regarding a wholly different matter. At the time, I was assisting the Lubavitcher Movement in its efforts to obtain a priceless collection of Jewish manuscripts from the communist government. Hidden away during the war, these documents—rabbinical writings, sermons, and decisions on Jewish law, some as old as six hundred years—had been discovered in a government library. On one such trip, finding I had some free time on my hands, I made a side trip to Gdansk to meet for the first time with the electrician whom everyone was talking about.

We were friends from the start. At bottom, Lech and I were really quite alike, just a couple of working-class Poles suddenly thrust onto the public stage. To my happy amazement, he knew all about me. "You are the American," he said, smiling and shaking my hand. "May I call you Uncle?" I laughed, and the name stuck.

To say that Lech impressed me is the most egregious understatement. At once, I saw in him the same kind of charisma and vision that I so admired in Karol Wojtyla. His mind was brilliant, lacerating. Though just a "humble electrician," he was able to frame the unrest at the Lenin Shipyards in historical context, while simultaneously giving his argument a brilliant, simple clarity.

"For years the Communists have been telling us, 'You own everything, everything in our country belongs to the people.' Look at Lenin! Look at Marx! Men of the people, they say." He laughed, but with a painful irony. "Well, we *are* the people. We can do a better job than this. Do you know why communism cannot succeed? Because it asks us to know one thing but believe another. Perhaps it can work, for a while, but only through fear. And we are tired of being afraid."

We were strolling together through the streets of Gdansk. As we walked, people greeted Lech—men coming home from work, women doing the shopping, even children playing in the dusty streets; everybody knew him. I was stirred by his words but also felt a chill of fear. Such ideas, uttered in the open, were treason. Hungary and Czechoslovakia had learned this lesson the hard way. If Poland went too fast, what would prevent Russian tanks from pouring across the border? I remembered what Jim had said to me at our first lunch a decade before: the Soviets could invade Poland merely by sending a postcard that read, *We'll be there on Friday*.

"All true," I said. "But change can't happen overnight. The Russians have too much to lose."

"Oh, we know that, Uncle," he told me, and pointed a finger at his chest, raising the thumb and cocking it like the hammer on a pistol—the first time, in my experience, that he ever did this. When he saw the fear in my eyes, he laughed and clapped my shoulder.

"Don't worry, Uncle. I have no intention of becoming a martyr. Not yet, anyway."

Our friendship was an hour old, but already, I knew he was the bravest man I would ever meet.

When I look back on those years, particularly the three-year period between 1979 and 1982, I see them now as the essential turning point in my life, the place to which every man must eventually come, where his spirit is held to the fire and the truth of his character is made known. Unconsciously, I knew this or, at least, now believe I did. Dreams are a doorway into a certain kind of wisdom, and my dreams, in those days, were trying to tell me something. I had always been a reluctant sleeper, a man who retired late, woke early, and rested lightly in between, but in those days I found myself preoccupied by a series of nocturnal disturbances that left me to prowl the halls and rooms of Emlen House well before dawn. Always, the experience was the same: I would awaken suddenly, drenched with sweat, my heart twisted with fear, but I would have no memory of what had frightened me. I would close my eyes again, try to see the dream, but I never could; the dream had gone. At last, unable to return to sleep, I would rise and brood till dawn.

It was maddening. For a period of about six months the dream returned at odd intervals, leaving me with only the taste of fear in my mouth but with no memory of its source. I kept this a secret from Oddie, who sensed nothing. In all the years of our marriage, I had never slept well, and the sight of Ed Piszek drinking coffee at the kitchen table at 4:00 A.M. was hardly unusual. Besides, what would I have said?

In the meantime, I was exceptionally busy. Events in Poland had begun to assume a breakneck pace; it was clear that a showdown was brewing between the government and Solidarity, whose leaders had begun to speak openly about the possibility of a general workers' strike. Tough talk had begun to come from Moscow, heightening the tension. There was talk that Soviet president Brezhnev was in ill health and that communist hard-liners were poised to step in. Then, in December '79, Soviet troops poured into Afghanistan, backing a pro-Soviet military coup. In protest, President Carter announced that the United States would boycott the summer Olympics in Moscow; the Selective Service, mothballed since Vietnam, began to register all able-bodied American men between the ages of eighteen and twenty-five. No one thought that anything like a superpower confrontation was in the offing, certainly not for the sake of Afghanistan, a country most Americans couldn't even find on a map. But the image of Soviet tanks pouring over a foreign border, any foreign border, had a chilling effect. The era of détente was over.

Although back and forth to Poland, I was also managing, at the same time, to run Mrs. Paul's, just as I always had. At some level, the company almost ran itself. Our core enterprise seemed as close to bulletproof as anything in American business. Although the American economy, as a whole, was in terrible shape, our annual sales still topped one hundred fifty million dollars a year; even the economic slowdowns of the early and mid-seventies, which had crippled many larger companies, had barely mussed our hair. Had I sold the company right then, I could have walked away with a handsome fortune. But I never took such feelers seriously. The very idea of selling actually made me laugh. Why would I sell?

Then came the four disasters.

It took me twenty-five years to build Mrs. Paul's. In the end, it took me barely twenty-four months to lose it. How this happened is difficult to say, precisely. Perhaps I was distracted; perhaps my mind was on other things; perhaps a twenty-five-year hot streak had made me overconfident. But sometime in early '79—dashing to catch one plane or another, thinking about Walesa, and Poland, and all the rest—I made a quick decision that would ramify like a cancer cell and bring down the company with lightning speed.

My decision was this: to buy a company called Arthur Treacher's, a fast-food chain specializing in seafood. In theory, it was the smartest decision I could have made, a natural move for us. Mrs. Paul's had reached a point where it simply had to expand to continue its growth. Across the industry, the word was the same: the two-income household was the new reality of American life, and people weren't cooking at home. Everyone believed that the next great wave in the food industry was in the restaurant business, with fast food leading the way. Giants like McDonald's and Burger King had long established themselves as a fixture on the landscape. In order to stay competitive in the food business, it was clear that Mrs. Paul's had to diversify.

But the idea was mere theory until the next year, when I was approached by a friend who told me that Treacher's was for sale, or could be. I knew the name well enough; Treacher's was, in fact, the largest fast-food seafood operation in the country. It was also losing money, and he thought that its parent, Orange Co., might be interested in unloading it at a discount. I agreed to the meeting, and a week later visited with the company's owner in Florida.

The Treacher's–Mrs. Paul's marriage seemed a natural. Though one of my bankers warned me that I was venturing into an entirely different kind of business, I pooh-poohed his words of caution. Arthur Treacher's sold cooked seafood for takeout; wasn't that exactly how I had kept Mrs. Paul's alive all those years ago, selling takeout from our first factory on Third and Cambria? And who knew more about the seafood business than we did? If Treacher's was in trouble, we would quickly turn it around. Orange Co.'s chairman had even capitulated to all my demands—a list of seventeen items—as long as the sale concluded quickly enough to announce on his quarterly report. So in the last week of November '79, the sale went through; Mrs. Paul's purchased Arthur Treacher's, some one hundred fifty stores owned by the company itself and the parent rights to six hundred operating as franchises, seven hundred fifty stores total, for five million dollars. On paper, it looked like the sweetest deal imaginable.

It took us just days to realize our mistake. On the Monday after Thanksgiving, four days after the sale had gone through, I sent Frank Keenan, Mrs. Paul's vice president of finance, out to the Treacher's company headquarters in Columbus to meet with the company's controller and look over their books. I waited all morning to hear from him. Finally, at two o'clock, Frank called me.

"Mr. P," he said gravely, "I think you need to come out here."

The news was bad. Frank sketched in the situation. Treacher's books were in a complete mess. The company's financial statements were at least five months behind. The last statement we had seen was for June '79; we had seen no more, it had turned out, because there *weren't* any more. He would see what he could dig up, Frank said, in the next twenty-four hours.

I met Frank the next day at an Arthur Treacher's store in downtown Columbus. The truth was, I had been in such a rush to buy the company, I had never actually been in one. It suddenly struck me; what had I been thinking, buying a restaurant chain where I had never eaten?

What Frank told me that day—and again, in more detail, over the next two months as the Treacher's financial picture was made clear—was nothing short of a worst-case scenario. From the murk of Treacher's financial statements was emerging a pattern of gross financial mismanagement. In effect, Treacher's was not functioning as a single company at all; most of the franchisees were in open revolt, refusing to pay any royalties to the parent company or provide a uniform menu, the hallmark of any brand name. The business was in chaos. I asked Frank how bad the royalty situation was.

"All told? I'm just guessing now, really. But it looks as if the franchisees owe the company at least thirty million, and maybe as much as forty."

It was an astronomical sum. "Can we recover it?"

"Legally, sure. Practically? Not a chance. You'd have to sue every franchise separately. It'd take forever and cost a fortune. I'm afraid I've got to tell you, Mr. P, you just took on six hundred partners. And not one of them plans on giving you a dime."

There was more bad news. Hidden away in the paperwork, he said, was a figure he could not believe. In order to grow the business quickly, Orange Co. had guaranteed the leases for all seven hundred Arthur Treacher's shops. The leases were long, too—twenty years.

It was a crazy move, unheard of in the food business, and I knew right away that we had been tricked. All told, Frank explained to me, the leases amounted to a potential liability of some two hundred million dollars.

For a moment I was dumbstruck. Two hundred million, on a business that had cost me just five! A business that was supposed to be a sideshow, barely a hobby for an operation like ours!

Finally, I managed to speak. "How come we didn't know this?"

Frank sighed. "The truth, Mr. P? We moved too fast. We never asked."

I knew he was right. In my stomach, I felt a hollow space open. Not "we"—me. *I* had moved too fast. "And it's legal?"

Frank removed his glasses and rubbed his tired eyes. "It shouldn't be. But technically, yes."

I sent my executive vice president and house council to visit some of the larger franchise owners, seeking a truce. Most were abusive, hardened by years of hostile relations with Orange Co. They returned, shaking their heads. We had bought ourselves a two-hundred-million-dollar insurrection. Treacher's was headed for disaster.

The first Treacher's franchise failed. Then another, and another, each time sticking us with the balance of their lease, payable in full immediately. By the second quarter of 1980, Treacher's was unraveling at three outlets a month.

Our sales figures came in: in 1979, we'd had no sales increase, the first year ever that Mrs. Paul's had failed to move ahead. It would have been a mere setback under ordinary circumstances, easily attributable to a faltering American economy, but with Treacher's on the ropes, the news was an utter catastrophe. Now we would have to wage a war on two fronts.

The third disaster struck: the price of fish, our one basic commodity, soared through the ceiling. In fact, this came as no surprise. The two-hundred-mile limit, preventing foreign vessels from fishing the rich waters off the American coast, had been signed into law by President Ford four years earlier. We had known for some time that we would be paying more for fish, and under ordinary circumstances, this fact would have presented little or no problem for us. We would have simply adjusted our prices, taken the dip in sales, redoubled the advertising, and set things right in a quarter or two. We might have even gotten a nice write-off in the process. But the two-hundred-mile limit was to have some unforeseen consequences that would bring us to our knees.

Our chief supplier at that time was Rybex, a Polish company. Our relationship had been good up to this point; I had, in fact, lobbied the American Congress on Rybex's behalf to secure for Poland a fishing quota in American waters even after the two-hundred-mile limit was imposed. Their ships were some of the world's most modern, with onboard processing facilities and holding tanks to keep the fish fresh. I considered Rybex in every way a valued partner in our enterprise.

But suddenly, as the price of fish ticked up, Rybex began to withhold shipments. Our customary order was two million pounds delivered every three months—twelve million pounds total, or roughly a quarter of the fish we used each year. Beginning in late '79, for a total of nine months, Rybex delivered no fish to us at all. Each time the excuse was different, and I watched with blackening dread as our supplies dwindled. Then, on a day I will always remember, we got the call: ten million pounds of frozen, filleted pollack was on its way to us from Rybex, nearly a year's supply in a single shipment. If we wanted it, we had to pay for it all at once. Otherwise, they would sell it elsewhere.

We didn't have the money, and they knew it. Their strategy was obvious: get us to break our contract, then sell the fish on the open market. I felt utterly betrayed. For a time, I even wondered if their motives were political, some kind of payback by the communist government for my increasingly open support of Walesa and Solidarity. We asked them if we could put the fish in a bonded warehouse, withdrawing and paying for two million pounds at a time over the next year. Hadn't I always been a good customer? I pleaded. We asked them, then begged them.

Their answer was simple: no.

Our situation had become truly desperate. After three decades of unmarred success, Mrs. Paul's was experiencing a total hemorrhage. I needed $8.5 million just to continue production, let alone begin to unravel the Treacher's mess. And my books, which had always looked spectacular, were suddenly a disaster to behold. In earlier times, my bankers would have worked with me, simply on the basis of my reputation. But my credit line at Girard had reached its legal limit; before I knew it, two other banks were called in on the deal, Fidelity and Continental, out of Chicago. I found myself negotiating for my financial life with total strangers, a troika of hard-nosed financial analysts who weren't particularly interested in the kind of man I was or the sort of business I had run for years. Until the Treacher's acquisition and the construction of the Tabor Road plant, I had never borrowed a cent of long-term debt; like most food businesses, we used a line of credit to cover the costs of seasonal inventory restocking, but all of it was short-term debt, and we paid only prime rate. Now, the first time I was actually in trouble, I found little sympathy. After much hemming and hawing, the banks agreed to loan me the money to buy the Rybex order, but at two points over prime and with a pair of additional conditions. I would have to spin off Arthur Treacher's. And I would have to divest myself of Chrysler stock.

The first condition was a pipe dream; Treacher's was worthless. The second was sheer lunacy. To sell my Chrysler holdings would be my ruin.

Over the previous few years, I had gradually become the single largest individual stockholder in Chrysler, with nearly a million and a half shares bought at an average price of eight dollars. Most of this had been bought on margin—a risky venture but basically sound. Although Chrysler was in a slump, I believed in the company. The automobile business was a cyclical industry, and when Chrysler turned things around, I stood to make a great deal of money. History would prove me right about the company, but in the meantime, the stock had slid even further, to $3.50 a share.

To sell it now would be insanity, I explained. Only a fool sells at the bottom, I said. But the banks wouldn't budge. Sell it, they said, or no loan. No loan, no fish. No fish, no Mrs. Paul's.

I sold. Disaster number four.

By early 1981, with no apparent buyer for Arthur Treacher's, it was clear that we had only two options remaining: file for bankruptcy or sell the business. Clearly, bankruptcy was the prudent choice. It would give me the chance to reorganize, and whatever stigma bankruptcy had once possessed in the public eye was long gone. But I could not see things that way. Bankruptcy was failure; it was disgrace.

But even more, I had the terrible, hopeless feeling that some cosmic or divine force simply didn't want me to be in business anymore. So many disasters, all at once! I could have withstood one or two or even three setbacks, but not four. And the more I considered my situation, the more I saw a new, dispiriting truth emerging. The last great age of the family-run company was drawing to a close, replaced by something more impersonal—a new, cutthroat era of junk bonds and hostile takeovers, computerized spreadsheets and high-flying Wall Street MBAs. Gone were the H. J. Heinzes of the world. The new face of American capitalism was a twenty-nine-year-old investment banker, lighting his cigar from a flaming one-hundred-dollar bill. All around, companies that had been fixtures of the American landscape were disappearing into corporate behemoths, ransacked and sold off for parts like old cars, while CEOs floated to earth on the cushioned air of golden parachutes. Maybe Mrs. Paul's was obsolete, I thought. Maybe I was, too.

I was facing the deepest personal crisis of my life and was seized by something uncharacteristic: an inability to act. Around me Mrs. Paul's was collapsing, yet, I could do nothing. Everyone was worried about me, but I was only dimly aware of their concern. Jim Michener phoned me: *Was everything all right?* he asked. Sure, of course it was, I said, some bumps in the road but nothing to worry about. *Was I certain?* he asked again. *He had heard the news.* . . . Everything's fine, I reassured him.

But by late winter of 1981, I had begun to speak openly about selling the business. At the time, four of my kids were working for Mrs. Paul's— George and Bill in sales, Ed Jr. in manufacturing and purchasing, and Helen as director of our test kitchens—and I wanted them to be ready. Our offices on Henry Avenue, once the happiest place I knew, had the atmosphere of a protracted and hopeless siege. For years, I had been the first man in the office every morning. Now it was all I could do to make myself set foot there.

Then, at home on the evening of May 14, I turned on the television and heard the news.

Karol Wojtyla, Pope John Paul II, had been shot.

The outcome was unclear; I heard at first that he had died. Then more reports came in: a single wound, not mortal. He had been greeting a crowd in St. Peter's Square when a man stepped forward and fired. The suspect, a Turkish dissident and Muslim fanatic named Mehmet Ali Agca, had been arrested by Italian authorities. It seemed likely he had ties to the Bulgarian KGB. From the Vatican came reports that the pope was resting comfortably. Relief flooded me. Michener had been right. At least the Communists were lousy shots.

Still, the assassination attempt left me even more troubled and uncertain. It, too, felt like a message. For the second quarter of the year, Mrs. Paul's managed, barely, to keep its head above water. But I knew that the end was coming. A few weeks after the shooting, Cardinal Krol called me at home.

"I know what you are thinking," he told me. His voice was stern. "I think you should consider reorganizing. There's no shame in it, Ed."

Through the entire crisis at Mrs. Paul's, I had never approached the cardinal with my troubles. I was deeply touched that he would call. But I also knew that bankruptcy was out of the question. It was simply anathema to my character.

"You've done a lot of good," he said. "Mrs. Paul's has helped you do that."

"I know," I said.

"Is it too easy to say, this too shall pass? I want you to understand, Ed, that whatever happens, I believe you'll come through this. The good you've done—it isn't just Mrs. Paul's. It's your spirit that has done the work."

"I appreciate that."

"I will pray for you. One more thing, Ed. If you sell?"

"Yes?"

"Don't sell cheap, Ed."

The next day, I held two meetings, one for Mrs. Paul's top people, one for the family itself. I was approaching a decision, I told them. If I chose to sell the business, I said, I would do everything I could to make sure no jobs were lost. Life would go on. That night, Oddie spoke to me before bed. What would I do without Mrs. Paul's? she wanted to know. But I had no answer.

At the same time, matters in Poland were reaching a crisis. The summer before, disastrous flooding in the south of the country had created terrible food shortages, exacerbating the general atmosphere of unrest. In July, a workers' strike at the Gdansk shipyards had crippled the country; in concession, the government had agreed to a variety of Solidarity's demands, including the right of the country's workers to form independent trade unions. Now, in the autumn of '81, Solidarity was threatening another strike unless the government agreed to a national referendum on forming a noncommunist government. It was too much too soon; I knew that the Soviets would invade unless public order was restored. On December 12, 1981, the union publicly announced its demands. A day later, the government of General Wojciech Jaruzelski declared martial law, heading off a Soviet intervention; Solidarity's leaders, including Lech, were arrested.

I was at home the night of December 13 when I heard the news. Until that day, I had been involved with a three-way negotiation with the Polish government and the government in Washington to provide food relief to the country. All that was now ended, I knew; the U.S. would levy sanctions, travel would be suspended, Poland would slip into darkness. And where was Lech? At bottom, I understood Jaruzelski's motives well enough; martial law was far preferable to invasion. He had taken a great personal and political risk; history would probably blame him for crushing Solidarity, but he had saved the country from an even worse fate. I seriously doubted any harm would come to Lech as long as Jaruzelski remained in charge. But the situation was clearly very unstable.

Was it the image of Lech under arrest that finally broke my will? What I do know is this:

One day, not long after martial law was declared in a country thousands of miles away from Philadelphia, I awoke and found I had no spirit left to run the company that until that day had been my life. I moved through the morning and afternoon in a kind of haze. I know that I went to the office for a while, looked over some fresh sales reports from the third quarter of the year, and visited one of my bankers; but I recall none of these things clearly. It is as if they happened to somebody else, as if I had left my body entirely. I went about my day, amazed to be both doing it and not doing it at the same time; finally, without quite meaning to, I found myself in my car driving out to Northeast Philadelphia to the new Mrs. Paul's plant on Tabor Road.

Tabor Road was our company's triumph—a brand-new plant, with completely modern equipment. Tabor Road had been meant to carry the company well into the future, and I had borrowed a great deal of money to build it. When I pulled into the lot, it was just after five, the end of the first shift. A light, wintry rain was falling. My engine still running, I sat in my car and watched as workers left the plant, and new workers arrived to take their places on the line. Many were dropped off by their spouses who brought their children with them, bringing them along for the ride while Mommy or Daddy went to work. In the cold drizzle, they kissed their loved ones quickly, then dashed inside to the plant that hummed with light and noise. Christmas was a week away. I wondered: *What bright promises were made in those quick moments in the parking lot before a mother or father disappeared for the night?* I waited until the lot was clear of cars once more, then drove slowly home.

I awoke the next morning unusually late; the clock by the bed said that it was already 8:30. I had not slept so late in forty years. The space beside me in the bed was empty. I had slept so long, and still I was so tired! For some time—who knows how much—I lay there on my back, looking at the ceiling, my mind floating. I thought of my father, gone so long, and my mother, now gone, too; I thought of Oddie and the Quakertown farm and of a sunny afternoon in 1946 when I had stood on the banks of the old millrace and told her that I wanted to go into business. I remembered the bar in Kensington, the tight space in the back where John Paul and I had cooked, our bodies shimmering with sweat in the close heat; I thought of his hand on the back of my neck in our yard in Drexel Hill on the night I had told him that I wanted to buy him out and of the smoke from his cigar on the morning he sat on the steps with me across from our Manayunk plant and told me the business was mine. I thought of the days when each of my children was born and of the lights from the lanterns that had led me down the long road from Wladek's farm to the highway. All of this and more; I lay in bed and remembered my life, and by midmorning, I knew what I was going to do.

I rose from bed, and from the telephone on Oddie's dressing table, I called the office and asked for Frank.

"It's over," I told him.

"Ed?"

"It's over," I said. "I want to sell. The whole company. Get whatever you can for it."

Then I hung up the phone and went back to bed.

Chapter Sixteen
Home

In the end, I barely had anything to do with the sale of the business; I simply couldn't face the prospect. Companies that had been lining up for a chance to buy us in prior years suddenly weren't all that interested. The overall business climate was poor, interest rates were high, and Mrs. Paul's wasn't the only food company with troubles. We spoke to Heinz, then Kellogg's; with Pillsbury, we came within a whisper of reaching an agreement before the deal went sour. It was a bitter time. In the end, irony of ironies, it was my old employer, The Campbell Soup Company—the same business that had fired me forty years before—that bought Mrs. Paul's.

The sale went through in June 1982. For seventy-eight million dollars, Campbell's acquired three of our four plants, all our manufacturing equipment, the totality of our raw and finished inventory, our research and development facilities, the Henry Avenue office building, and of course, the brand name itself. The last was the most painful of all. Seventy-eight million was a lot of money, but by the time all debts against the company had been satisfied at settlement, just twenty million dollars remained. Conservatively, it represented just a tenth of what the company had been worth only a few years before.

The one part of the business Campbell's did not want to buy was Arthur Treacher's. They had seen too many companies like mine get into trouble with franchised restaurant operations, they said. We looked around and finally found a buyer, a group of franchise owners from Ohio.

We sold Arthur Treacher's for a single dollar.

For a while, I was despondent. The blackest depression descended on me, as if I had lost everything. But money was not the greatest loss. I simply didn't know what to do with myself now that Mrs. Paul's was gone.

I couldn't even bring myself to clean out my office on Henry Avenue, and when my daughter, Helen, finally offered to pick up my things, I thanked her, relieved.

I consoled myself with the thought that the sale of the company hadn't put anyone else out of work, at least immediately. Like a giant sponge, Campbell's absorbed the entire enterprise. It is altogether likely that for some of my employees, the packers and handlers and truckers, the change of ownership was no more than a momentary distraction, if that—just a new name on the boxes. Closer to home, my sons George, Ed, and Bill all went across the river to Camden to lend a hand in the change in ownership; although Ed stayed with the company only six months, George and Bill took different jobs with Campbell's after the transitional period was over and stayed seven years. Helen, who had worked for me as head of Mrs. Paul's product development, could have gone anywhere she wished. I was glad that she chose to stay with me, helping me on day-to-day matters. It was a Herculean task she took on, sweeping up the wreckage.

I was pleased that my disaster did so little harm. It was even nice, in a way, to see my children venture out in the world on their own, out from under their father's shadow. But I wanted to hear nothing of Campbell's, nothing more of Mrs. Paul's. A few years later, I read in the newspaper that the plant in Manayunk, vacant since the sale, was scheduled for demolition. A different man might have gone to see it happen: to hear the wrecking ball make contact, taste the dust as it rose around him, perhaps take home a brick or two as a souvenir to be placed, with mournful ceremony, on the fireplace mantle. But I stayed home.

It took less than fifteen years for Mrs. Paul's to be sold again. In 1996, Campbell's sold it off to a start-up company based in San Francisco, Aurora Foods, that was buying up "neglected" brand names and trying to revive them. So, Mrs. Paul's, like a lost child, spun further away from me, into an ever-wider orbit.

But that, of course, was later. Of the darkest period, the long, desolate months between late 1980 and the winter of 1982, I can only say that those were days when my deepest faith was tested.

I look now on that time with a wince; it is embarrassing even to acknowledge that I could have sunk so low. The pity I saw in others' eyes was a reflection of my own self-pity, the worst of human emotions, and intellectually, I understood this. What harm had occurred, really? No one had lost his job (except, of course, for me); the world had not been deprived of some necessary commodity; no one would starve or die from disease or suffer a moment's loss of liberty as a consequence of the sale of Mrs. Paul's. In the larger picture, all that had happened was the transfer of ownership of a medium-sized, historically profitable company from my hands to another's. In other words, nothing. In the preceding decade, I had become awfully good at seeing things in terms of their larger importance; I had yoked myself to causes far larger than personal success and found the greatest sense of satisfaction in my life by doing so. The bitter irony was that now, with Mrs. Paul's gone, I could only see myself as an unemployed former CEO, without a purpose he could name. I was sixty-six years old, and my empty days stretched before me like a vast, treeless plain. I thought of the word "retired." I chewed it over, like a piece of hard gristle. *Retired.* I didn't even play golf.

It was time, of course, that cured me, as it cures so many others. I know now that I was lucky. For some, depression is an abyss that can never be escaped. It is a darkness that consumes everything. But mine was more like a single, darkened room in an otherwise bright house. I only needed someone to show me the way out.

So, a story:

December 1982, a Sunday afternoon, six months after the sale of Mrs. Paul's; in the passenger seat of my son-in-law Erik's van, I passed through the gates of Emlen House, headed for the airport. The day was as gray as my mood. I was flying that night to Rome, where, the next evening, I was scheduled to meet with the holy father for a private dinner at his Vatican residence. The prospect actually embarrassed me; I felt like a fraud. The invitation, which had come many months before, said nothing about the sale of the company, and I assumed that the holy father was unaware of it. We were friends, but our relationship was also business; I imagined that he expected to be receiving an important and wealthy benefactor, the head of a major American company. Now I was neither.

As the day of my trip had neared, I confessed to Oddie that I didn't have the heart to go and wanted to cancel.

"Never mind that," she had said. "He may not say it, but I will. He asked you to come because he needs you, your input, your ideas. And besides," she scolded, "who turns down an invitation from the *pope?*"

I had agreed, but now, as the van pulled through the Emlen House gates, past the marker I had seen a thousand times but not read in years ("Here in the Emlen House Washington had his headquarters from Nov. 2 to Dec. 11, 1777, just before moving to Valley Forge . . ."), I suddenly felt a biting chill unsnake around my spine—the same chill, I imagined, that Washington himself must have felt, riding his horse down this very road to join his ragtag, underfed army for its long, winter encampment. *Dark days,* I thought, and I glanced at Erik, thanking him in my heart for keeping silent at the wheel.

We drove on through the descending, early winter dusk. I had spent my whole life in Philadelphia, but in those days, even the landscape seemed strange to me, worn out and slightly off-kilter, like something in a dream. I touched the glass of the window, chilled by the winter air streaming by. The sky hung low and looked to be holding snow. It was as if I wasn't living my life at all but remembering it. We made our way through Fort Washington into Springfield Township, crossed Fairmount Park at Bell's Mill Road—a lovely, winding descent into the Wissahickon Gorge and up the other side—and headed east through the outskirts of the city toward the Schuylkill Expressway. It was a route I had traveled hundreds—no, thousands—of times in the past. It was then that I knew what troubled me so deeply, this gray day in December. Not the cheerlessness of the weather, nor the fact that I would soon have to face my dear friend with news of my defeat; not even the thought of the long, empty hours on the plane, hours that I would spend in brooding contemplation.

No; what bothered me was far more immediate. The route we were following would take us right past the old headquarters on Henry Avenue.

I don't think that Erik was even aware of what we were doing, but as we approached the building, I felt the van shudder; involuntarily, Erik had tapped the brakes at the last moment. But it was too late for him to turn off onto a side street, and the gesture would have been obvious in any event. We glided past, pretending nothing had happened. I hadn't seen the place in six months, not since I had signed the final sales agreement handing the company over to Campbell's Soup. The windows were dark, of course; no one would be working on a Sunday so close to Christmas. But I also knew that Campbell's had plans to vacate the building, because they would be moving the Mrs. Paul's wing of their operation to their company headquarters across the Delaware River in Camden. So, perhaps the place had already been vacated. What a strange, desolate feeling it was to see the building once more, knowing that I would never set foot in it again.

At the next intersection, Erik stopped the van for a red light.

"Sorry," he said, breaking the silence. He lifted his shoulders in an embarrassed shrug and glanced across at me. "I should have thought."

I waved the thought away. "That's all right," I answered. "It was the natural way to go."

"I feel like we should have held our breath or something. You know . . . like kids do in a car when they pass a graveyard?"

I had to laugh. "Actually, I think I did."

At the airport unloading zone, I pressed Erik's shoulder, and he nodded and drove off. I carried my one bag inside, through international check-in, then to the gate, where my plane, a TWA 747, was waiting. For the first time in twenty years I would be flying coach. I wedged myself into my tiny seat (how did people stand it, I wondered, spending ten hours crammed into something so narrow?), and waited for takeoff. Minutes passed as passengers boarded. The flight was nearly full, and a woman about my age took the seat next to mine, nodding a curt hello as she stowed her bags, which I saw were Christmas presents wrapped in bright paper. I turned my gaze to the window. Outside, a light rain mixed with flecks of snow had begun to drizzle on the tarmac.

Then—irony of ironies—I saw it. *Could it be . . . ?* But it was. Taxiing down the tarmac past our plane was the sleek company jet that had belonged to Mrs. Paul's. I was dumbstruck. I could make out my former pilot, Wally Dapron, in the Lear's cockpit; for a moment I thought, absurdly, that if I waved and banged on the cabin window, I might get his attention. But, though he was just a few hundred feet away, the distance between us—blanketed by the roar of jet engines—might have been a thousand miles. I had traveled all over the world in that sleek little plane with Wally at the controls. But he was piloting somebody else now, while I sat above him, unseen, in tourist class.

It was too much. I wanted to laugh, to cry, to bang my head against the cabin window. The world had slipped into parody. Finally I did laugh, and when the woman beside me gave me a quizzical look and asked what was so funny, I pointed out the cabin window.

"See that plane?" I said. "Until just a few months ago, that plane was mine."

"Ah." Her mouth open, she nodded uncertainly; I could tell she didn't believe me. And why would she? What would a man who once owned a Lear jet be doing back here in coach? "I see," she finally managed.

"It's true," I insisted.

"Well." She smiled, humoring me, as one might humor a child with a charmingly overactive imagination. "It's a very pretty plane. You must miss it."

A flight attendant came by, checking that everyone was buckled in, and the woman asked her quickly if there were any other seats available.

"Just a couple," she said. "But they're back by the restrooms."

"That's fine," the woman said. "Anything will do."

She rose and gathered her packages in something close to panic. I didn't say anything.

"It's my back, you see," she explained to me, balancing her boxes and shopping bags. "I need more room to stretch out. I'm just glad they had some open seats."

"It's all right," I said. "You don't have to explain." I shot her a frown. "It was my plane, though."

We landed at Da Vinci Airport just after dawn. Somehow I had managed to sleep most of the way and debarked feeling strangely rested—better, actually, than I had felt in days. Though it was still early, the airport was busy and chaotic, teeming with holiday passengers and business travelers trying to wedge just one last deal into their schedules before Christmas. In line at customs, beneath the watchful gaze of the *carabinieri*, I waited behind a group of American college students, armed with maps and backpacks and talking in the loud, happy voices of young people on the eve of a great adventure. One by one, they made their way through, then asked the customs officer to stamp their passports—proof that it was all real, that they really were in Italy at last. The world was a book just beginning to open to them, and I felt my spirits lift. What business did I have to be so glum?

At a small bar in the airport I drank a quick cup of dark, strong espresso, then ventured outside to find transportation into the city. Usually a limo and driver would be waiting for me, but not that day; I had decided to skip it, thinking it was about time I figured out such things for myself. But as I stepped outside into the dank morning air, I realized that I had not thought this plan through at all. I didn't have a clue how to negotiate Rome's public transit system, and I spoke barely enough Italian to find a restroom or make change. I was about to spring for a taxi—an expensive and dicey proposition, I guessed—when a young man stepped up to help me. I recognized him from the group of students in the customs line: a handsome kid, with tiny wire-framed glasses and a golden haze of new beard on his chin and cheeks. He was wearing jeans and a sweatshirt that said "Property of Harvard University Athletic Department." From his broad shoulders hung a backpack that must have weighed fifty pounds. He wasn't much younger than my own son Bill.

"The easiest way into town is to take one of these busses," he explained, pointing at a line of modern-looking coaches parked at the curb. "You can buy a ticket on board. That'll take you right to the main subway terminal. From there, you can get anywhere. I've done it a bunch of times."

"Thanks," I managed.

"It's OK," he said, grinning. "*Fa niente.* You just looked a bit lost there."

"I think I was, a little."

With his thumb, he pointed over his shoulder at the enormous backpack. "If you're looking for a hotel, I've got a good guidebook with me. I could even make the call for you if you don't speak Italian. I only speak a little, but Italians are happy just to hear you try."

"That's all right," I said. "I've actually got a reservation. It may be the *only* thing I've got."

He smiled warmly and put out his hand to shake. "I'm Daniel. You need any more help, just ask, OK? Our plane got in early, so we're going to be stuck here waiting for our ride for a while."

I looked over at the busses. "Does it matter which one I take?"

He laughed ironically. I could tell that he was an old pro at this sort of thing. "Probably. But, hey, this is Italy. You can't try to control everything over here. For all we know, there'll be a strike in the next ten minutes. When you get on board, say to the driver, 'Stazione?' That means the station at the center of town. You can get a subway map there."

I thanked him again and boarded the bus. Just as Daniel had promised, it let me off at the train; from there, an English-speaking attendant at the tourist kiosk directed me to the underground, which whisked me to within a few blocks of my hotel. I hadn't been on a bus or subway in decades; but here I was, using both, just like everybody else. Like my subway ride, the hotel where I was staying, The Alicorni, was new to me; just a hundred yards from the Vatican, it was used primarily by visiting clerics and had an austere economy to it. I ordered breakfast up in my room, ate ravenously, phoned Oddie to let her know that I had arrived all right, then lay down on the bed and was instantly asleep.

By the time I awoke it was already 6:00 P.M., so I quickly showered, dressed, and walked across St. Peter's Square. The night had turned out to be pleasantly warm and clear, like an evening in spring, and tourists milled around the plaza, talking in a hundred different languages and hamming it up for pictures. Clergy strode purposefully through the throngs, carrying briefcases like American office workers back home. At the security checkpoint, I gave my name to the Swiss Guards, and they waved me ahead, into the Vatican City that few tourists ever see: down a cobblestone opening onto a small square, another security checkpoint beyond, and the private elevator that with heavenly efficiency whisked visitors up to the pope's residence. Polished marble floors, breathtaking statuary and stained glass and frescoes, gold leaf everywhere: I am certain there could be no other residence to match it in all the world, yet most awesome of all is the deep quiet of the place, a silence so encompassing that you wonder if your very thoughts can be heard. My escort led me to the vestibule outside the pope's private dining room, where his secretary, Monsignor Stanislaw Dziwisz, whom I knew from his earlier days in Poland, was waiting for me. We greeted one another, then a minute later, the doors opened, and the holy father beckoned me in.

We were old friends, of course, but that didn't mean that I was any less susceptible to experiencing something like awe in his company. In fact, I think it was because I knew him so well that I felt the power of his presence so keenly. I reminded myself to be cool and calm, as if nothing unusual was happening.

But I couldn't manage it; my charade was too much. No sooner had we sat ourselves at the table than he rose again, and came around to my side. He reached out and put his hand on my shoulder; his face was stern, unyielding. I know I trembled, thinking I had offended him. He had found out about Mrs. Paul's and would scold me for not telling him the truth. *He's seen right through me*, I thought, and my face began to burn again with humiliation.

"I don't want you to worry," he said. "You're going to get back all the things you have lost, everything important in your life. Your life is going to be more meaningful, because of this."

"You knew—"

He nodded. "Of course. That's why you're here. I know you. You'll get it all back. You will get it all back, like Job, so don't worry."

And I put my face in my hands.

Walking back to the hotel that night, I decided to take the long way to enjoy the balmy air. The streets beyond the Vatican pulsed with life. I took it all in: old folks sitting in front of their buildings, the young lovers strolling arm in arm, the clatter of cups and the sound of conversation floating onto the sidewalk from the cafes that cluttered the ancient sidewalks. He had *known*; my old friend had known, and that was why he had asked me to come. I felt a tremendous weight rising from me, a weight I hadn't even known was really there: the weight of being alone. At a small trattoria, I took a table on the sidewalk, ordered a coffee and grappa, and watched the great Roman parade flow past. My father had been dead for nearly fifty years, but I think it was his grip I felt that night when the holy father had placed his hands on my shoulders and told me not to be afraid. And I thought he must have known that, too.

What else could I do? How better to celebrate? I married Oddie, my wife of forty-six years.

The notion was, indirectly, Cardinal Krol's.

"Edward," he said to me one day, "I've waited for years for you to come up with the idea by yourself. I simply can't wait any longer. Why don't you become Catholic?"

Always the pragmatist, John Cardinal Krol had more than my soul on his mind. A mutual friend had nominated me for membership in the Knights of Malta. Because I lived in the cardinal's diocese, the letter had come to him. But the fact that I wasn't Catholic—had never received the sacraments—would force him to block my nomination.

I could see that the prospect pained and embarrassed him. But initially, I was relieved. It was a great honor to be nominated, of course, and membership in the Knights of Malta carried considerable cachet in Catholic circles. But I had never been a "joiner." A certain independence had always been my trademark, in business, in philanthropy, and most of all, in private life. I didn't even belong to the auto club.

So, the fact that I wasn't Catholic seemed like an airtight alibi. But then, I thought about what Cardinal Krol was really asking. Why *not* become Catholic? For decades, I had worked side by side with some of the most influential Catholic clergymen in Europe and the United States. The men I respected most and counted among my closest friends were churchmen, nearly to a one. Didn't this say something about my values, and what I believed? And of course, I approached the matter from a spiritual point of view as well. The destruction of Mrs. Paul's had taught me a powerful lesson; without faith in God and the belief that everything happened for a purpose, some things simply could not be withstood.

With Cardinal Krol's help I began my religious education, so I could receive the sacraments that would formalize the truth I already felt in my heart. My commitment to the process was total. But one hurdle remained: I would have to convince Oddie to marry me in a Catholic church.

Throughout the years, Oddie had stood by me as my philanthropic and political involvement with the church had deepened. Certainly she did not doubt the value of the work that the church was doing, especially in Poland, and she had visited the pope with me on a number of occasions. Cardinal Krol was a fixture in our household, a trusted family friend. Though she was not Catholic herself, she was Christian, attending worship services most Sundays at the Lutheran church near our home.

The problem as I understood it was not spiritual but emotional. I feared that she would misunderstand my desire to renew our vows in a Catholic church as a retroactive negation of our original ceremony and the contract it implied. If I wanted to marry her *now*, wasn't I also saying that we had not really been married in the first place?

So I waited, without saying anything, to detect a sign from her, one way or the other. But I couldn't tell what she was thinking. And of course, I now know that this was precisely what she had in mind. The problem was mine, not hers, and she was waiting for me to work it out.

Finally, on a Saturday evening, I led her into the sunroom, and I told her everything—what I wanted to do and what I feared it might mean to her.

"Ed, you really surprise me," she said. I thought she might be about to laugh. "We've been married almost fifty years. Why do you think it would even occur to me that this would change anything?"

"I guess I hoped it wouldn't."

"Unless of course *you* think it would. That somehow, doing this now would mean we weren't married in the first place. You're the one who brought it up."

"Well, I don't think it at all. I promise you that."

"So let me ask you this. What do you think *God* thinks?"

Her question surprised me. "Wouldn't it be a little presumptuous of me to say what God thinks?"

She smiled gingerly. "Maybe. But probably he wouldn't mind this once. Well?"

The answer was easy to give. "Well, we love each other. We've loved each other for nearly fifty years. We've raised a wonderful family. We've been through everything two people can go through together."

"And?"

I had to smile. "I guess I'd say he thinks that's a marriage, as much as anything could be."

She smiled and took my hand. "Then I'd say we all agree."

I looked at our hands, twined together—an octopus of flesh and bone. It was hard to say where one hand ended and the next began. We were seventy years old, the parents of five grown children, grandparents to eleven more. On Oddie's finger was the plain gold band I had given her almost half a century before, driving across the river to New Jersey, our future a story yet to be told. *Here we were,* I thought, *just a couple of old flames.* It had all passed so quickly.

"So? What do you say?"

At last, Oddie laughed. "Come on, Ed. How about a little *ceremony* here? A girl doesn't get a proposal every day of the week, you know."

I nodded. "Seems fair."

I rose from the sofa and tried to kneel before her. But my knees were stiff, and I had to settle for balancing myself on the edge of the coffee table. The whole thing struck me as vaguely comic, like a scene from a movie, and I wanted to laugh. But the urge passed, and I took her hand again.

"How about it? Will you marry me, Miss McFadden?"

"Of course I'll marry you, Ed Piszek."

No doubt Cardinal Krol would have happily provided the grandest cathedral for the occasion. But Oddie and I agreed that the last thing we wanted was anything like a spectacle. "You start small, you end small," she joked. "Besides, who would want to watch a couple of old geezers like us getting married?" We chose a small parish church just a few miles from Emlen House and limited the guest list to close family and friends. My son-in-law, Erik, was the best man, and Carmen, our housekeeper and dear friend, was matron of honor. Oddie wore a tan suit with white trim and carried a bouquet of white calla lilies. In a sense it was a day like any other. We rose, ate breakfast, got dressed, went to church, came home. In the midst of it, as if by chance, Oddie and I were married.

But it also wasn't, of course. It was our wedding day.

As we drove away from the church, Oddie took my hand. "How many people get this chance?" she said. "Isn't it wonderful, to be starting over like this?"

And she was right. That's exactly what it was.

Chapter Seventeen
The American Uncle

The cloud had lifted; I began my life again, a seventy-one-year-old newlywed and former CEO, as free as I was that long-ago autumn day, when Oddie and I had driven my little car across the river to New Jersey. And the timing could not have been better. Was it simply coincidence or part of some larger synchronicity? I emerged from the wreckage of my old life just in time to see Poland do the same.

Lech's incarceration, as it turned out, was mercifully brief. After a year of house arrest, he emerged heavier and pale but his spirit unbroken. At the time, few people in the media seemed to completely understand the meaning and circumstances of his release. Even I did not appreciate all the details, until many years later.

Lech's release was simply politics, Polish style: held as an unofficial hostage against the threat of a Soviet invasion, he was let go the moment the crisis had passed. Certainly American sanctions—and the veiled threat of a closer U.S.-China relationship—went a long way toward leveraging his freedom. In international circles, martial law had been universally condemned, and for a brief time, Poland was perceived as the new ideological battleground between East and West. But a subtler truth was operating, and it was one with which I was already well acquainted: for the Communists, the ideological battle for Poland was already lost. Poland was no longer an ideologically driven nation at all, and when Wojciech Jaruzelski had declared martial law and outlawed Solidarity, his primary motive was to keep Poland's reform engine from overheating—in other words, to keep the Soviets out, not to banish reform per se. The world may remember him differently—as the man who jailed Walesa—but the truth is, Jaruzelski was a brilliant politician and a smart student of Polish history, and the momentous changes that followed in the 1980s couldn't have happened if martial law had never been declared (or lifted when it was).

Jaruzelski was also keenly aware that control in Poland was a three-way affair. Wedged between Solidarity and the Communists (or worse, the Russians) was the Catholic Church, which amounted to a kind of swing vote. Late in 1980, as a showdown between striking Solidarity workers and the government threatened to push the nation into chaos, Jaruzelski made a quiet, urgent appeal to the new Polish church leader, Primate Joseph Glemp, who had succeeded Wyszynski. If the church would use its influence to maintain civic order, Jaruzelski offered, then the government would lift its ban on church construction. Assuming a peaceful resolution to the present difficulties, the Catholic Church would be permitted to build all the new churches it could afford.

Though this received little attention in the West, it was probably the single largest concession Jaruzelski could have made. In effect, in return for a temporary truce, the general made the church the guardians of the public welfare, breaking the back of official state atheism once and for all. The construction of new churches would go a long way, too, toward guaranteeing an elevated visibility and stature for the Catholic Church in the long term. Now, Glemp could go to the people and say, "Don't rise up, because you're only going to be killed for your efforts. Instead, see what we have won for you. New churches means new schools and a better way of life for your children." In essence, Glemp could take credit for being both the voice of reason and a tough negotiator with the Communists.

Though most of the world viewed the Solidarity experiment as a failure, in fact, the groundwork had been laid for far more significant and lasting change, not only in Poland but across the Soviet satellites. In Walesa, the reform movement had its first major, international figure in twenty years. Walesa left his detainment a much beloved figure; though he had no Solidarity to run—the union was officially outlawed and would remain so until 1989—the power of his personality and the hunger for reform had not abated, and his short year in captivity had only enhanced his standing.

I did not see Lech again until much later, when the sweeping changes of the eighties were almost complete. But I was fortunate to advance his cause in a number of ways throughout the decade.

The greatest of these actually began in the summer of 1981, in the very thick of the Arthur Treacher's disaster. Though matters in Poland were quickly spiraling out of control—martial law was, in fact, just around the corner—at the time, I thought of Solidarity's stunning advances in almost purely positive terms. Though Mrs. Paul's had begun to collapse around me, I took heart in Lech's success and admired the tremendous courage he showed in standing up to the Communists.

The risks involved were just one more thing that, back then, I was not seeing clearly. Still, I was excited by what was happening, and I wanted to do something to be useful, to advance the cause as best I could.

As it happened, these machinations coincided with a weekend trip to visit Jim Michener at his home on the Eastern Shore of Maryland. For nearly a decade, Jim and I had traveled all over the world together, and there wasn't a man alive I trusted more. But one thing I knew about Jim: you didn't tell him what to write about. Our friendship was based, in part, on the unstated agreement not to tell each other too specifically how to conduct our professional affairs. I hadn't mentioned the possibility of a book about Poland for many years. Not since our initial meeting all those years ago had the subject come up in any concrete way. But with things in Poland moving so quickly, I felt the time was right to say something.

Jim had moved to the Eastern Shore to research his novel *Chesapeake* and had liked the place so much that he had chosen to stay on. It was a lovely, late summer's day, and I had flown down to the little Easton, Maryland, airfield in the company plane—one of the last trips I would ever take in it. Jim and I were sitting on his patio, overlooking the placid bay, when I finally broached the subject.

I said, "Tell me what's next, Jim."

He was seventy-five years old—an age when most men are ready to hang up their careers for good. He gave me a happy smile, as he always did when he was ready to write a new book. "Ed, it's very exciting. Texas. It looks like it's going to be Texas."

"How long will it take?"

He said it was going to be a long novel—perhaps his longest. It would take three years.

My heart sank. I knew—and I think Jim knew—that it could be his last book. There would never be a novel about Poland. If I didn't speak now, I never could.

"Jim," I said, "I have a petition. Under ordinary circumstances I'd never tell you what to write about, but I have to say this. We've traveled Poland together over and over. You know the country inside out, as well as any man could. Jim," I said, "if you don't tell the story, who will?"

For a moment he said nothing. Then he nodded. "I'll think about it."

I got on the plane the next morning. Jim had said nothing at all about the idea since I'd spoken the night before, and I had no idea how to interpret his silence. I had crossed a line—an important line—in our friendship, but the cause was worthy, I thought. Still, I was nervous all that day, worrying that I had offended him.

The next day my phone rang at 8:00 sharp. I had already been up for hours; so had Jim, I suspected. The hour was surprising, because Jim neither made nor received phone calls before noon. The morning was his writing time, sacred and inviolable.

"All right," he said tersely. "I've been up all night, damn it, thinking about this. I'll do it."

I was so surprised I practically spilled my coffee all over myself. "What about Texas?" I stammered.

"Ed, you talk like I'm going somewhere," Jim said with a laugh. "I'm only seventy-five, you know. Texas isn't going anywhere."

On the spot, he gave me a list of about fifty different things he would need: access to libraries, meetings with officials and church leaders and Polish historians, certain documents he would need to see.

"Did you get all that?" he asked me when he was done.

I looked at my list, five pages long. "Holy mackerel, Jim. Are you sure this is *all?*"

"Don't worry," he said. "There'll be more. This was your idea, you know."

James Michener's *Poland* appeared in November 1983, and although it only briefly registered on major American best-seller lists (and never, alas, at the top), it showed a phenomenal longevity that ultimately made it one of Jim's most successful books, rivaling *Hawaii*. Internationally, it became a blockbuster of epic proportions; the combined hardcover and paperback sales amounted to an astonishing three million copies in the U.S. and two million overseas. Even now, a year after the author's death, it remains one of his best-selling titles. In Warsaw's American bookstore—across the street from the Presidential Palace—*Poland* still sells one hundred copies or more each year.

The novel was a mass-communications bonanza for the country, and it couldn't have come at a better time. With Solidarity outlawed, Poland could have slipped from the forefront of America's consciousness. But suddenly, on beaches and aboard airplanes, in bedrooms and on park benches, in libraries and dormitories and drawing rooms, Americans by the hundreds of thousands were losing themselves in the tale of Polish history.

And then a miracle happened.

Lech Walesa was awarded the 1983 Nobel Peace Prize.

The paradox was that, from a certain point of view, Lech was an agitator, a firebrand. It was not peace he was working for, not overtly, but democratic reform, and such transformations are rarely tranquil. That he ultimately triumphed without so much as a shot fired testifies to the persuasiveness of his personality, the force and coherence of his appeal, and in the end, not a little luck besides.

And yet: when I thought about what was happening in Poland and what it might mean for the rest of the world, I began to see Solidarity's struggles in a different light. Democratic reform and social justice were more than mere theories of effective governance. Democracy was a notion that took its strength from the simple moral urgency of its argument. Democracy was an expression of the best of the human impulse and an encouragement to that impulse; only in a system that valued the individual could real peace—not a mere silencing of guns but a peace of mind and spirit—take place. And in that sense, all democratic movements, from the shots across Lexington Green to the strikes at Gdansk, were part of a vast continuum, chapters in a single human struggle spanning centuries.

How ironic. I lived in a house once inhabited by George Washington in a city known as the birthplace of modern democracy, and I was nearly seventy years old before I saw any of this clearly.

I had to express this new idea somehow; what was happening in Poland was too important, too *connected*, to ignore. And, for me, my new understanding answered a question that had long been lurking under all of my work: the question of what it meant to be both Polish and American.

In more recent years, the idea of the "hyphenated American" has received considerable attention, by scholars and in the popular press. What used to be called "ethnic pride" has been renamed "multiculturalism," but the core idea remains essentially the same: far from the paradigm of the melting pot, America is a nation united for the most part by difference. Except for Native Americans, whose claim to the continent is thousands of years old, we are all from somewhere else and so see the world at least in part through the sentimental lenses of our near-ancestral pasts—through the hazy memory of Polish being spoken in a dark Quakertown kitchen, or the taste of a grandmother's recipe for a Christmas strudel, or the recollected sound of worksongs, rich with African rhythm, floating across a field at dusk. To speak more abstractly, America is less a place than an experiment, an idea in progress. To be born in America is to inherit this paradox as one's patrimony; to live here is to fathom what it means.

I had spent two decades fathoming my own Polishness, and more than once, I had been the recipient of comments and observations that only lightly concealed an irritating truth: many people felt that it was impossible to be as "Polish" as I was and still be an American, too. Why, for instance, did I spend so much money and so much time trying to improve life in a foreign country, when there was so much that needed to be done at home? And in fact, the question gave me pause. Why did I? It was nothing I had examined too closely, but still, the question gnawed at me.

Now I had my answer. Poland *was* America or, at least, was trying to become America. Borders were arbitrary; it was ideas that mattered. And the idea of democracy had become Poland's, too.

For at least a year, I mulled the matter over. What could I do to express this new connection? Then I found my answer right under my nose behind a glass case in Philadelphia's Independence Park.

No American symbol is so potently connected to the very idea of democracy as the Liberty Bell, hung in Philadelphia's Independence Hall in 1753 and rung on the occasion of the signing of the Declaration of Independence, on July 4, 1776. I had seen it myself countless times; whenever I hosted out-of-town guests, invariably it was the bell, of all Philadelphia's revolutionary period artifacts, that they asked to see. And the bell is in many ways the most perfect of symbols, not least of all because it is so outwardly ordinary. It is, after all, just a bell, and not even a very good one; cracked beyond repair in 1846 (not in 1776, as most people think), it hasn't rung a note since. The bell means what it means because of what it *did*, not what it *is*, and the fact that it can never ring again seals its meaning forever. Looking at it, one cannot help but feel that encased in its smooth finish, still humming through its molecules, is the very vibration of freedom itself.

I named my new public charity the Liberty Bell Foundation in its honor and because I felt so keenly the tug of that moment, two hundred years ago, when the signers of the Declaration of Independence had taken one of the greatest gambles of modern history. (No doubt, many of them wholly expected to be hanged for their troubles, just as Lech expected an assassin's bullet.) The purpose of the foundation was primarily educational, and the need was obvious. All the studies showed that most Americans knew far more about what programs were on television than about the content of their own Constitution. Civics, as a course of study, had all but vanished from the public school curriculum, and the colleges were not making up for the deficit; it was not unusual for someone to spend four years of higher education without once encountering the major documents and ideas that have shaped American life. Beginning in 1986, the Liberty Bell Foundation began a program of distributing, to every high school and college in the country, texts and reference books on the United States Constitution and Bill of Rights. Surprisingly, they often were not welcomed— more than once I found myself in the queer position of defending the Constitution as a course of study—but more often than not, our efforts were met enthusiastically.

A number of years before, I had commissioned a working replica of the Liberty Bell to serve as part of our Americana Jubilee exhibit in Philadelphia during the bicentennial celebration. Now, nearly eleven years later, Liberty Bell II (as we called it) was officially invited by the U.S. Constitution Bicentennial Committee to serve as a centerpiece during the next year's celebration of the U.S. Constitution and Bill of Rights. On September 17, 1987—the two-hundredth anniversary of ratification—Chief Justice Warren Burger rang the bell during a ceremony at Philadelphia's Independence Hall. The bell would later travel to eight of the original thirteen ratifying states, a centerpiece to their own ceremonies marking the anniversary of ratification, before returning to Emlen House grounds. But that day, listening to the bell's lucid peel rebounding across the old city, I wasn't thinking about the future at all. Those who heard it all said the same thing to me: it was a moment when the past itself seemed to hang in the air. And I thought: *Wouldn't it be something, if the bell could go to Poland?* But of course that was impossible; the bell was, after all, an American symbol.

Impossible, I said to myself. It is impossible.

And I was right. The bell did not go to Poland.

Poland came to the bell.

Nineteen eighty-eight: Things in Poland had begun to happen with remarkable speed. Across Eastern Europe, communism seemed to be losing its footing. Mikhail Gorbachev, the reform-minded successor to Konstantin Chernenko, had been in power as Communist Party leader since 1985; that year, under a restructuring of the Soviet civilian government, he would be named Soviet president and chief of state. The changes he had wrought in just three years were mind-boggling: modified free elections, market reforms, a more open Soviet press. Soviet troops had begun their pullback from Eastern Europe, and just as significantly, from Afghanistan. The INF Treaty, banning intermediate-range nuclear weapons from Europe, was signed and sealed, waiting for the American Senate to ratify. That year alone, he would meet twice with American President Ronald Reagan, once in Moscow and once in the U.S., where he also addressed the United Nations. The two were reported to be friends—unthinkable just a decade before. Gorbachev himself was almost impossible to dislike: educated, stylish, and reasonable; dressed in tailored suits and speaking with a confident, easygoing manner; he seemed the very epitome of a Western political leader.

In hindsight the situation was far more volatile than anyone actually believed at the time. Old habits of thinking die hard, and communism had held Eastern Europe in a headlock for more than forty years. But in fact, no more Soviet invasions were coming soon, if ever. Eastern Europe was ripe to break free. The only question was who would try to go first. One successful test case, and the rest would shortly follow.

Early in the year, the Polish government finally relented to public pressure for some form of shared governance and agreed to hold round-table talks with Solidarity leaders, as well as members of a number of splinter parties. At first, I was less than optimistic; the whole thing felt like a put-on, and I had worked long enough with communist officials to know that they would never bet on any game that was not rigged. But as the talks wore on, it became ever more apparent that the only way the Communists could maintain control of any new parliament would be if they could depend on the allegiance of one or more splinter groups. On the other hand, if the opposition parties could settle their differences and band together, the Communists would find themselves voted summarily out of office. Day by day, it began to look like this could indeed happen.

The Communists' last chance to salvage the situation came in the form of a public debate between Walesa, speaking on behalf of Solidarity, and Alfred Miodowicz, chairman of the OPPZ (or Polish Government Trade Unions), late in '88. Either out of overconfidence or desperation, the government permitted the debate to be televised nationally, and not surprisingly, every Pole with access to a TV tuned in. I was in Warsaw with Jim Michener at the time of the debate and got to watch it firsthand. From my point of view, it was a clear Solidarity victory; where Miodowicz spoke ominously about law and order—the old communist saw—Walesa spoke in calm, persuasive tones about the necessity of a multiparty system. He asked: How could Poland move ahead, with only one point of view? It was hard to disagree.

Still, I had no idea how Poles themselves would react to the debate. Just the idea of a debate would be something completely new to them. The evening after the broadcast, Jim and I were dining at the home of Archbishop Bronislaw Dabrowski, when a young priest rushed in. He was so excited he had to drink a glass of water before speaking. By then, everyone was silent, waiting to hear from him.

"It's out in the press," he said finally. "Everyone thinks it was a massacre! Walesa bested him on every point!"

Rejoicing spread across the room. Then, a few minutes later, we were interrupted a second time by a great commotion outside. Suddenly, Lech himself burst into the room, surrounded by his closest associates.

I was completely astonished. I looked at Jim. "What in the world—"

But I didn't have time to finish. Lech embraced the archbishop, then picked me out from the crowd. He rushed over to where I was standing and threw his arms around me.

"It is good to see you again, Uncle," he said, grinning. "When I come to the United States, I shall expect you to keep me out of trouble."

I was smiling from ear to ear. "You can count on it," I said.

He nodded, embraced me again, and was off into the throng. I watched him go, certain that I was looking at the next president of Poland.

In April 1989, Solidarity was officially relegalized, and in June, Solidarity candidates all but swept the country's first parliamentary elections. For the first time, a noncommunist government held power over a Soviet satellite state. Hungary and Czechoslovakia, already in the throes of their own prodemocracy movement, quickly followed suit. On November 9, as the world watched, the Berlin Wall—communism's most heartbreaking symbol—was dismantled by joyous throngs. Bulgaria, Romania, Estonia, Latvia, Lithuania: one by one, each captive nation rose and stood. Unable to contain the spirit of reform, Gorbachev watched as his own country began to break apart; by the end of the next year, all fifteen Soviet republics had declared themselves at least partly autonomous.

It was a feverish, frantic time. Most Americans could only watch it on television and read about it in the newspapers. I was luckier. Ten days after the Berlin Wall fell, Lech Walesa, soon to be elected president of the free Republic of Poland, came to see me.

The occasion was an official visit by Solidarity leaders to the United States, where Lech would address a joint session of Congress. True to my word, I had agreed to keep him out of trouble and help to manage his itinerary, which culminated in a visit to Emlen House.

Lech and his entourage arrived on the evening of November 18. The place was in chaos, swarming with press and members of the state department's diplomatic security service. We would be his final stop; I could tell the trip had already exhausted him. But we had planned a ceremony for the next day. I asked him: Was it still all right to go ahead?

"Of course, Uncle," he said. "For you, of course."

I awoke early the next morning. Fifty guests were scheduled to come for breakfast at the nearby Copernicus House, where Lech was staying, on the Emlen House grounds; after, we would gather on the lawn outside, where there would be a short program of music by the University of Pennsylvania Glee Club, the Valley Forge Trumpeters, and speeches by a number of visiting dignitaries. I dressed in the predawn darkness, thinking: *Here is a day I will remember the rest of my life. Right now, one of the most important men in the world is sleeping under my roof.*

Suddenly it was all too much. I gave Oddie a gentle nudge, where she slept. "Hon?"

Her eyes fluttered, then opened wide. "Ed? What time is it?" Before I could answer, a look of exasperation crossed her face. "Good God, today of all days you didn't let me oversleep—"

I shook my head. "It's all right. It's still early."

"Don't scare me like that." She sat up in bed, then eyed me curiously. "Are you OK?"

"Of course I'm OK." I felt myself smiling. "I'm better than OK." I shook my head. "I guess I just wanted someone to tell me it was all real."

Oddie smiled, stifling a yawn. "Yes, it's all happening, hon. Do you want me to get up now?"

I nodded. "Yes, I think so."

"All you have to do is ask. Do you want to know something else?"

"Anything."

"None of this surprises me at all, actually."

By the time Lech came downstairs, fifty guests were waiting for him for breakfast. Cars and press vans clotted the driveway to Copernicus House; secret service agents prowled the house and grounds; members of the Penn Glee Club wandered around the patio, humming and clearing their throats. A small dais had been erected on the lawn outside, and beside it, our replica of the Liberty Bell had been rolled into place. How strange it was, to see my home transformed! For just a few hours, it would be the ceremonial centerpiece of one of the twentieth century's greatest dramas.

We all said grace, holding hands—a lovely moment. We ate, then went outside into a cold, clear morning in fall, beneath flags snapping on a chilly breeze, where more guests waited by the dais, and the Penn Glee Club opened the ceremony by singing the Polish national anthem. Warren Burger spoke, then Jim Michener, then Lech himself. I barely heard any of it. All I could think was: *Imagine!*

The program would close with the ringing of the Liberty Bell. Thirteen local schoolchildren joined Lech and myself on the dais, each to ring the bell once—with an extra ring for Poland, and one for the world.

Fifteen rings in all.

They made the most beautiful sound I had ever heard.

Chapter Eighteen
Farewell

Success, money, fame; in the end, how fleeting they all are. In living one's life, caught up in the hum and energy of it, it is easy to believe that we are only the sum of our accomplishments. But in the end, the body tells the final chapter of the tale.

All my life I had been blessed with excellent health, and even in my early seventies, my days were long and full. I continued to travel abroad—to Poland and Rome and Ireland and elsewhere—and was still consumed by a variety of philanthropic undertakings. I worked each day from dawn until well past dark. Each year I passed my annual physical exam with flying colors, and I had never felt better. I planned to live to be a hundred.

But Oddie's health had begun to suffer. Three hip replacement operations had slowed her down considerably, and diabetes, first detected in her late fifties, had taken its toll on her vision and strength. Then, in March 1991 on a visit to our home in Florida, Oddie slipped in the bathroom and badly broke her ankle. She had gone down to Florida reluctantly, and at our urging, the previous January—we all had thought it would be good for her health. Now, she was stranded; her ankle, slow to heal because of the diabetes, required not one but two operations, confining her to the hospital in Florida for months. The doctors told us that even if the ankle healed properly, Oddie would need to use a walker.

Caught up in my various projects and worrying about Oddie, I barely gave myself a thought. But the truth was, something was wrong with me, too. All during that long, difficult winter, I had begun to notice a shortness of breath during my morning walks, accompanied by a mild tightening in my chest. In hindsight, it was obvious what was happening to me, but I put it out of my mind; not *that*, I thought, not to Ed Piszek. I told no one, waiting for the problem to go away. But finally, one February morning, I returned from my walk around the Emlen House grounds so breathless I could barely get the words out. I was terrified, and reluctantly confessed to my kids what was going on.

Despite all the evidence that I was in trouble, I still balked at seeing a doctor. I simply didn't want to hear more bad news. Eventually, Helen called Oddie in Florida, where she was still in the hospital, to tell her what was happening and ask her to make me see a doctor.

"It's no big deal," I said.

"No big deal. Listen to you. You can't *breathe.*"

"I'm really feeling much better," I lied. "It was probably just something I ate."

"Hon, do you think the pope wants a live Ed Piszek or a dead Ed Piszek?"

"No one's going to die."

"Not if he goes to the doctor, he isn't. Hon, *please.*"

I finally agreed, and a day later, our family physician, Dr. Gerald Shomer, examined me. His reading of the situation was cautious. He didn't hear any problems with my heart, he explained, not specifically, but the symptoms I described worried him. It was quite likely that I had some partial blockage of the coronary arteries. If so, I would need an angioplasty, at the very least. I didn't know very much about it—angio-*what?*—but it sounded harmless enough: a balloon inserted into the affected arteries, then inflated to widen them and increase the flow of blood. Still, he wouldn't know anything more until I had a stress test.

A few days later, Erik drove me to see the cardiologist that Shomer had recommended, Dr. Gilbert Zuckerman, whose office was just a few miles away in Flourtown.

"I'm really feeling much better," I said, which was true; after a couple of days of rest, the shortness of breath seemed to have evaporated completely. "This is probably just a big waste of time."

"That's what we always hope for," he said, and gave me a little encouraging smile. "Mr. Piszek, it's just a little walking. If everything works out, you'll be home in time for lunch."

Dr. Zuckerman gathered his paperwork together and motioned for us to head over to the testing area.

"You know," I said, "I've heard stories about men who die in the middle of these things. Perfectly healthy one minute, then—poof!"

Dr. Zuckerman chuckled. "Well, we try not to let that happen. But just for the record, a cardiologist's office is about the best place to have a heart attack, if you're going to have one."

"I'm not happy about this at all."

"No one is." He placed a firm hand on my shoulder. "But it's the easiest test in the world to pass. Let's just wait for some good news, shall we?"

The testing room was down the hall from his office and reminded me of a high-tech gymnasium. A bank of treadmills and rowing machines lined the wall; parked next to each was a contraption I took to be a heart monitor, with a screen and an ink printout. As Dr. Zuckerman's office had instructed, I arrived wearing a pair of loose sweatpants and tennis shoes. The technician asked me to remove my shirt and affixed a battery of wires to my bare chest and back with suction cups and tape. He then directed me to one of the treadmills.

"All right, Mr. Piszek," the technician calmly instructed, "we're ready to go. Just a light walk, if you please."

Off I went—first just walking, then picking up the pace bit by bit, until I was moving at a bouncy jog. I waited for the tightness to return, ready to stop at the first hint of trouble. But several minutes passed, and all I felt was the pleasing tiredness of mild exercise. Just a false alarm, I thought. A warning, perhaps, to take better care of myself, to slow down a little perhaps, as befitting a man my age. But a heart attack? No way. I was not at all surprised when Dr. Zuckerman halted the test just halfway through.

"I've seen enough," he said.

"Great." I wiped my face with a fresh towel and put my shirt back on. Zuckerman briefly left the room, then returned with Erik, who had been waiting outside. "C'mon, Erik," I said, motioning for the door. "I've graduated. If we hurry, we can be home for lunch."

"I'm afraid that won't be possible, Mr. Piszek," Dr. Zuckerman said. "I'm sending you to Chestnut Hill Hospital right now."

"Wait just a minute. You said you'd seen enough."

"That's right. And I think there's reason to be quite concerned. I'm sorry for the bad news, but you could be in real trouble, Mr. Piszek. There's no waiting around."

"But I feel fine."

Dr. Zuckerman frowned. "To tell you the truth, that's what worries me." He turned to my son-in-law. "Erik, I'd like to send him by ambulance. I'm pretty sure I can have a bed waiting when he gets there. I can be there within an hour or so myself."

Erik agreed, and Dr. Zuckerman made a call to the hospital, while Erik copied down the information. Perhaps it was fear, but I felt myself grow hot with anger. No one was listening to me. Hadn't they heard? I felt *fine*. An ambulance? There was nothing wrong with me.

Then I felt it—the shortness of breath, the tightness, a tingling in my hands.

"No ambulance," I said. "But I'll go."

At Chestnut Hill, more tests revealed just how serious the situation was, and it was decided that I should be transferred to Jefferson Hospital in Center City for a catheterization, which was performed the next morning, a Friday. The procedure was painless; a tiny wire was inserted into the arteries that fed the heart, so the cardiology team could see precisely what was going on. I had given up thinking they would find nothing, but could no longer distinguish my feelings of anxiety from any real shortness of breath caused by a heart problem. A few hours after the procedure, Dr. Zuckerman visited my room and laid out his grim report. Just as he had expected, I had a significant blockage—90 percent—in three arteries that fed the heart with blood. My heart was receiving just one-tenth of the blood it needed to work properly, and though I hadn't had a heart attack yet, one was certainly lurking in the weeds—months, even just days, away. An angioplasty would not do. I had been scheduled for a triple bypass at 6:00 A.M. Monday morning.

The weekend stretched before me like a long deathwatch. There wasn't much for me to do, no treatment to receive; I knew without being told that they were keeping me at Jefferson just in case I had the heart attack that everyone was so certain was headed my way. Zuckerman's joke was not a joke anymore. Nurses came and went, taking blood and reading my blood pressure and pulse. I hadn't spent so much as a day in the hospital in my life, and I felt for the first time the weird, unpleasant sensation that my body, for the time being, was not entirely my own.

But over the next two days, the feeling of captivity was transformed, gradually, to something else. In twenty-four hours my body would be wheeled down the hall, my chest opened and laid bare, my heart—that organ that seems, whatever the scientists tell us, to be the seat of so much of who we are—massaged, reworked, rewired. The thought initially terrified me. But by Sunday afternoon, fear yielded to a new feeling, comforting and strange—a great sense of calm, as if I were somehow separate from my body, this broken old body that seemed to be causing such a fuss. I thought: *My body is like a car, and I am its passenger.* Odd to think it, but I did, and it made me want to laugh. The car would be taken into the shop to be fixed or not, while I waited elsewhere to hear how much the repairs would cost. When the surgeon met with me on Sunday night to describe the details of the operation to me and my children, I found I wasn't even interested. The information would do me little good, one way or another, after all. I only wanted this cocoon of ironic detachment to last.

"You know," I told him, "this is all the last thing in the world I really want to hear right now. Just wheel me in and do your stuff. I have no problem putting me in your hands."

The surgeon, whose name was Dr. Edie—a renowned heart specialist, as it turned out—seemed momentarily taken aback. But then he nodded and shook my hand.

"Sleep well, Mr. Piszek. It's a big day tomorrow. We'll see you bright and early."

Later that night Helen came by the room. We had planned to call Oddie together, at the hospital where she was staying down in Florida.

But the call could not go through. No one answered at Oddie's room, and when we called the desk at her hospital, we were told that she had already gone to bed and that the phone line had been temporarily disconnected so as not to disturb her. Helen began to explain—*Didn't they understand, her husband was going in for open-heart surgery tomorrow morning?* But I waved her off.

"Dad . . ." She stopped, her hand over the mouthpiece of the receiver. Her face was creased with worry. "Dad, shouldn't we, you know, just in case?"

"It's all right," I said. "Her doctors know best. I'll talk to her tomorrow."

Of course, that wasn't what happened. No one had told me (or had they?) that even when you survive open-heart surgery—sail through it with flying colors—that you do not do much of anything afterward, not for days. Somehow I had gotten it in my head that when it was all over, I would stand up from the operating table and dance. Silly. The reality was far starker; I felt like a car had landed on me. Tubes and wires flowed in and out of me like tangled Christmas lights. But I was alive, fresh arterial blood filling my tired heart muscle once again.

Three days later Oddie and I finally spoke on the phone.

"You OK?" she asked.

"Never better. You should see the scars."

"This is some stunt you've pulled," Oddie said.

Day by day, I began to feel stronger. Friends I had not spoken with in years wrote and called me to wish me well. Jim Michener called to regale me with tales of his own bypass three years earlier and to remind me to take it easy.

"I knew a fellow had the same operation. He felt so good afterwards that he insisted on going skiing a few weeks later. He hadn't missed a season of skiing his whole life, and he said he wasn't about to miss one now."

It seemed like a happy story. Imagine, being able to ski just a few weeks after open-heart surgery! *He must be a remarkable man,* I thought.

"That's amazing," I managed to say.

"Amazing?" he chuffed. "I don't think so. Foolish is more like it. Fellow went out on a plane and came home in a box. So go slow, Ed. That's what I'm telling you. Go *slow*."

I took his advice. They say a triple bypass is good for seven to ten years before it needs repair. I'm in year seven now, eighty-two years old. Dr. Edie's handiwork, as far as I know, still beats soundly beneath my chest. Maybe I will live to a hundred, after all. But if I do, I will do it alone.

On the evening of April 23, 1994, Oddie and I went to a barbecue night at the local Lutheran church. Her health had continued to deteriorate since her fall in Florida, and even such a simple outing had become quite difficult for her. She was confined to a walker, and though cataract surgery the year before had helped her vision somewhat, she still had a great deal of trouble with her eyes. Her spirits had been poor, but she had made a point of reserving that night for the barbecue, and I was pleased that she would want to go out. She wanted to watch the dancing, she said.

It was a pleasant evening, and we returned home early and went to bed. Then, in the middle of the night I was awakened by a crash. I sat up quickly in bed and saw that Oddie was not beside me. From the floor on the far side of the bed, I heard what sounded like Oddie's voice, muttering something I couldn't make out.

I scrambled out of bed. Oddie was lying on the floor. My mind, still half-asleep, struggled to surmise what had happened. Her lips moved in the darkness, forming strange, half-intelligible words. Her eyes opened and flickered at me.

"You're dreaming, hon," I said. "You've fallen out of bed."

She nodded, and seemed to gather hold of herself, satisfied by my explanation. The diabetes had made her a restless sleeper, and it wasn't the first time she had fallen. I asked her if she had hurt herself, and she shook her head no. I called for Carmen, our housekeeper, and together we helped Oddie back into bed. She was murmuring—the last remnants of her dream, I supposed—but then fell silent again, her breathing deep but a little raspy. *Perhaps she has a cold coming on,* I thought, and made a mental note to call the doctor the next day before I, too, fell back to sleep.

In the morning I awoke early, went downstairs for breakfast, read the Sunday papers, and then went back upstairs to get ready for church. It wasn't unusual for Oddie to sleep in, and I supposed that the evening's festivities had probably tired her out. In any event, I thought I would wake her up soon enough. She wouldn't want to miss the whole day.

I had just finished dressing when Carmen knocked on my dressing room door. Her face was pale and frantic with alarm.

"Something's wrong with Mrs. P," she said.

Oddie could neither move nor speak. Half of her face and her right arm and hand were paralyzed. At the hospital, the doctors explained everything. Sometime in the middle of the night, Oddie had suffered a stroke. The strange murmuring—she had been trying to tell me.

The prognosis was mixed. With rehab, it was likely she would regain some powers of speech and mobility. With strokes, it was hard to tell; sometimes the brain could repair itself, the doctors said, sometimes not.

For the next six weeks, the rehab people worked to restore some movement to Oddie's right side and to improve her speech. Probably she would never walk again under her own power. It was a Herculean effort she put forth, but heartrending, too. There was simply too much damage. I felt, for the first time, the sensation of missing her, as if Oddie were going somewhere without me.

Oddie was released from the hospital in the first week of June, on a clear sunny day that was like the first real day of summer. It would be our last warm season together.

When I remember that long, sleepy summer and the autumn that followed, I remember not only how hard it was, taking care of her—Oddie didn't want a nurse, and neither did I—but also the bittersweetness of it, for it was our long goodbye. All the years together of work and struggle, of raising a family and building a business—all seemed to fade now. I wanted to make up for lost time. I hadn't always been the most lovingly expressive of husbands, I knew. I had done the right things, but I hadn't always articulated them, saying the words out loud. In the last months of her life, I began each day by singing to her, the old love songs of our youth, whose titles I wasn't even certain I remembered, but whose phrases, I found, were waiting just at the tip of my tongue.

"*A day without you is a day without love,*" I sang, "*. . . and a day without love is like a night without stars . . .*"

The words came from something called "The Cuban Love Song." She would smile, perhaps laugh a little. Through the bunched muscles of her clenched jaw, she would say, "Ed, you are the world's worst singer."

Bit by bit she regained some of her strength and powers of movement, as the doctors had foretold, though much was gone forever. Then, in early February, a season of snow and ice, she suffered a second stroke. It was considerably milder than the first, but it managed to undo all the progress she had made. The doctors agreed that there was no point in keeping her for a protracted stay in the hospital.

A few days before she was scheduled to be released, I had to leave the country for an important meeting in Warsaw. I wonder now how it was I could have gone, when it was so clear that the end was near. But the truth is that, despite all the signs, I had no feeling that she would die—not then, not all that year, no matter how sick Oddie was. We had been together nearly sixty years; it was simply beyond the power of my imagination to envision a life without her, *beyond* her. And I'm certain Oddie knew this. When I offered to reschedule the meeting, so that I could be with her and help get her resettled at Emlen House, she refused.

"You go," she said. Her powers of speech were badly compromised, but we had been together so long that words were hardly necessary. Oddie and I could have a conversation simply by looking at one another, and in her eyes I saw a firm resolve that I should get on with things. Perhaps she was protecting me from something she already knew.

"You go," she repeated. "I'll be here."

Helen made the arrangements to bring Oddie home from the hospital on February 14, Valentine's Day. Helen later told me that she barely spoke at all; she only smiled, to tell her she was happy to be going home. Her eyes seemed to be gazing at some faraway place, as if she were already looking at the angels. She passed away that night.

Helen reached me by phone in Warsaw the next morning—late afternoon, Warsaw time. I am told that, even when Helen gave me the news—neatly, succinctly, as such news must always be relayed—I acted as if I didn't believe her. Over and over I asked, "Where is she? Where is she?" The answer couldn't satisfy me. *Gone.* It was no place.

One idea fixed in my mind. I wanted Oddie buried on the grounds of Emlen House. It was her home, the place she had loved more than all others, and I could not imagine her leaving there. Some of my children thought the idea was eccentric, but even when everyone finally agreed, we ran into trouble with the township; in this day and age, even death is subject to zoning laws. There were papers to be filed, bureaucrats to be satisfied, inspections to be made. Finally, after a six-month interment in another family vault, Oddie was moved back to the garden where, all those years ago, Radcliffe Cheston had bestowed his blue-blooded estate on us, and Emlen House had become our home.

And that is where she is—just beyond my window, where I can see her, and even talk with her. I get up in the morning, eat breakfast, do my work—and always, Oddie is near.

"Good morning, sweetheart," I say each day. Or else, a bit of patter from our years of life together: "You are the greatest woman in the world, bar—"

And Oddie, laughing, would always finish the sentence: "None."

I still hear her saying it.

Epilogue
A Game of Catch

Summer 1998, an evening at twilight; I stand at the window in Oddie's sunroom, looking out to the lawns and garden beyond. To my right, the old millrace gurgles with July's slow, green water. The heavy white light of midsummer fades toward a cool dusk. Two years ago, I turned eighty years old. I am still here.

But many others are gone, besides Oddie. Primate Wyszynski, Cardinal Krol, even Clyde Potter—so many have passed away. To live a long life is a blessing, but it comes with a price. To be the last, one must watch the final thinning of the herd.

My old companion, Jim Michener, is gone, too. Jim had been on kidney dialysis for six or seven years, and as his health had begun to fail, he rarely ventured from his adopted home in Austin, where he had settled after writing the Texas novel that Poland had interrupted. He often joked good-naturedly about the dialysis (at a public appearance, a woman had once asked him if he found dialysis "annoying," to which Mich replied that "death would be far more annoying"), but I knew the limitations it imposed weighed heavily on his mind. He had always been the most hale and vigorous of men, and the last thing he wanted was to reach a state where he was merely existing, a prisoner of the body. Quietly, in the fall of 1997, Jim made the decision to take himself off dialysis and let nature take its course.

Just a few of Jim's closest friends were informed of his decision, and I flew down to Texas to visit him in his last days. With me was the great ball player Stan Musial, with whom Jim and I had become the closest of companions; a trip we had taken together to Poland and Rome in 1988 had, in fact, served as the basis for Jim's memoir, *Pilgrimage*.

The three of us were together just a few hours in Austin. We didn't speak a word about what was happening; we talked about what was going on in the world, as we always had, and then when he seemed to be growing too tired, we said our goodbyes, knowing it would be the last time.

"See you 'round, Jim," I said.

He gave a little wave. "I'll call you," he said. He died a week later.

But of course, life goes on. In the last few years, more and more of my time has been spent on a curious pursuit: baseball.

The fact was, I almost never played baseball as a kid. Such green space as the game requires was rare in North Philadelphia, and I was too clumsy besides to play very well. But a few years ago, the International Little League, through my friend Stan, approached me about raising the funds to establish a training and play-off center in Poland. The center would serve all of Europe, North Africa, and the Middle East, and be located in Kutno, about forty miles from Warsaw on the road to Poznan.

As soon as Stan explained it, I fell in love with the idea. Here was something Poland could do for the rest of the world, a way for Poland to be number one at something. And Little League baseball—what could be more fitting? It was a deeply American game but also a kind of international language. Three million kids played the game around the globe, and the lessons it taught were the best, simplest kind: teamwork, effort, the bright physical pleasure of the game itself. A boy or girl who is playing baseball is simply more alive than one who isn't. I wrote a check and got on the phone to find more people who would do the same.

By early 1998, the center was well under way. In addition to regular playing fields, a stadium had been constructed, with seating for two thousand spectators and lights for night games. Groundbreaking for the training center itself, with dormitories and cafeterias, was scheduled for sometime in late '99. Play-offs had been held there for two years running. (Middle Eastern powerhouse Saudi Arabia won both times.) It had been a long, difficult road convincing potential donors of the importance of such a project, but the details were finally coming together.

"It seems like a small thing," Stan said to me once, "but it really matters to these kids. I think it matters more than anything."

We were seated in the stadium bleachers on a sunny autumn day, watching Romania play Saudi Arabia. It had been an exciting game so far, with spectacular power hitting and several close plays at the plate. The two teams were never separated by more than a run or two.

I passed him the popcorn. "I think that's right."

"It's enough just to do some good in the world, isn't it?"

Some good in the world. I was struck with a feeling of déjà vu, and I realized I had heard the phrase before. My old friend Cardinal Krol had used it, back in the dark days when Mrs. Paul's was slipping away and I thought my life was over. *You've done some good in the world, Ed Piszek,* he'd said.

When the game was over, Stan and I milled around for a while to meet some of the players and coaches. It was Stan, of course, who was the real celebrity, and when the kids found out who he was, they mobbed him for autographs. Kids were holding up baseballs, gloves, popcorn containers, the backs of their hands—anything signable—for Stan to etch with his name. What a sight it was: kids from Romania, Saudi Arabia, Poland, Italy, speaking in a cacophony of different languages but all speaking the same language of boyhood and the love of baseball. It was one of the greatest pleasures of being Stan's friend, seeing the way that kids responded to him. It made the world seem less complicated somehow and seemed to contain a truth that, in the end, might be the one that saves us all.

"You all right over there?" I asked over the din. I was standing ten feet away on the sidelines of the chaos.

Stan winked at me. "Sure. Never better."

I slipped away. I had no destination in mind, just a desire to walk and enjoy the day. I found myself on one of the empty practice fields, where earlier that morning I had watched part of a consolation round game. By the sidelines, somebody had left a ball and glove, and after a moment's hesitation I picked them up. The glove fit snugly but not uncomfortably, and as I pressed it to my face, my senses were flooded with the scent of green grass and sweat and leather—the scent of the game, of childhood, of memory itself. I turned the ball around in my right hand, gauging its compact weight. How long had it been since I had held a ball and glove?

"Rzuc tutaj."

I turned toward the voice. A young boy, perhaps eleven or twelve, was standing not twenty feet away, along the first base line. He was wearing the uniform of one of the local Polish teams, and a shock of blond hair peeked from beneath his cap, which he wore at a jaunty angle. I wondered how long he had been standing there.

"Is this your glove?" I asked, but of course it was not; he had his own.

He shook his head. "Throw it here," he said again, in Polish.

I did. Not a bad throw, either. He took just one step to the side and nabbed it cleanly. As he wound up to return the ball, I realized I had been drafted for a game of catch.

"You're the American?" he said.

The American. I wondered, *Which one?* I thought perhaps he had me confused with Stan. But I allowed myself to imagine that he knew who I was. I tossed the ball back to him.

"*Polski Amerykanski,*" I said. "Polish American."

He looked around. "You built this."

"Oh, not me. Many people. I just helped."

He smiled and threw me the ball. "*Dziekuje,*" he said. "Thank you."

In March '98, I flew back to Poland to receive the *Polonia Restituta,* the Commander's Cross—one of that country's highest awards, and the highest it bestows upon non-Poles. The ceremony was held at the Presidential Palace in Warsaw, with a full battery of press and members of the diplomatic corps in attendance. The award itself was a handsome, suitably modest-looking medal, emblazoned with a single white star. Milling about later, the medal pinned on my chest, I was asked by the press how it felt. I didn't have to think long to come up with an answer.

"Like a graduation," I said.

It was a time of celebration in more ways than one. The U.S. Senate had just voted to grant Poland membership in the North Atlantic Treaty Organization (NATO)—a graduation of its own, really, bringing that long-imprisoned country under the protective umbrella of the West. I had been lobbying for NATO membership ever since democratic government had been restored, with my efforts intensifying in '96 through '97, as the Senate vote approached. The situation looked excellent, but even I was surprised when the vote came down: 80 to 19 in favor, a veritable landslide. That I had lived to see it seemed like one of the greatest, most unlikely triumphs of my life.

The irony, of course, was that Lech Walesa was no longer Poland's president. Like Winston Churchill and Charles de Gaulle, Lech had done momentous things for his people only to find himself turned out of office, replaced after one term by former Communist Aleksander Kwasniewski. On the subject of his fall from power, he was deeply philosophical; history had taught the lesson, time without number, that the agent of change was rarely the agent of rebuilding. I knew that the NATO vote was in many ways a personal triumph for him, the result of many years of careful lobbying. "It is inevitable," he always warned about Russia. "The bear will come out of its cave." NATO membership made that prospect all the more unlikely and further inched Poland's momentous changes toward permanence.

Still, I would have liked to receive the medal from him.

About a month later, a second ceremony was held at Kosciusko House,

welcoming me back to Philadelphia and marking the medal's official place-
ment on display there. It was a warm, blustery day in early April, a time of
year when the city is at its finest. On such a day, it is easy to imagine the
streets of Old Philadelphia as they were two hundred years ago, when the
likes of Thomas Jefferson and George Washington walked there. The street
in front of the house was cordoned off for the ceremony; besides family and
friends, the crowd contained members of the press, city officials, and even
Philadelphia Mayor Edward Rendell himself, who made one of his famous
blitzkrieg appearances, bolting from his car to take the podium and say a
few words.

A wonderful day: yet, something nagged at me all that day and the
next night, too. No one said anything specific, but the tone of the occasion
suggested something like finality. That fall I had turned eighty-one. The
phrase everyone used was "a time for recognition." And yet, it seemed
there was so much left undone.

After the ceremony and the lunch that followed, I drove alone three
hours to State College, where I was scheduled to give an address to a convention on volunteerism being held at Penn State, then drove the three
hours home, returning around ten in the evening. It had been a long day;
I drank a glass of milk and went to bed, and in the morning, awoke early,
full of a surprising and unexpected energy. With nothing on the calendar,
I decided I would drive down to Brigantine, on the Jersey shore, to visit
my sister Cecilia. In all the commotion at the ceremony, I had barely had
the chance to speak with her, and since Oddie's death, I had made a point
of visiting her at least once a month. I waited until 9:00 A.M. to phone her,
then got in the car and set out, thinking nothing of one more long drive.

Traffic had thinned since the rush hour, and a light drizzle dappled
the windshield, not quite enough rain to warrant turning on the wipers.
The car, a new Cadillac sedan, made barely a sound. I drove through
Manayunk (an upscale restaurant, the Arroyo Grill, had recently gone up
on the island where the old Mrs. Paul's plant used to be), nosed onto the
Schuylkill Expressway, drove through Center City, and took the Walt
Whitman Bridge, vaulting across the Delaware River into New Jersey and
pointing myself east toward the shore, an hour and a half away. The rain
stopped, then resumed, then stopped again. The landscape flattened in
the haze, as I made my way onto New Jersey's coastal plane.

I am told I barely made it ten miles past the Delaware before the
accident. My memory of what first occurred is imprecise, like something
in a dream, which it almost certainly was; I recall moving into the left lane,
to pass a truck, then returning to the right lane, then being jolted into
consciousness by the sound of the Cadillac's front end striking the guardrail. Probably, for one brief moment, I had fallen asleep.

Post after post struck the front end of the car, the force of the impact so violent I was momentarily stunned into inaction; I jammed on the brake then, and watched as the car spun completely around, and the ground fell away. For a brief moment the car was airborne, like a sled going off a ramp. Then it crashed back down, coming to rest backwards in a dense thicket.

Everything was very still. Just for a second, I sat there, wondering if I was still alive, and if I was, how this was possible. Beyond my face, the windshield was smashed in a spider's web pattern, and I touched my head, searching for blood, but found none; at least I hadn't hit the windshield. Vines and bushes blocked the driver's window, and when I scooted over to look out the passenger side, I saw that, below me, the ground fell off sharply into a four-foot drainage ditch. Just a few moments had passed since the accident. Beyond the ditch, traffic zoomed by, heedless. No one had noticed; I had flown off the road and simply disappeared.

And then I knew. My father hadn't died at the wheel of his car. For so many years I had thought this; perhaps my mother had told me. Suddenly I remembered that wasn't how it had happened at all. When his car went off the road, it had ended up cocked at a forty-five-degree angle off the edge of the ditch. When my father had gotten out, somehow the change in the distribution of weight had caused the car to topple on its side, crushing him beneath it. If he had stayed in the car and waited for help, or simply gotten out the other side, he would have walked away without a scratch.

The force of the impact had crushed the Cadillac's front end, bending the frame and wedging the front doors tight. The driver's side was blocked in any event, and remembering my father, I wasn't about to try to get out of the car on the side where the ditch was. I scrambled into the backseat, and somehow got the left rear door free. My body pressed against the Cadillac, I inched myself through the thicket, climbed over the car's rear trunk, jumped the ditch, and found myself standing at the edge of the highway. A hundred feet or so further on, a white sedan had pulled into the breakdown lane and stopped. Its reverse lights came on, and it began to back toward me. Only then did I see that it was an unmarked highway patrol car. Probably the officer had been hiding on the median, clocking speeders, and had witnessed the whole thing.

I turned then and saw the car in its entirety, for the first time. The front end was completely demolished, caved in like paper; the windshield was smashed, and steam was pouring from the front grill, mixed with sputtering coolant. The front tires were splayed like a dog's paws. Behind me, down the highway, lay the twisted remains of thirty feet of the cement-and-steel guardrail, tangled and smashed beyond recognition by the force of the impact.

Dad, I thought, and at that instant I was eight years old again, shouting his name and chasing his car as he pulled down the Quakertown drive, dust boiling from the tires. *Dad, I almost caught you. Today was almost the day.*

Eventually, the EMTs would come, and my neck would be put in a brace—a mild whiplash—and I would be taken by ambulance to the hospital, where six thousand dollars' worth of tests would find nothing at all; no reason for the lapse in consciousness that had caused the accident and no consequences beyond a few bruises. The Cadillac, the only real casualty, would be towed away to the junkyard. (The wrecking yard attendant, when he learned that the Cadillac's driver had survived, reportedly shook his head in amazement and remarked, "That guy must know the pope.") My son, Ed, would race from Fort Washington to find me arguing with the doctors, who wanted me to spend a night in the hospital (which I had no intention of doing, and didn't).

But that was later. Now, I stood by the highway, watching the white taillights of the patrol car backing toward me. Cars streamed by, braking at the last minute for their drivers and passengers to peek at the car in the ditch and at the old man standing by the side of the road. Beyond, the highway stretched on eternally, flat and straight and fast, leading to a thousand destinations unseen in the April morning mist. I stood looking at it, happy to be alive.

It just kept going.